D1474221

WITHDRAWAL

Innovation, Human Capabilities, and Democracy

Innovation, Human Capabilities, and Democracy

Towards an Enabling Welfare State

Reijo Miettinen

OXFORD
UNIVERSITY PRESS

OXFORD
UNIVERSITY PRESS

Great Clarendon Street, Oxford, OX2 6DP,
United Kingdom

Oxford University Press is a department of the University of Oxford.
It furthers the University's objective of excellence in research, scholarship,
and education by publishing worldwide. Oxford is a registered trade mark of
Oxford University Press in the UK and in certain other countries

© Reijo Miettinen 2013

The moral rights of the author have been asserted

First Edition published in 2013

Impression: 1

British Library Cataloguing in Publication Data

Data available

Library of Congress Cataloging in Publication Data

Data available

ISBN 978–0–19–969261–3

Printed in Great Britain by
MPG Books Group, Bodmin and King's Lynn

Contents

Contents

Preface and acknowledgements

This book has a three-phase prehistory of a decade. I wrote a small book entitled *National Innovation System; Scientific concept or political rhetoric* in 2002 published by the Finnish Innovation Fund (Sitra) and the publisher Edita. The book emerged from one of the projects of the Sitra Research Programme on the Finnish innovation system. The term 'national innovation system' (NIS) became a foundational term for Finnish science and technology policy in the early 1990s. I wanted to analyse the background of the concept and its adoption to the Finnish science and technology policy. My viewpoint was that of an 'outsider' as I am neither an economist nor a political scientist. However, I had worked for the Group for Technology Studies of the Technical Research Center of Finland, where my colleagues were active in introducing the evolutionary economics of innovation to Finland. I myself was involved in studying innovation processes and networks inspired by science and technology studies and sociocultural psychology. This provided a foundation for a fruitful critical dialogue.

In 2006 Yuji Mori of University of Chizuoka suggested to me in a conference that the 2002 book be translated into Japanese. This initiative led me to write an updated and enlarged version of the original book. During its translation process in 2007–2008 Yuji made many invaluable comments and suggestions to improve the manuscript. The book, entitled *Finnish National Innovation System; From technology to human capabilities*, was published in Japanese in 2010.

In Spring 2009 Kari Lilja of the Helsinki School of Economics invited me to a workshop of an EU-funded project on Nordic business systems. At the workshop I met Professor Charles Sabel, who later kindly invited me and Jarkko Hautamäki to join a Sitra-funded study on the development of the special education of the Finnish comprehensive school together with AnnaLee Saxenian ja Peer Hull Kristensen (Sabel *et al.* 2011). This project decisively influenced the contents of this book. I learned the concept of an enabling welfare state and the idea of tailored capability-cultivating services. The analysis of the development of the Finnish comprehensive school and its special education system presented in this book owes much to the project. The project also stimulated the dialogue between the sociocultural and pragmatist conceptions of learning, institutional change and democracy that constitute the theoretical backbone of this book.

Many of my colleagues have given valuable suggestions and comments on the versions of the chapters of this book. Particularly I want to thank the following persons for important and valuable comments that greatly helped in developing the ideas of the book: Paul Adler, Reijo Ahola, Mathieu Albert, Pirjo Aunio, Ant Elzinga, Ritva Engeström, Ilse Eriksson, Benoît Godin, Jarkko Hautamäki, Jyrki Kettunen, Tarmo Lemola, Raimo Lovio, Lars Mjoset, Charles Sabel, Hannu Simola, Sami Paavola, Helena Thuneberg, Kari Toikka, Jaakko Virkkunen, and Eero Väätäinen. Also the doctoral students at the Center for the Research of Activity, Development and Learning (CRADLE) have given me valuable comments. Anne Laitinen helped in the translation of the tricky original quotations from Finnish into English. My wife Maija Miettinen made the work possible by helping to acquire the documentation needed for the work and tirelessly providing her time and support in order to create the conditions for the writing work.

Reijo Miettinen

May 2012

1

Introduction: The Finnish model of innovation and welfare

1.1 National models confront the contradiction between global competition and the maintenance of welfare

In the 2000s Finland has with other Nordic countries been at the top both in the lists of national competiveness as well as in the lists evaluating the various aspects of the quality of life of the citizens (e.g. Balzat 2006). In the *EU Innovation Union Scorebook 2010* Denmark, Finland and Sweden were included with Germany in the group of four "innovation leaders" whose innovation performance was 20% or more above the EU average. The Nordic model is evaluated as being able to deliver both equity and efficiency (Sapir 2006) as well as combining collective mechanisms of risk sharing and openness to globalization (Andersen *et al.* 2007). Until recently, however, the Nordic social democratic welfare states were not regarded as a viable model in the tightening international economic competition. Their high level of taxation was thought to lead to a lack of incentive for innovation. Moreover, the large public sector was thought to limit the functioning of the free market, which was regarded by the liberal tradition as the main road to equality and prosperity.

In the 2000s several developments have led to a re-evaluation. The economic crisis of the late 2000s has again shown the dark side of unregulated competition. Taxpayers' money is being used to support the banking systems to resolve the problems caused by speculation in the financial market. The increasing income differences and poverty in Western societies have manifested themselves in the form of exclusion, lack of trust in politics, and even in riots. To counter this development the European Union introduced the social dimension to its development plan as a part of the Lisbon strategy. All these developments have contributed to a renewed interest in the Nordic welfare societies as an alternative which might suggest how competitive edge, social equality, high quality education, and trust in institutions may be combined. Within the Nordic countries Finland has been regarded as a model case of knowledge economy or information society because it was able in the 1990s to create a strong information and communication technology sector. Finland has also been regarded as a model country for its educational system. Finnish 15-year-old students have repeatedly been on the top in the OECD PISA studies that measure reading, writing, and maths skills and knowledge in natural sciences. In addition, among the OECD countries the differences between schools are lowest in Finland. Finally, Finland has been regarded as a model of systemic innovation policy because it was the first to adopt the national innovation system approach as a foundation for its science and technology policy.

Manuel Castells' and Pekka Himanen's *The Information Society and the Welfare Society; The Finnish model* (2002) found that the key feature of the Finnish system was a "virtuous cycle" between strong education, welfare society, and economic development. The success of the information society makes the continuous financing of welfare society possible, which in turn is able to generate well-educated people capable of developing the information society further. The idea of a "virtuous cycle" between welfare and economic efficiency was at the heart of social democratic welfare state policy. Castells' and Himanen's analysis suggests that this idea may, in a renewed form, be a viable alternative model in a globalizing network society and in a knowledge-based economy. By elaborating a model of an enabling welfare state I will study in this book whether and in what way such a virtuous cycle may be achieved.

It has been suggested that as a result of globalization – and in Europe as a result of European integration – national specificities will disappear and systems will increasingly converge. However, researchers who have compared varieties of capitalisms as well as varieties of business and national innovation systems (e.g. Amable 2003; Whitley 2007; Fagerberg *et al.* 2009) have mostly rejected this possibility. Natural and historical specificities persist and competition itself constantly gives rise to new ways of organizing economic activity.

A discussion of national models may seem paradoxical in a globalizing world in which capital, firms, and people move across boundaries and transnational collaboration constitutes an essential foundation for innovation. The continuous comparisons of regional and national institutional settings are, however, an integral part of the new global competition (Kettunen 2004: 303):

The discussion on 'models' is dominated by the encounters of transnational capital and national institutions, indicating the increasing reflexivity as an aspect of globalization. Reflexivity is nourished by the imperatives of competitiveness, which include the need for continuous comparisons in order to learn universal 'best practices' or to find 'difference', one's own particular competitive advantage, the edge. European integration provides an important context for the discussion on models.

The European Council declared in Lisbon in 2000 that Europe should become "the most competitive and dynamic knowledge-based economy in the world". As a part of this goal it introduced a new governance strategy, the Open Method of Co-ordination (OMC). The idea of benchmarking national practices played a central role in OMC.

In economics and social sciences national "models" of innovation and types of national economies have been analysed by several research approaches such as "varieties of capitalism" approaches (Hall and Soskice 2001; Amable 2003), the comparative business systems approach (Whitley 2007) and national innovation systems approaches (Nelson 1993; Fagerberg *et al.* 2009), as well as by comparative studies of welfare states (e.g. Esping-Andersen 1990; Pierson 1991; Pierson and Castles 2007a). All these approaches study the makeup, complementarity, and interaction between national institutions in order to explain the differences in the economic development or welfare between the industrialized countries.

The first three of these approaches are firm-centred. They focus on firm activities and analyse the impact of the institutional environment on them. The challenge for them is to define the important "subsystems": actors or institutional domains of a national system that should be included in the analysis. Amable (2003), for example, defines five major institutional areas the complementarity of which he analyses to define the types of capitalism: product-market competition, labour-market institutions, financial sector, social protection, and education. The national innovation systems (NIS) approach has focused on the interaction between firms, universities, public research institutions as well as government agencies involved in science and technology policy and funding (Nelson 1993). A broader interpretation of the NIS approach underlines the interactive learning between firms or producers and users, and wants to include education as well as learning within firms as key processes in a national system (Lundvall *et al.* 2002).

The starting point for welfare state theorists has been the problem of "protecting" citizens from the risks of the labour market and ensuring minimum living conditions for all citizens. The welfare state comparisons have therefore primarily focused on the relationships between labour market institutions and social policy. More recent discussions of the "crisis" and future of the welfare state ask whether and how welfare can be maintained in the conditions of global competition, changes in the labour market, family structures, and the age composition of the population (e.g. Esping-Andersen 2009).

Although the analysis of institutions and their interactions are the main focus of comparative approaches, there is no consensus on how institutions are defined and why and how people behave and learn within institutions. Institutional economics (e.g. North 1990) defines institutions as systems of rules that create a framework and incentives for the decision-making of individuals. Historical and sociological institutionalists often define institutions as rule systems or systems that persist because of rituals, habits, and routines that the members follow. Such a concept of institution is too static to make sense of the relationship between the historical continuity of institutions and institutional change and learning.

The change and development of institutions has become a central theme during the last decade both in the political economy (e.g. Streeck and Thelen 2005; Mahony and Thelen 2010) and in neoinstitutional organization theory (e.g. Greenwood *et al.* 2002). If institutions play a key role in explaining national innovativeness, the understanding of how institutions develop constitutes an important foundation for policy making. To contribute to this issue I will adopt the concept of institution as a multiorganizational field from neoinstitutional organizational studies (DiMaggio and Powell 1991) and analyse human activity within them by using a non-individualistic view of human activity, the sociohistorical approach, or, more specifically, the cultural-historical activity theory (Vygotsky 1979; Engeström *et al.* 1999b; Miettinen 2009). The definition of an institution as an organizational field allows an analysis of heterogeneity, multiple distributed agency as well as horizontal and vertical learning across organizational boundaries of an institution better than the concept of an institution as a system of rules or habits.

The basic concepts of the cultural-historical approach are the social origins of mind and cultural mediation of human activity by signs and tools (Vygotsky 1979). An individual, a local community, and a culture co-evolve and individuals learn when they participate in solving the problems of the activities in which they are involved. Learning takes place through "remediation", that is, through collaborative adoption and development of new intellectual and practical tools to meet the demands of a changing environment and to solve the emerging contradictions of an activity or an organizational field. In this view, instead of and in addition to rules, shared tools, concepts, and instrumentalities are seen as constitutive for the development of an institution.

In this book I aim to put innovation studies, political economy, welfare state research, organizational studies, and socio-cultural psychology in dialogue with each other. All of these disciplinary traditions speak about such phenomena as knowledge, capabilities, learning, and institutions. Each of them defines and understands them in different ways. By bringing their viewpoints and concepts into critical dialogue I aim at taking a step towards a multidisciplinary understanding of the conditions of innovation, welfare, and institutional change. The dialogue also includes reflection on the relationship between innovation, institutional learning, welfare, and democracy, which are often discussed as separate issues.

1.2 From innovation system to an enabling welfare state

Finland was the first country to adopt the concept of a national innovation system (NIS) as a basic category of its science and technology policy in the early 1990s.[1] The national innovation system approach was developed by the evolutionary economics of innovation to explain the differences in economic development between nations (e.g. Lundvall *et al.* 2002; Sharif 2006; Godin 2007). Several developers of the approach also functioned in the 1980s and early 1990s as advisers of the OECD and contributed to the formation of the OECD's innovation policy. Finland adopted the concept from the OECD and Finland was an active contributor to the OECD's NIS projects in the 1990s. As a policy paradigm the NIS approach studies how the institutional environment of firms can be developed to contribute to their innovative activity. It also proposes a horizontal policy: education, regional, industrial, foreign, science, and technology policies should converge to contribute to innovativeness.

The language of NIS was successfully used in Finland to create a national consensus around competitiveness through innovativeness. Virtually all political parties agreed on this vision and hardly any objections were presented. This consensus has been characterized as depoliticization of policy making because it presented the innovation policy as an economic necessity and tended to inhibit the formulation of

---

[1] The terms "national innovation system" (NIS) and "national system of innovation" (NSI) are synonyms that are used interchangeably in the literature. For the sake of clarity, I will use the term "national innovation system" (NIS) throughout the book.

alternative policy visions. This was a fundamental change that took place in the vocabulary and mindset of policy making in the late 1980s. It has been analysed in terms of a transition from a welfare or a planning state to a competition state. The basic values characteristic of the welfare state discourse such as equality or solidarity were replaced by values and vocabularies anchored to the aim of succeeding in the global economic competition (Heiskala and Luhtakallio 2006).

It is debatable, however, whether the new innovation policy introduced novel policy institutions or practices. Rather it reproduced and developed further the instruments created by the industrial, science, and technology policies of the previous decades. The most visible result of the Finnish science and technology policy has been the consequent and uninterrupted increase of funding in science and technology from the beginnings of the 1970s. The share of R&D input of the GNP was 0.9% in 1971, rising to 1.7% in 1980 and achieving the level of 4% in 2009, which is among the highest in the industrialized countries. The foundation of this policy was laid already by the industrial policy of the 1970s. The investment in R&D funding was seen as an important means of modernizing the one-sided Finnish industrial structure that was heavily based on the forest industry.

The technology policy of the 1980s introduced a strong focus on technological research, support for the R&D of firms as well as national technology programmes. The National Technology Council (Tekes) was established in 1983. It became the key planner and executor of technology-oriented policy. The national technology programmes funded by Tekes were prepared, applied, and realized jointly by universities, firms, research institutions, and industrial associations. This procedure contributed to an exceptionally high level of collaboration between firms, universities, and research institutes in Finland.

The limitations of the national innovation system approach in Finland became visible in the 2000s. It was criticized for being too exclusively focused on technology. The concepts of social innovation and a broad-based innovation were introduced. This extension of the definition of innovation gave rise to three contradictions. First, if innovation refers to reforms and development in all spheres of society including public services, can the firm-centred model developed by the evolutionary economics of innovation be a sufficient model any more? Would it be important to understand the specificity of these reforms and to mobilize theoretical, professional and practical knowledge accumulated in these activities in order to enhance innovations?

Second, the idea of involving the users in the innovation process contradicted the elitist nature of innovation policy making and the exclusive nature of the major institutional reforms in the 1990s and 2000s. The foresight projects were done by a limited group of people composed of the representatives of R&D funding organizations, ministries, and big companies complemented with selected researchers. The academic community, professional and civic associations, the parliament as well as the municipalities were largely left outside of the process. In the preparation of important institutional reforms, such as the university reform, the committee procedure with an extensive participation of stakeholders was replaced by a rapporteur procedure, in which trusted people or small groups were asked by a minister to prepare a suggestions for a reform. This led to a democracy deficit in innovation policy: the expertise of the well-educated professionals in different levels and spheres of society were not included in policy making.

Third, the merging of industrial, science, and technology policies into research- and innovation policy and the increased funding for applied technological research – mostly funded without a peer review procedure – caused deep concern for the fate of basic research. Evaluations revealed signs of a weakening of the university research compared with other European countries in terms of the number of publications and citations. Several actors made initiatives to revitalize science policy as an independent policy in charge of the quality and international level of scientific research.

The alternative view to innovation and welfare policy making I will elaborate in this book takes the cultivation of human capabilities as starting point. They are an increasingly important foundation both for innovativeness and for welfare of citizens in a knowledge-driven society. In addition the development of capabilities is intrinsically connected to the extension of democracy in society. Various values such as equality, the possibility of human development and flourishing, welfare and democracy, need to be taken into account in policy making without subsuming them as conditions of global competitiveness.[2] In this view the development of individually tailored capability-cultivating services is a central means of enhancing welfare, innovativeness, and full participation of citizens in society. To ensure the quality of these services local experimentation in multi-professional communities as well as horizontal learning across professional groups and organizational

---

[2] Many of the students of the concept of the global competitiveness have concluded that it must be defined as an ability to create welfare (e.g. Aiginger 2006:170). Neither should the often-used indicator of competitiveness, productivity, be detached from other values (2006: 170) "Productivity can be high at the price of unemployment, a low participation rate, social inequality, and ecological deprivation."

boundaries is needed. The state assumes a new role of ensuring that the dialogue and institutional learning needed for the development of the quality of services takes place.

Investment in education, learning and skills has been a central idea in welfare theory, the economics of innovation and in innovation theorizing. A turn from the protective concept of the welfare state towards an "active" and "enabling" welfare state took place in the 1990s with the idea of investment in human capital playing a key role in this transition. According to Anthony Giddens (1998: 117), for example, the central guideline for the new social democracy in the UK is "investment in *human capital* wherever possible, rather than the direct provision of economic maintenance." Education was meant to respond to the demands for a flexible workforce in a post-Fordist economy.

The terms "investment in human capital" and "production of general and specific skills" have dominated this discourse. However, the concept of human capital does not discuss the qualitative differences between educational systems. It has difficulties in dealing with the capabilities most needed in the invention of new realities, namely critical thought, creativity, and imagination. Developmental psychology has shown that early childhood is a critical period for the formation of personality and cognitive capabilities of an individual. It has also shown that play is instrumental for the development of the imagination and creativity that constitute the foundation for adult innovativeness. That is why play pedagogy needs to be developed in pre-school education and in the first grades of basic education.

The concern over the provision of capability cultivation services brings to the fore the problem of forms of governance of basic services. The PISA studies issued four times in the 2000s by the OECD have measured the reading, writing, and maths skills and knowledge in natural sciences of 15-year-old students in the member countries. The Finnish basic school students have come top in all of these studies and the share of low achievers and the differences between schools have been the lowest among the OECD countries. One of the explanations for this success is that Finland has stubbornly resisted the internationally dominating neoliberal educational policy. It has continued to develop its public unitary school system inspired by educational equality.

None of the main features of the neoliberal education policy, privatization, creation of educational markets or the establishing of an accountancy system based on the results of high-stakes national testing have thus far realized in Finland. Virtually no privatization of schools has taken place in Finland. There are no national tests in the country, except for the student matriculation at the age of 18. The responsibility of student evaluation is given to school communities, because they are thought to be most able to help the students and take the necessary developmental measures. The centralized evaluation is sample-based and the authorities prevent the publication of the comparisons of the student achievements between schools. Coordination primarily takes place by the Educational Act and national curriculum for the comprehensive school that defines the general goals and contents of education, through in-service education and experimental projects. Extensive collaboration and institutional learning take place across horizontal and vertical boundaries between the organizations in the organizational field. The PISA comparisons undeniably show that a public service system is able to produce excellent results with reasonable costs and is able to ensure equality better than market-based systems that tend to increase social segregation.

The concept of an enabling welfare state was suggested as a solution to the crisis of the old welfare state and as an outline for a new welfare society able to adapt to globalizing and a rapidly changing working life, while simultaneously being able to ensure the welfare of citizens (e.g. Curtis 2006, Kristensen 2011a; Sabel *et al.* 2011). It refers to a transition from a redistributing to an active enabling welfare state based on the provision of capacitating services which enable citizens to handle risks, shifts and changes in their lives. Education is the central instrument in assuring employment, a creative contribution to working life and in preventing exclusion from social life. Because individuals are different and the risk situation varies, services must increasingly be tailor-made and individualized.

Local experimentation and learning in hybrid communities and developmental associations are essential for the development of quality services in an enabling state. This calls for a decentralized system of governance which, however, is supported and coordinated by the state. In an enabling welfare state "the second-order enabling role" of the state becomes essential (Curtis 2006). It entails advancing a dialogue with market and civil society actors, as well as enhancing experimentation and learning, which make the constant redefinition of standards and shared goals possible.

An enabling state can be regarded as the next stage in the development of the Nordic welfare state for several reasons. The "old" Nordic welfare state created strong public enabling services including day care, basic, vocational, and adult education as well as public library services. An enabling welfare state will develop further these capability-cultivating and "civilizing" services. The creation of basic services was accompanied with the education of professional groups (e.g. teachers, special education teachers, school psychologists, school social workers) that together provide services, as well as with the organizing the research related to these services. As a result of this development, for instance, in Finland today highly competent multi-professional communities take care of education in schools. They are connected through further education and different projects to universities, research institutes, and professional and civic associations. These communities and their developmental networks constitute a foundation for the further development of the quality of enabling services.

The educational institutions created by the welfare state have radically changed the educational level of the population. A well-educated population provides a huge potential for theoretical, professional, and practical knowledge to be distributed across all spheres of society. This potential needs to be mobilized through innovative activity. It underlines the need to democratize innovation. Fourth, the Nordic countries have a strong tradition of local municipal governance. The decentralized provision of services based on wide national goals constitutes a good starting point for developing the "enabling governance" that stimulates local experimentation and the constant updating of national goals and standards around good practices.

Finally, the idea of an enabling welfare state can also be regarded as a reformulation of the idea of the virtuous circle of equality, economic development and democracy central to the ideology of the Nordic welfare state. One of the major theorists of the social democratic welfare state, economist Gunnar Myrdal, found that the major goal in the virtuous cycle was to release people's creative forces (Kettunen 1997: 170): "This was a precondition for social equality and welfare, but still more, promoting social equality was seen as a means by which human resources would be released."

Education and cultivation of individual capacities also decisively contribute to the innovativeness of a nation in three ways. They create the foundations for the absorptive capacities of firms and other organizations. Second, universal education contributes to the development of social capital and trust, making economic transaction easier and more reliable as well as enhancing creative collaboration between different professionals and social groups. Third, a high-quality and versatile vocational and tertiary education ensures that collaboration with firms and service providers can be fluently adopted to support even unexpected structural changes in the economy.

1.3 An overview of the book

This book is divided into two parts. The first five chapters analyse the foundations, emergence, and development of the national innovation system approach and its adoption in the Finnish science and technology policy in the 1990s and 2000s. The crisis and limitations of this policy framework in the 2000s is discussed. In the second part of the book an alternative viewpoint to innovation and welfare policy is outlined. It is based on the idea of capability-cultivating institutions as a key foundation both for national welfare and competitiveness. The development of the Finnish comprehensive school and its special education system is studied in order to clarify the nature of institutional change and learning and the conditions of governing and developing the enabling services. The concept of an enabling welfare state is developed to answer the challenges of the Nordic model of welfare in a globalizing knowledge-driven economy.

Chapter 2 reviews the rhetorical approaches that have been used in the study of technology policy language and paradigms. Specifically, it discusses how such concepts as *boundary concept, social representation, diagnosis of the era, and economic imaginary* have been used to explain the nature and success of policy buzzwords that have been developed interactively in research and policy making. The key role of the OECD as a central transnational institutional link between innovation research and policy making is examined. In addition, the rhetorical strategies used in the OECD technology policy documents to convince the national policy making audiences are analysed.

Chapter 3 reviews the emergence and development of the concept of a national innovation system in innovation and technology policy studies. Christopher Freeman introduced the term in 1987 in his analysis of the institutional reasons for the "developmental gap", that is, the differences in the rate of economic growth between Japan and the USA and between Japan and Europe. The other source of NIS comes from the idea of interactive learning, which was found to be important in the study of the national specificities of the small economies in the Nordic countries. The NIS approach is poorly connected to general or dynamic systems thinking and it is controversial as to whether it is able to provide an alternative to market failure theory that has served as a key foundation for science and technology policy making.

Chapter 4 analyses the adoption and use of NIS in the Finnish technology policy of the 1990s and 2000s and specifically in the triannual reviews of science and technology policy prepared by the Science and

Technology Policy Council of Finland. The term was used to create a favourable climate for R&D and innovation activity and a consensus around a national goal of competitiveness through systematic development of the Finnish NIS. The turn to social innovation and the extension of innovation into public services in the 2000s made innovation almost a synonym of a reforming society, challenging the firm-centred national innovation system approach.

Chapter 5 analyses the impacts of innovation policy and concludes that the Finnish economic miracle of the 1990s – rapid economic growth based on the rise of the Finnish ICT sector – cannot be explained by the "Finnish model" of innovation policy. Rather this development was due to the liberalization of financial markets, the fortunate decision of the Nokia management to focus on digital technology and cellular phones at the right time, as well as a sufficient supply of well-educated Finnish engineers. The innovation policy became directed by an innovation policy elite composed of representatives of R&D funding agencies, ministries, and big companies. The scientific, professional, and civic associations as well as service providers were largely excluded from the strategic decision-making. The last two sections of Chapter 5 develop an epistemology of transdiscursive terms. They argue that many of the policy buzzwords are powerful organizers of policy discourse and they direct the attention of various social groups to important social developments. However, to be performative, that is able to create social reality, they need to be complemented by relevant policy instruments and tools. These instruments are often not derivable from the policy concepts. Rather, they emerge out of the specific knowledge and expertise available in different domains of society. The experts and practitioners of these domains need to be mobilized and involved in the development of these instruments.

In Chapter 6 the development of the Finnish comprehensive school and its special education system is analysed as an instance of institutional change and development. The analysis also looks for explanations of the success of Finnish 15-year-old students in PISA tests. Among the main explanations are trust-based decentralized governance of the school, the esteem and popularity of the teaching profession, and a unique special education system. Research-based development of diagnostic and pedagogical tools constituted an essential foundation for professional expertise in school communities.

Chapter 7 argues that the further development of capability-cultivating universal services created by the welfare state in the 1970s and 1980s constitute an essential foundation for innovation and welfare policy in a knowledge-based economy. The financial crisis of the welfare state endangers the provision and quality of enabling services. The prevailing concepts of human capital, dynamic organizational capabilities, and the cognitive concept of individual intelligence and skills are not sufficient for developing a capability policy. A socio-cultural concept of self and creativity is needed in order to contribute to the construction of a sustainable capability policy and for the development of the quality of enabling services.

Chapter 8 summarizes the argument of the book through outlining a model of an enabling welfare state. This model can be seen as a new stage in the development of the Nordic welfare state. It reconstructs the old ideal of a virtuous cycle between economic development, increased welfare, equality, and the enlargement of democracy. The enabling welfare state develops further capability-cultivating services, assuming the role of organizer of institutional learning and local experimentation. It will be argued that public service provision is better able to enhance institutional learning than a system based on the market and competition. In addition, the limitations of a national view must be recognized. The basic moral principles of the welfare state such as equality of educational opportunity need to be extended to principles of global governance.

Chapter 9 presents the conclusions of the book in the form of policy recommendations for an enabling policy. Family policy, day care, basic and secondary education are vital areas to ensure the inclusions of all citizens in society. The professional and civic associations need to be included in policy making to mobilize relevant expertise, to ensure the implementation of reforms, and to deepen democracy. Local experimentation as well as horizontal and vertical learning in multiorganizational fields must be enhanced to ensure and develop the quality of services.

2

Institutional rhetoric between research and policy making

How do policy concepts and paradigms such as the NIS approach emerge and distribute, and how are they able to redirect policy making and finally be institutionalized in national policy making? To answer these questions, this chapter first reviews the rhetorical turn in the study of language and politics, with examples of the recent uses of rhetorical approaches in the study of science, technology, and politics. It will analyse how policy concepts emerge and develop in the borderline between research and policy making. Specifically it will discuss the role played by the OECD in the emergence and development of the national innovation system approach.

2.1 Rhetoric in science, technology, and innovation policy

The approach of classical rhetoric to language use and argumentation was developed as a part of the philosophy of antiquity. Rhetoric was one of the liberal arts that constituted the curriculum in the European universities until modern times. In the early 1900s it was left in the shadow of analytical philosophy and formal logic. It was then rehabilitated in the 1960s, and the new wave of rhetorical studies is often characterized as "new rhetoric" (Burke 1969; Perelman 1982). Whereas logic focused on the rules of logical inferences, rhetoric studies how a speaker or writer argues to convince an audience of the value of her/his position or of an alternative way of action. Historically, rhetoric was related to policy making. In the Greek *polis* the skill of convincing others, often characterized as eloquence, was an essential part of policy making and much esteemed. On the other hand, Greek philosophers developed theories of rhetoric for responsible language use in community life. Their work was further developed by several philosophers and orators in Roman and medieval times and it was a key part of philosophy studies in the curricula of early European universities. Several approaches of the "new rhetoric" were developed in the second half of the 20th century. Stephen Toulmin (1958) and Chaïm Perelman (Perelman and Olbrechts–Tytecal 1971) contributed to turn rhetoric from a study of eloquence into a study of reasoning and argumentation. Instead of focusing on logical inferences oriented to show that something is true, rhetoric focuses on argumentation that tries by rhetorical techniques and persuasion to win the support of an audience. In the 1970s and 1980s Quentin Skinner (1978) developed a rhetorical approach to the study of the conceptual change in politics. Concepts are resources to be used in political struggles. Political innovators manage both to give new extended meanings to them and change the contents and direction of the policy making. Another researcher of the development of policy concepts, Reinhart Koselleck, expressed this idea by saying (1982: 413): "concepts no longer merely serve to define states of affairs, they reach into the future." The tradition of critical discourse analysis in sociology (Fairclough 1992) and its variants in social psychology (Billig 1987; Potter 1996) have also studied language use in ideology and politics (for a review, see Finlayson 2004).

A rhetorical approach has been used in the study of persuasion and argumentation in scientific publications (Gross 1996; Ceccarelli 2001). Even in science, arguments and words cannot be understood merely in terms of their validity or their connection to empirical data. They are also "loaded" to serve an author's purposes and are addressed to particular audiences. Leah Ceccarelli (2001) has analysed the rhetoric means that Theodosius Dobzhansky used in his magnum opus *Genetics and the Origins of Species* (1937/1964) in order to get the separate communities of geneticists and biologists to work together toward the development of the modern evolutionary synthesis. Ceccarelli shows how Dobzhansky's book was a major intellectual achievement in its ability to synthesize the main achievements of the two disciplines and elaborate them in a forward-looking research programme.

The study of rhetoric in technology has been revitalized in recent years (for a review, see Godin 1997). Charles Bazerman's (1999) masterful analysis of the role of rhetoric and persuasion in Thomas Edison's creation of the electric light system is an apt example. Sulfikar Amir (2007) studied how technological nationalism was used to legitimate the development of Indonesian aircraft production. The production of aircraft in turn was used as a vehicle for fostering national identity based on pride in a technologically independent "modern" Indonesia. In the mid-1990s, technological nationalism was used to legitimate the transfer of money from the Reforestation Fund of Indonesia to complete a project of constructing a 30-seat aircraft.

In its analysis of the European innovation policy, an expert group of the European Commission on science policy (Taking European Knowledge Society Seriously 2007: 24) found what it called a "regime of technoscientific promise". According to the group (2007: 25), the first principle or rhetorical move operative in this regime is: "the creation of a fiction in order to attract resources (. . .) that the emerging technology (biotechnology in the 1980s, nanotechnology now) will solve human problems (health, sustainability, etc.) through a wide range of applications." This move was complemented by others, among them an argument according to which, in the world of competition, Europe does not have options (e.g. a social, less competitive model of society): "we must move forward if we are not to fall behind" (2007: 26).

Magnus Eklund (2007) has applied the Skinnerian approach of conceptual change to the study of the adoption of the innovation system concept in Sweden. It seems that the concept was not extensively used in the Swedish S&T documents and discussions in the 1990s. The S&T discussions were framed by other concepts, such as industrial networks, developmental blocks, and social relevance. The system of innovation concept was adopted as a rhetorical resource in 2000 in a political debate over the funding of sectoral research. It was used against the suggestion that control of the funding for sectoral research should be given to the research councils and in order to justify the foundation of a new funding organization, VINNOVA (the Swedish Governmental Agency for Innovation Systems). The new agency was to direct the funding so as to foster technological change and contribute to the innovativeness of industry instead of making grants on the basis of the scientific quality of the research proposals.

Shirley Leitch and Sally Davenport (2005) use critical discourse theory to analyse the change in the science and technology policy language in New Zealand between 1995 and 2000. They analyse how market concepts were gradually adopted and developed by the New Zealand Foundation of Science and Technology. The main term used first was "excellence", which gave way to "relevance" and finally to "horizon", which was originally introduced by McKinsey and Company, a consulting group (2005: 905). The terms "basic research" and "applied research" were replaced by four economic horizons that were used in making funding decisions. The broadest terms used in the policy language of the foundation were "knowledge society" and "knowledge economy".

Robert Jessop (2008) and Gnai Lim Sum (2010) have developed an approach for the study of policy buzzwords or paradigms that they call "cultural political economy" (CPE). It combines discourse analysis and Gramchi's idea of hegemony to critical political economy of capitalism. The epistemic starting point for the approach is that "the actually existing economy" as chaotic sum of all economic activities must be distinguished from *economic imaginaries*. The actually existing economy is so complex and chaotic that it cannot be made an object of calculation and management. Instead economic imaginaries – such as NIS or knowledge-based economy – select a subset of economic relations as an object of calculation, management, and intervention (Jessop 2008: 16). The approach shares with the evolutionary economics of innovation the ideas of variation, selection and retention of the economic imaginaries. The proponents of economic imaginaries try to achieve a hegemonic position for them as a policy paradigm and as an account of the present economy.

Ngai-Ling Sum (2010) presents an illuminating analysis of the development of the concept "competitiveness". According to Sum, Porter's model of competitive advantage and his concept of cluster represents the most recent phase in the discussion of competitiveness. She analyses how, by whom and by what mechanisms Porter's model became widely used in Asian countries. Among them was the Institute of Strategy and Business established in 2001 at the Harvard Business School (HBS) to disseminate Professor Porter's ideas. Several other institutes and consultancy firms associated with HBS were established in Europe and Asia. Because of the strong commercial aspect in dissemination of Porter's model, Sum calls it a *knowledge brand* that is promoted as a policy-making instrument at the national, regional, and local levels.[1] Several international (e.g. World Economic Forum), regional (Asian Development Bank), national, and city organizations actively participated in the promotion of the model in Asia. In addition to high-esteem seminars and consultancy, the model is also distributed by benchmarking reports and indices such as the *Global Competition Report* designed by the World Economic forum based on Porter's model. It ranks and score countries in relation to the presence/absence of certain factors of competitiveness. The publisher of the report, Macmillan, advertised it as a "unique

---

[1] "In this context a knowledge brand can be defined as a resonant hegemonic meaning making device promoted by the 'world-class' guru-academic consultants who claim unique knowledge of economic world and pragmatically turn them into transnational policy recipes and tool kits" (Sum 2010: 191).

benchmarking tool in identifying obstacles to economic growth and assist in the design of better economic policies" (Sum 2010: 192).

Jessop underlines that economic imaginaries are not only rhetorical devices to convince an audience. They have a performative and constitutive force. Economic imaginaries (Jessop 2008: 18) "identify and seek to stabilize some economic activities among the totality of economic relations and transform them into objects of observation calculation and governance." In order to do that a set of resources and instrumentalities are used, such as statistical indicators, benchmarks, and league tables, as well as producing a set of useful concepts, slogans, and policy prescriptions.

2.2 Making sense of concepts that transcend the boundaries between science and policy making

Science and technology studies and the social sciences have suggested several concepts in an effort to understand the nature and power of the concepts that transcend the boundaries between science, policy, and public discourse. I (2002) called the concept of a national innovation system a "transdiscursive term", because it only can be understood as developing simultaneously and interactively in innovations research and policy making. It is both a scientific concept that is elaborated and discussed in communities of innovation researchers and a political term used by national and international (OECD and EU) policymakers. To understand its dynamics, different meanings and uses in both of these contexts must be analysed as well as the transitions from one context to another. Other concepts used to analyse this kind of term include *director of attention* or *an umbrella concept* (Godin 2006), *boundary concept* (Löwy 1992), *social representation* (Moscovici 1984), as well as *Zeitdiagnose* or diagnosis of the era (Mannheim 1943; Noro 2000).

Benoît Godin (2006) finds that the introduction of the label "knowledge-based economy" is indistinguishable from larger attempts to develop indicators in order to measure science and technology development. In 1996 the OECD started to develop a set of indicators to measure knowledge-based economy. However, most of the indicators collected were indicators that the OECD had already measured for years. They were now reorganized under the concept of a knowledge-based economy. They do not, however, Godin thinks, measure satisfactorily knowledge distribution or use which were central to the concept "knowledge-based economy". Godin therefore concludes that the concept should be primarily understood as a director of attention or an umbrella concept (2006: 17):

> I suggest that the concept of a knowledge-based economy is simply a concept that serves to direct the attention of policy makers to science and technology issues and their role in economy and, to this end, a concept that allows one to talk about any issue of science and technology and generate a large set of statistics under one roof. This kind of concept I will call an umbrella concept.

In a study of the history of immunology, Ilana Löwy stated in 1992 that whereas well-defined scientific concepts guide the work of coherent scientific groups, an emphasis on fuzzy or loose concepts is necessary for the investigation of relations across disciplinary boundaries. Löwy refers to Ludwig Fleck (1979), who noted that a certain scientific term often has different meanings in different communities or "thought collectives". Fleck further suggested that the variance in the meaning of terms that circulate among different thought collectives might lead to scientific innovation. Löwy thinks that fuzzy, imprecise terms can be regarded as "boundary concepts".[2] They permit partial agreement on the usage of a term, thus allowing participants from different collectives to maintain their original professional cultures. It is the very fuzziness of a term that permits it to function as an interdisciplinary organizer, thus enabling different groups to articulate a roughly shared direction of interests and moral commitments and still maintain their own identity and interests.

Löwy's analysis is focused on boundary crossing between scientists and physicians. Her idea, however, may well be applied also to inter-actions between scientific, policy, and business communities. In his analysis of institutional change in policy arena, Christopher Ansell (2011: 48) introduces the concept "metaconcept". A metaconcept is a boundary object that facilitates communication and interaction across boundaries and maintains a space for localized practice. Metaconcepts facilitate transaction between local, national, and international policing. In addition, they entail a teleology (2011: 50): "as multivocal

---

[2] The concept of the boundary object was originally introduced by Star and Griesemer in 1989. Bowker and Star (1999: 297) define the concept as follows: "Boundary objects are those objects that both inhabit several communities of practice and satisfy the informational requirements of each of them. Boundary objects are thus plastic enough to adapt to local needs and constraints of the several parties employing them, yet robust enough to maintain common identity across the sites. They are weakly structured in common use and become strongly structured in individual site-use. (...). Such objects have different meanings in different social worlds but their structure is common enough to more than one world to make them recognizable, a means of translation. The creation and management of boundary objects is a key process in developing and maintaining coherence across intersecting communities."

boundary objects (...) metaconcepts can often serve as a powerful rallying point and banner for large-scale institutional change." The multivocal and boundary spanning nature of metaconcepts help to knit different projects and goals together. Their ambiguous nature is an advantage because it enables them to have a wider appeal. The national innovation system may well be regarded as a metaconcept that is operative in several different contexts. Charles Edquist (1997: 16), for example, suggests that the systems innovation approach has a three-fold function of "a means for studying innovations, as a conceptual framework for government policy-making, and as a basis for formulating the innovation strategies of firms."

Another researcher of science, Peter Galison, has studied how the representatives of subcultures in physics (theorists, experimenter, and instrument makers) develop locally a pidgin in order to coordinate their actions (1997). Sometimes these pidgins disappear, sometimes they extend into creoles that gain an established position in a field of research. Although the concept of pidgin deals with the emergence of a local vocabulary in one discipline, it may be extended, like a boundary object, to cover the transactions between research, policy, and public opinion.

A boundary concept may also fail to reconcile the contradictory expectations and interests of social groups and stakeholders. Luigi Burroni and Maarten Keune (2011) have analysed one of the concepts that plays a central role in the European Union Employment strategy, *flexicurity*. Flexicurity is an attempt to reconcile and combine two traditionally opposite trends: fostering labour market flexibility on the one hand and providing security to individual on the other. Some of the commentators find that complementarity between the two can be achieved. Some authors think it remains an aspiration or a "composite resolution", a linguistic combination of opposites that can be applied to virtually any policy mix. Most of the flexicurity researchers agree that flexicurity is an ambiguous and vague concept. Some authors find this a strength since the term "can be used to address a range of sometimes contradictory policy goals" (Rogowski 2008: 86). Burroni and Keune (2011: 78–79), in turn, view the conceptual ambiguity as a weakness for two reasons. First, the concept is so vague that fundamentally different views of labour market problems with different policy implications can be aligned with it. Therefore, its utility as a guide for policy is questionable, they think. Second, employers and unions disagree on many aspects of the flexicurity debate in the European Union. This leads to a situation in which the flexicurity concept has become widely accepted but where at the same time a struggle takes place in which different actors try to impose their favourite interpretation.

The French social psychologist Serge Moscovici (1984) has studied what happens to a concept when it is transferred from science to policy or popular use and becomes part of everyday thinking. He analysed the transfer of concepts and ideas of psychoanalysis to media, popular books, and the everyday language of the public at large. Moscovici defines two mechanisms of how ideas become social representations or "commons-sense objects": objectification and anchoring. In anchoring the new concept is connected to the prevailing system of concepts and beliefs. In objectification ideas are made material and we distance ourselves from them (2008: 55):

> Ideas are no more perceived to be products of intellectual activity of certain minds and are seen as something that exists outside. Something that was known has been replaced by something that is perceived. The gap between science and the real narrows, and what was specific to a concept comes to look like a property of its counterpart in the real world.

The process of reification is connected to objectification: a human construction becomes a natural entity. In reification an abstract and tentative concept is made into a "given", a self-evident and tangible entity, which, therefore, exists in reality without any doubt. In the case of NIS, reification seems an apt characterization. In policy discourse NIS has become a tangible entity and an object of planning instead of just a tentative concept of making sense of complex social and material realities.

In sociology, the visionary concepts of present society have been analysed in terms of a particular genre of theorizing that one might call a "diagnosis of the era". The term comes from the German word *Zeitdiagnose* and does not have an established counterpart in the English language. A good early representative of this genre is Karl Mannheim's *Diagnosis of Our Time* (1943), written during the Second World War. It analyses the use of social technology by the totalitarian states and the crisis of the values in the society. Mannheim believed that a *Zeitdiagnose* can show a way to a new social philosophy. The Finnish sociologist Arto Noro (2000) has analysed the *Zeitdiagnose* as a specific genre of sociological theorizing. It differs from general social theories and from research theories oriented to empirical study of societies. Analyses of an era cannot be directly used or tested in empirical research, although they are based on results deriving from it. We need diagnoses of our time in order to make sense of what kind of a society we live in and what is happening to us. They orient us to the future by characterizing the present. They generate research questions and stimulate the development of more elaborate concepts and theories. According to Noro, a diagnosis of an era is "a performative message sent out of the sphere of scientific communication" (2000: 324). The genre of the diagnosis of an era operates in the social territory between research, public discourse, and politics.

2.3 Statistics, indicators, and policy document writing practices

One of the assumptions of rhetoric is that arguments and concepts can bring about changes in human practice. By focusing mainly on written and spoken texts, rhetorical analyses are seldom able to analyse the practical implementation and consequences of promises, arguments and or ideas. In this sense they cannot fully substitute for ethnographical studies, where actual practical activity is observed in the context of the language use related to it. The only substantial study of the practice of policy document writing and policy making I have come across is "Representing biotechnology: An ethnography of Quebec science policy" (Cambrosio *et al.* 1990). The authors interviewed civil servants of the Quebec administration, observed staff meetings, and had full access to "raw texts" (memos, drafts, etc.) relating to biotechnology policy making.

Their data revealed two key policy-making procedures. The first was the creation of a "folder" for the new object to be planned. This folder included a classificatory system with legitimate categories of biotechnology and its subfields that covered the external world of biotechnology, its main representatives, etc. It steered the collection of relevant data and existed as a file of information with relevant documents that could be circulated within the administration. The second procedure they call "intertextual webs". They found that the policy documents were "literally packed with explicit or implicit references to, or borrowings from, other documents" (1990: 216). The intertextual practice, that is, referring to and quoting from documents, took the following forms:

1) References to previous government decisions and plans. Constant mention of the texts embodying previous public commitments of the government, decisions of the cabinet and action plans. "These formal references clearly aim at showing how the new actions proposed follow, or agree with, previous government decisions" (Cambrosio *et al.* 1990: 216).

2) References to documents of other governments or international organizations such as the OECD. Other formal references are made to the documents embodying decisions taken by other governments or to recommendations of such well-established organizations as the OECD.

3) References to a government's own regulatory documents, such as laws pertaining to financial administration or ministerial responsibilities.

4) Constant use of published information from government sources that gives readers basic concepts, facts, and statistics so that they can make sense of the issue and that is "conductive to the understanding of the actions suggested as opportune – nay, necessary" (1990: 217).

5) Tacit borrowings, often word for word, from a broad range of sources, documents written by other civil servants, from other sections or sometimes even other ministries.

As will be seen, the concept of intertextuality will be useful in analysing the distribution of OECD-mediated policy terms such as "National innovation policy".

Mathieu Albert and Suzanne Laberge (2007) have studied how and why the science and technology administration of Quebec in Canada adopted the NIS approach. They interviewed the civil servants who participated in the formation and implementation of the innovation policy. They have also asked why the innovations system approach has been adopted by public administrations around the world so rapidly and what role the OECD has played in the process. Lundvall *et al.* (2002: 214) asked the same question: "It is interesting to speculate why the concept has diffused so rapidly among scholars and policy makers."

The answer that Albert and Laberge provide to this question is twofold. First, by virtue of its cultural authority as an international organization, the OECD has been able to use scientifically distinguished scholars in their programme work. With their involvement the systems approach acquires the authority of science and was thereby legitimized as an authoritative approach to national policy making. In the study done by Albert and Laberge most of the interviewed civil servants recognized this authority without reservations. As one of them explained: "The OECD is bit like a global forum for economic thinkers. (. . .) I think that if we are quick to accept OECD recommendations, it is because we feel that they come from committed professionals who base their findings on studies from leading scientists" (2007: 229).

Another explanation for the rapid adoption of the systems approach is that the Oslo Manual provided a tool for policy making both at national and regional levels. The indicators for measuring the efficiency of an innovation system are presented in the Oslo Manual. In the words of one of the policymakers interviewed by Albert and Laberge (2007: 231), "We try as much as possible to evaluate the efficacy of our innovation system using the indicators from the OECD Oslo Manual, to compare ourselves with other regions and countries." Two regional bodies had developed their own frameworks for analysing the regional innovation system based on the Oslo manual, as well as specific management report cards, progress reports, and benchmarking schemes (2007: 238–239). By analysing the weaknesses and strengths of the system they hoped to be able to create a more favourable environment for innovative business activities. Albert and Laberge think that the absence of indicators can explain why other policy concepts, such as new production of knowledge (Gibbons *et al.* 1994) or triple helix (Etzkowitz and Leydesdorff 2000) have not generated nearly as much interest as NIS among public administrators.

2.4 OECD task forces as international fabrics of technology policy language

The OECD has played a central role in advancing science and technology policy institutions in its member countries, in organizing the creation and unification of science and technology statistics as well as in making comparisons between the member countries. The introduction of the concept of national innovation shows that the OECD is also a producer of policy language. Godin (2006: 3) calls the OECD as "a research think-tank that feeds policy makers". It is an international arena in which technology policy language and tools are produced, maintained, and distributed. It is a hybrid forum composed of the representatives of national policy-making agencies (such as ministries, funding organizations, and civil servants), of OECD and EU officials, and of science and technology policy researchers. It is this structure that makes it an efficient producer and distributor of new concepts and tools. Within the OECD, the task force for Technology and Innovation Policy (TIP) under the Commission of Science and Technology Policy (CSTP) has been particularly active in organizing projects, seminars, and conferences dedicated to innovation policy.

In 1995, the TIP task force initiated a project devoted to national innovation systems. The first phase of the project focused on the comparison of national innovation systems aiming to create a set of quantitative indicators for that purpose (OECD 1997a). In the second phase, the project was divided into a number of focus groups in such areas as innovative firm networks, clusters and mobility of human resources. Three publications emerged: *Managing National Innovation Systems* (1999a), and two proceedings related to cluster policy (1999b and 2001c). A further project produced two more reports on NIS policy in the early 2000s (OECD 2002 and 2005). Simultaneously with the OECD's NIS project the European Commission published its *Green Paper on Innovation* in 1995 and initiated a project on innovation policy entitled Targeted Socioeconomic Research. A report summarizing the results of the projects for policy purposes expressed the core idea of the work (Lundvall and Borrás 1997: 3): "One basic objective of the exercise has been to provide policy-makers a reasonably coherent 'world view' and with basic principles of policy making on innovation in the new context."

Finnish participants have characterized the mission of the OECD TIP group as follows:

> On the general level, the goal of TIP is to review the science and technology policy measures of different nations, make international comparisons and give, on their grounds, good policy practice recommendations. The work of the group is focusing on three areas: a) regard on national innovation systems, b) the development of good practices of technology and innovation policy and, c) international issues of technology. (Husso and Kangaspunta, 1999: 584)

The researcher participants come from specialized science and technology policy units (such as the Science Policy Research Unit in England), universities, and business schools. There is close collaboration between these three groups. All of them participate in the preparation of OECD policy documents by organizing programmes, projects, and regular meetings, as well as seminars where papers and manuscripts are presented and discussed.

As an example we can take the four-year study by the TIP task force on the relevance of national innovation systems in 1996–1999. After the presentation of country reports in the form of the descriptions of the national systems of the participating countries, several focus groups were formed "to conduct in-depth studies of particular aspects of the innovation system" (OECD 1999b: 7). One or two member countries with a special interest in and knowledge of some particular topic functioned as organizers of the focus-group work, assuming responsibility for preparatory work, coordinating the research and organizing the meetings. Among the groups was the group on clusters (the leading country being the Netherlands), another on innovative firm networks (led by Denmark) and the third on human resource mobility (led by Norway and Sweden).

In this respect NIS constituted a new type of activity within the OECD (1999a: 3): "Many countries volunteered to lead the work in the focus groups; and their significant financial and intellectual resources made the exercise possible." Sixty-one representatives from 16 countries participated in the NIS project. Most of the 32 representatives were civil servants from ministries or research councils of the member states. Ten of them came from national research institutes, such as the Institute of Economic Research (Austria), The Flemish Technology Observatory (Belgium) and the Center for European Economic Research (Germany). Ten participants came from universities (1999b: 171–172). There were also some consultants in the national groups. Evidently, country reports and focus studies were done by research institutes funded by national agencies.

Such a collective preparation mechanism assures that ideas are quickly transmitted to national policies. The administrations of the participating countries are involved in the work through their own contributions, and the documents produced are disseminated to all participants. The project produces a pool of textual raw material to be used in the writing of policy documents in the member countries. Thus, several national research institutions are involved in studies that follow the guidelines laid down in the OECD groups. In this regard, the researchers have multiple roles. They provide the early ideas and preliminary results of their own studies for inclusion in the documents, collect comparative data for reports, and, to a certain extent, participate in writing the OECD reports. Above all, the institutional procedure supplies the civil servants of the national science and technology administrations with a window on the recent results and ideas of the international innovation and policy research and an invaluable source material for drafting national policy documents. This corresponds with what Finnemore (1993: 586) found in her study of UNESCO: "Studies often were coupled with meetings of government science officials from member states. Governmental participation in producing the recommendations of these studies ensured that these recommendations were reaching the desired audience."

2.5 Rhetorical features of the OECD NIS policy documents

The policy documents produced by the OECD and the EU (for example, OECD 1992, 1997b, 1998; for EU contributions, see Lundvall and Borrás 1997) have a constitutive role in the formation of an internationally shared policy framework. To be able to provide "a reasonably coherent 'world view' and basic principles of policy making" to policymakers, these texts surely must adopt rhetorical strategies which differ from those of other types of texts. As suggested by Moscovici, in order to create a world view, it is important to be in contact with science, which produces constantly the new conceptualizations on which policy language is dependent. The reference to science is also important for the trustworthiness of the knowledge used to substantiate the policy recommendations.

The use of the concept "intertextuality" by Cambrosio *et al.* may be applied to an analysis of the creation of policy documents by OECD science and technology policy bodies. For this purpose, a distinction must be made between two kinds of OECD policy documents: actual policy documents, which are anonymous, unitary programme reports, and more heterogeneous collections of papers. The first are self-contained, unitary policy documents, typically the end products of the major TIP programme. They supply definitions of basic concepts, background information, and policy recommendations (OECD 1997b, 1998, and 1999a). Each of them, therefore, constitutes an attempt to define a "world view" in a single document. The other type of publication consists of OECD proceedings that collect papers presented in seminars organized by OECD focus groups and projects. These papers are written by researchers, OECD officials, and civil servants of participating nations. In the latter instance, these papers are often descriptive reviews or accounts of a country's policy experiences, often without substantial basis in empirical research or references to literature. The *STI Review*, published since 1980, has the same kind of heterogeneous profile. Most of its items resemble papers published in the scientific journals, but opinions and country reviews are also included.

In the following, I will outline some features of the policy documents produced by major OECD projects. I will use the two major OECD reports on NIS, *National Innovation System* (1997) and *Managing National Innovation Systems* (1999a), as my examples. Without undertaking any systematic analysis of the contents of these reports, I will make some general comments on their most obvious common features as texts: 1) anonymity; 2) a tendency to use clear-cut and converging definitions of basic concepts; 3) self-referentiality; 4) extensive use of unpublished papers prepared for the OECD, selective use of books and fairly scanty use of papers from scientific journals; 5) dependency on economic literature; and 6) background knowledge and results of studies that are presented in the form of separate text boxes, tables of statistics and figures that are largely independent of the text and might be called "knowledge windows".

The first distinguishing feature of the OECD policy documents is that they are anonymous. Since there is no author, the reader does not know who is speaking. This might be designed to give the text an appearance of greater objectivity, as it is presented as the work of a collective of experts. Because of the purpose of the document, viz. the creation of a shared world view for policy makers, the basic concepts are defined clearly, concisely, and definitively. When various definitions are presented, they move in the same direction and are complementary. No critical or adverse points of view are presented. Hilkka Summa (1989) found similar features in her study of planning rhetoric in the documents of Finnish public administration: two key elements were the use of the passive voice and the almost total absence of self-reflection.[3] Both NIS reports (1997: 10 and 1999a: 24) contain converging definitions from the literature. Both documents use the definition of NIS by Metcalfe (1995), taken from the *Handbook of Economics of Innovation and Technical Change*:

> A set of distinct institutions which jointly and individually contribute to the development and diffusion of new technologies and which provides the framework within which governments form and implement policies to influence the innovation process. As such it is a system of interconnected institutions to create, store and transfer the knowledge, skills and artifacts which define new technologies.

This definition is well suited to the purposes of the document, owing to its surface clarity and to its characterization of a national innovation system both as a social phenomenon and as a framework for policy making. In addition to converging verbal definitions, a pictorial model of a national innovations system (Figure 2.1) is presented that depicts

---

[3] "The planning prose has certain special features that distinguish it from, for instance, artistic, scientific and or journalistic text productions. Among these are the dominance of the passive voice in expressing activities and events which distinguish it both from the scientific and the journalistic expression. The administrative planning texts are distinguished from the scientific texts especially by the almost complete absence of self-reflection. The planning text does not situate itself nor reflect upon its own foundations, but gives an image of stating 'self-evident' facts" (Summa 1989: 179).

"actors and linkages in the innovations system" (1999a: 23). The source of this model is given simply as "OECD". The 1997 document claims that it is possible to trace the links and relationships in the system and that such an analysis "may ultimately lead to the ability to measure the knowledge-distribution power of a national innovation system, which is considered one determinant of growth and competitiveness" (1997: 11). As will be shown in the next chapter, the conclusions and results of the comparisons of national systems would not support such an assertion (e.g. Nelson 1993).

The most authoritative outcomes of this sort of work are anonymous policy documents (for example, OECD 1997b and 1999a). Although they contain ingredients from research results (partly from projects that were commissioned and funded by the OECD), the connection to research is not fully transparent. Some of the references in the documents point to unpublished papers given in different OECD workshops, and these are practically unavailable to anyone who was not a participant.

Table 2.1. References included in OECD Reports *National Innovation System* (1997), *Managing National Innovation Systems* (1999a) and *Dynamising National Innovation System* (2002) and *Governance of Innovation Systems* (2005) according to document type (given in percentages).[4]

	OECD 1997	OECD 1999a	OECD 2002	OECD 2005
1. OECD (reports, papers for seminars, STI Review)	37.0	40.9	62.5	50.00
2. Reports and documents issued by the EU and other international bodies	3.7	9.9	–	5.2
3. Reports of national ministries and bureaus of statistics	3.7	7.0	3.1	3.4
4. Reports and working papers of research institutions	14.8	5.6	8.3	15.5
5. Unpublished conference and symposium papers	14.8	2.8	9.4	8.6
6. Newspapers and non-scientific professional magazines	–	2.8	1.0	–
7. Books or book chapters	18.6	18.3	9.4	6.9
8. Papers published in scientific journals	7.4	12.7	6.3	10.4
Total	100.0	100.0	100.00	100.00
N =	27	71	96	58

[4] For the sake of comparison, I also analysed the references of a major OECD report entitled *Technology, Productivity and Job Creation* (1998) with 296 items in its bibliography. The distribution was very similar to that presented in Table 2.1. The references to OECD documents accounted for 35.1% and those to scientific papers for 10.5%.

Table 2.1 presents the distribution of the items in the lists of references contained in the four NIS reports according to the type of document. The degree of self-referentiality is fairly high: in the 1990s about 40% of these references pointed to other OECD publications or papers. In the documents of the 2000s this figure rose to more than half of all the references. About 60% of the references were to "political" documents (categories 1, 2, and 3). The share of the references to scientific journal papers was about 10%.

The most frequently cited journal is *Research Policy*, and the rest of the journal references are to economic journals. There are no references to journals devoted to the social sciences or the humanities. The last fact suggests that NIS language is primarily derived from economic theorizing. The documents present the customary account that the emergence of the innovation policy is generally contemporaneous to the transition from neoclassical economic theory to an evolutionary theory that focuses on institutional conditions of innovations and interactions between economic actors. The new growth theory and institutional economics are also included in the contributions (OECD 1999a). The systems approach can be seen as deriving from the interactive conception of the evolutionary approach in its focus on interactive learning among producers, researchers and users.

These texts generally have a particular way of presenting the results of preparatory studies and relevant research literature in the form of *text boxes, tables, and figures* that summarize the background assumptions of documents and the results of the preparatory work. They often include a mass of information and background assumptions that are not discussed further in the texts themselves. Little or no information is given about how they were produced. Consequently, they cannot be submitted to critical scrutiny. Detached from the context of their production and, partly, from the text themselves, they tend to become free-standing "knowledge windows". They supply examples, illuminate and accompany the main line of argument of the documents, giving them face validity by referring to the world of science and research.

In *Managing National Innovation Systems* (1999a), the "institutional profiles", which are various kinds of organizational charts meant to represent the national innovation systems as taken from the national reports, are such pictorial icons. Figure 2.1, from *Managing National Innovation Systems* (1999a: 23), depicts the contributing factors and their linkages in the innovation system.

The source of the model is given laconically as "OECD". The flowchart is largely self-sustaining. Its elements are discussed in the text only briefly. The model depicts structures but not interactive processes that

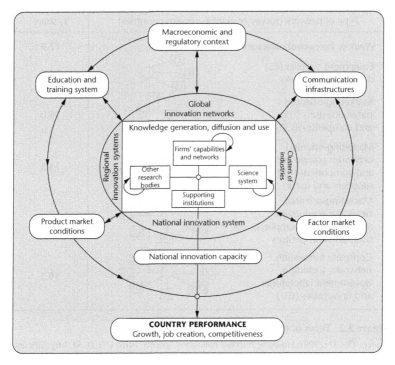

Figure 2.1. Actors and linkages in the innovation system

Source: OECD (1999a), *Managing National Innovation Systems*. Paris: OECD, 23. http://dx.doi.
org/10.1787/9789264189416-en

are essential for the system dynamics theory (Forrester 1968). It is complemented with a selection of verbal definitions of NIS and the exposition of the three levels of analysis of national innovation systems (micro-, meso-, and macro-), both presented in separate boxes. Most of the elements and the logic of the figure are not further explicated.

An example of the presentation of condensed study results as an icon is depicted in Figure 2.2, "Types of firm networks". It shows the distribution of such networks into five distinct types in eight European countries as presented in two documents (OECD 1998: 60 and 1999a: 54). Its labelling system seems also to constitute a kind of generalized, normative tool for evaluating the quality of the firms' network connections. How the data for the national comparisons were collected remains open, as well as whether real firms fit the categories. The figure and the accompanying text give references only to an unpublished draft paper (DeBresson *et al.* 1997) prepared by the OECD itself, which makes it

Type of network (survey of eight European countries)	% share
Weak or no network linkages	12.9
Equipment supplier (ES) dominated networks	14.4
Marketing-oriented networks: users (US) and competitors(CO)	16.0
Marketing-oriented networks: equipment and component (CM) suppliers and users	15.8
Marketing-oriented networks: equipment and component suppliers, users and competitors	21.9
Complete innovation networks, including government laboratories and universities (GU)	19.1

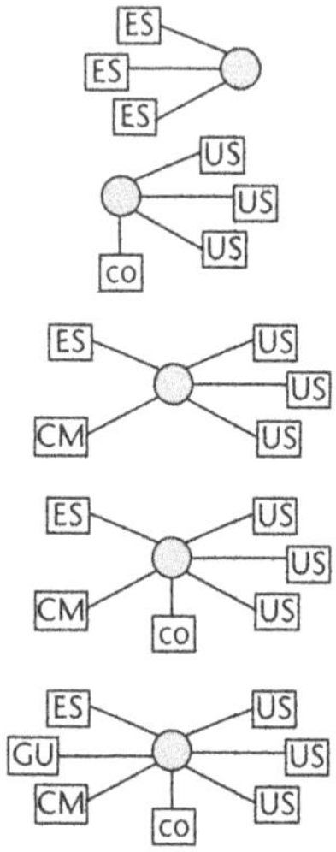

Figure 2.2. Types of firm networks

Source: OECD (1999), *Managing National Innovation Systems.* Paris: OECD, 54. http://dx.doi.org/10.1787/9789264189416-en

impossible to answer these questions or to learn more about the study. The figure is presented in a section where networking is dealt with as "an effective innovation technique in its own right" (1997: 53). The sentence that refers to the figure tells that "innovating firms generally interact with several partners rather than with a single one" (1997: 54). The implications of the results presented in the figure for technology policy are not discussed in the text.

Other features mentioned by Cambrosio *et al.* can be found in the documents. One of them is frequent use of comparative statistics. My intention, however, is to show the relevance of a rhetorical analysis of international policy documents. Such an analysis will serve to clarify the connection between the nature of the texts, the process and organization of their production and their intended use.

3

NIS in innovation and technology policy research

3.1 Two sources of NIS: An understanding of the institutional conditions of a technology gap and the idea of interactive learning

The first main source for introducing the NIS approach was an attempt to understand the reasons for the difference in economic growth rates between industrialized countries. Research in the 1980s sought to find out what causes technological gaps between nations and, especially, what made Japan's astonishing technological and economic progress possible. Christopher Freeman's study of the national innovation system of Japan, published in 1987, provided answers to these questions.

Bengt-Åke Lundvall is among the economists who wanted to develop an alternative to neoclassical economic theory, which explained economic development in terms of capital and labour accumulation. Lundvall emphasized interactive learning and innovation as the key pillars of economic growth. His theorizing on interactive learning constitutes the second main source of the term "national innovation system".

Several major attempts have been made to characterize the nature of NIS as a research framework and as policy tool. They include the work of Charles Edquist (1997 and 2005), of Richard Nelson (1993) and his colleagues, and Beng-Åke Lundvall's (2004) recent outline for a NIS approach.[1] After analysing these attempts, I will review the theoretical foundations – besides evolutionary economics – suggested for NIS. They vary from thermodynamics and general systems theory, new growth

---

[1] In an early review, Maureen McKelvey (1991) distinguished between the four NIS approaches of Porter, Freeman, Lundvall, and Nelson, and made comparisons between them. Her review does not discuss the political background or uses of NIS.

theory in economics, and biological theory of knowledge, to Nicklas Luhman's theory of social systems. The more policy-bound, practical definitions focus on the interactions of the national institutions that have promoted innovations.

In the early 1990s, two major books on national innovation systems were published. *The National Systems of Innovation* by Lundvall and the Aalborg group (1992) is a theoretical introduction to the subject. It introduced a conception that is often called an interactive learning concept of NIS. The other book, *National Innovation Systems: A comparative analysis*, edited by Richard Nelson (1993), includes empirical analyses of the innovations systems of 14 countries. Its theoretical orientation will be discussed in the following section. At the time these books appeared, there was no accepted or shared concept of NIS in the research community, but only a loose framework and projects that were oriented towards creating and testing one.

A background context for the new innovation policy was the globalization of economic competition between nations. Richard Nelson and Nathan Rosenberg characterized the new spirit as "technonationalism" (1993: 3). It combined the belief that the technological capabilities of a nation's firms are the key source of their competitive prowess, with a belief that these capabilities are, in a sense, national and can be built by national action. This is the general context within which the creation and further development of the new innovation policy and the concept of NIS took place.

Lundvall *et al.* (2002) noted that we should not place the emphasis on the intellectual origins of the NIS concept. Instead, its main background should be found in the needs of policymakers and students of innovation. These needs were found to be intertwined.

> The activities of national governments and international organizations like the OECD had during the 1960s and 1970s led to an immense interest in reasons why national growth rates differ and one of the explanations was differences in the research systems of the different countries. For researchers who tried to combine general economics with innovation studies, such explanations seemed just to scratch the surface of the issue. (Lundvall *et al.* 2002: 215)

The new knowledge needed for innovation obviously did not come from universities or technical research but rather from engineering, customers, marketing, and elsewhere. These sources needed to be included in an innovation system. This concept was also present in the comparative studies of national styles of innovation management exemplified by Freeman's study of the Japanese NIS.

In the 1980s, linear models of innovation were replaced by interactive ones, in which various factors and actors are all instrumental (Freeman 1979). Lundvall (1992) elaborated this idea when making learning in producer-user interaction a key issue for the study of national systems of innovation. The idea was further extended to cover the flow and synergy of ideas, knowledge, expertise, and combinations of resources of various public and private institutions. The transition to a new innovation policy could, therefore, be characterized as a transition from "the intellectual domination of the linear model" to the systems of innovation approach (Caracostas 1998: 308). In this context, it must be noted that The acceptance of the idea of interactive explanation, however, does not presuppose the acceptance of a systems approach in a strong sense, that is, as a system whose key elements and interactions can be defined on a reasonable theoretical and empirical basis. For instance, the actor-network theorists in the field of sociology of science and technology who developed the conception of innovation process as a network construction categorically rejected any systems description or explanation (Crawford 1993; Miettinen 1999a).

The concept of NIS was first used in empirical research by Freeman in his book *Technology Policy and Economic Performance: Lessons from Japan* (1987). The technological and economic development in Japan was rapid, and the leading position of the USA seemed to be waning. Freeman's book was an attempt to explain why this should be so. Freeman used the concept of a national innovation system to cover those features in Japanese economy and society that could explain the growth of their economy.[2] He found five factors:

1) the role of the government in the modernization of Japanese economy, and, particularly, the activity of the Ministry of International Trade and Industry (MITI),

2) education and training as key components of this modernization,

3) an intensive effort to import and improve the best technologies in the world (through reverse engineering),

4) close co-operation between the government and big industrial concerns, and

5) the formation of vertically integrated groups of firms known as *keiretsus*.

---

[2] In Freeman's view, a national innovation system is a "network of institutions in the public and private sectors whose activities and interactions initiate, import, modify, and diffuse new technologies." This resembles his interactive idea of innovations. Interestingly, he defines the system in terms of a network.

Freeman's study is an early example of the revival of institutional economics (see e.g. Hodgson 2004; Nee 2005). Whereas neoclassical economics is oriented toward modelling the equilibrium of economy using sophisticated mathematical methods and is based on the concept of an individual behaving rationally in the market, institutional economics suggest that institutions interfere with the workings of markets. A national bank system is not allowed to collapse, basic research and education are publicly funded, various institutional arrangements have been developed to stimulate innovation or university-firm interaction. Institutional economics also suggests that nations can derive competitive advantage from their institutional infrastructure (Hall and Soskice 2001). This is exactly what Freeman's study is making sense of. The institutional concept of NIS was further developed by Richard Nelson (2002), who initiated a research programme in 1987 to analyse and compare the differences in national innovation systems with the participation of several research groups.[3]

The second main source of the concept of a national innovation system derives from the studies of Bengt-Åke Lundvall. In a paper entitled "From producer-user relationships to national innovation systems" he (1988: 349) states: "The separation of users from producers in the process of innovation, being a stylized fact of modern industrial society, has important implications for economic theory." In the new economic theory, instead of the focus being on decisions made on the basis of a given amount of information, it would be on the processes of learning and interaction between actors. He further argues that a nation is a natural framework for user-producer interaction because of the geographical proximity of actors, national government, and historically unique technological capabilities, as well as that nation's shared history and culture (1988: 360).[4]

Lundvall's group developed a producer-user perspective already in the early 1980s and anticipated many issues that later became important for

---

[3] In his review Lundvall (1998: 16) suggests that the concept of national innovation system was first launched in the innovation literature in 1988 in an important collection of essays entitled *Technical Change and Economic Theory* (edited by Dosi *et al.* 1988), which included a chapter on national systems of innovation with contributions by Nelson, Freeman, Lundvall, and Pelikan.

[4] Other innovation researchers had also addressed this phenomenon. Eric Von Hippel (1976) analysed the dominant role of users in innovation process, introduced the lead-user method (1986), and in his book *Sources of Innovation* (1988) showed the significance of users' contribution for the emergence of innovations. In innovation studies, Roy Rothwell (1986) wrote about re-innovation by users. Subsequently the idea of producer-user collaboration in innovation has been an important issue in business studies and has been conceptualized as "co-configuration" (Victor and Boynton 1998), "co-production" (Normann 2001), and the "democratization of innovation" (Von Hippel 2005).

innovation studies. The group studied the impact of microelectronics on the Danish economy by focusing on the adoption and development of microelectronics in dairy production, the clothing industry, and in waste water treatment in local administration (Lundvall 1985). In all cases Lundvall's group found a tendency towards producer dominance in innovation along with a lack of competence on the user side. Lundvall concluded that this pattern of innovation might inspire a technology policy that would be more oriented toward strengthening user competence than the policy approaches of the 1980s and would bring users and producers together in new constellations (Lundvall 1985: 44).

Lundvall's studies are another step towards an institutional analysis. Based on empirical studies on the interactions between dairy machine manufacturers (producers) and milk producers (users), the producer-user relationship is taken up as the key phenomenon. This is also a step toward a microanalysis of institutional interactions: learning and interaction refer the real interactions between real people and organizations. The quality of this interaction matters. Here the object of study was shared by organization and business studies and with studies of learning and knowledge production.

In 1992, Lundvall repeated his call for an economic theory that "puts interactive learning and innovation at the center of analysis" (1992: 2). The concept of knowledge is now taken as a starting point, for "the most fundamental resource in modern economy is knowledge, and, accordingly, the most important process is learning" (1992: 2). These starting points led Edquist to characterize Lundvall's conception of NIS as a conception based on interactive learning theories (Edquist 1997: 5 and 7). Later, Lundvall (1994) developed a theory of the "learning economy" as an alternative to neoclassical economic theory.

In making sense of the "interactive learning theories" that constitute a basis for a new economic theory and for the concept of NIS, Lundvall referred in his 1992 paper to two sources: Kenneth Arrow's 1962 paper *The Economic Implications of Learning by Doing* and Nathan Rosenberg's 1982 paper *Learning by Using*. Arrow's paper elaborates learning-curve theories, first developed in psychology in the 1930s and 1940s and later applied in analysing organizational learning processes. In these theories, learning is described as a function of time and repetitions, and mathematical models are created to depict this relationship (Hartley 1966; Mazur and Hastie 1978). This is what Arrow does. In his paper, Arrow constructs a mathematical model that aims to take the growth of experience into account. The index of experience in this model is cumulative gross investment (1962: 157). Subsequently, cumulative output volume has been used as a standard measure of experience (Adler and Clark 1991).

The concepts of the learning curve and learning as an outcome of cumulative experience have been criticized by learning theorists, economists, and industrial sociologists as conservative conceptions of learning and, as such, are inadequate in explaining innovations. Albernathy and Wayne (1974: 118) regard the learning-curve model as part of a firm's cost-minimizing strategy, which is "an enemy of product innovation". Ghemawat (1985: 144) finds that the learning curve was originally a kind of economic abstraction, "a mathematical relation between the calculated output of product and its cost." The dynamics and differences between various ways of learning have not been the subject of analysis. Understanding these presupposes a focus on the mechanisms of learning as well as on a distinction between levels and types of learning.[5]

Rosenberg's paper is richer in content. He characterizes several learning processes prevalent in industry and focuses on learning by using.[6] This learning takes place in the utilization of the product by the final user. Rosenberg shows that the operating costs of a DC-8 airplane were radically reduced during its life span as a result of minor technical modifications. Nevertheless, even Rosenberg's conception of learning is a logical inference from long-term economic and technical information, and it remains in the tradition of learning-curve theories.

Bengt-Åke Lundvall's (1985, 1988) idea of interactive learning between producers and users transcended the limits of learning-curve theories in focusing on social interaction in networks. This idea was an important new insight that challenged the study of innovations. Lundvall, however, has encountered the problem of how to conceptualize and study learning in a sensible and fruitful way. The first solution to

---

[5] In their model, Adler and Clark posit a sort of second-order learning that comprises a) explicit managerial and engineering action to change the technology in response to design errors and b) training programmes (1991: 270–271). Bateson (1972) made a distinction between primary (modifying-routine), secondary (problem-solving), and tertiary (problem-reframing) learning. Engeström (1987) developed a theory of tertiary learning as expansive learning, in which the whole activity changes, including the quality of outcome and collaborative relationships.

[6] Rosenberg defines several kinds of learning processes related to the innovation process. At the basic research end of the spectrum there is 1) acquisition of knowledge concerning the laws of nature. At the development end of R&D there is 2) searching out and discovering the optimal design characteristics of the product. It involves also 3) discovering product characteristics desired in the market (Rosenberg 1982: 121). 4) Learning by doing is cumulative learning that occurs as a by-product of productive activity. It consists of increasing skill in production and is expressed as reduction in labour costs per unit of output. Finally, 5) learning by using takes place. Rosenberg suggests that all these forms of learning should be studied empirically.

this problem proposed by economists – Lundvall himself included – was to conceptualize learning by listing the universal kinds of activities that learning can be associated with: "learning by doing", "learning by interacting", "learning by searching". These characterizations, however, remain general and were not conducive to understanding the quality, conditions, problems, forms, or organization of learning.

The second solution suggested by Lundvall (1998: 9) was to link learning to four types of knowledge: "know-what" refers to access to information, "know-why" to causal relationships, "know-how" to capabilities of doing things, and "know-who" to access to the knowledge and capabilities of others. Since the speed of learning has become a key in the "globalizing learning economy", new knowledge that is not easily transferable to other localities becomes of special importance. Knowledge with strongly tacit elements (typically know-how and know-who) presupposes trust-based, reciprocal interactions between actors (1998: 10). Even in this version, learning still tends to remain an inferred necessity for explaining economic development. It tends to remain, itself, a black box. In order to understand the dynamics of interactive learning or knowledge creation, we need to study interaction between people: what was learned, how, by whom, and at what level of work and organization. This is what sociologists of knowledge, ethnographers of organizations, and scholars of organizational learning are doing (e.g. Engeström 2001).

A paradox of Lundvall's theory is that it postulates a central mechanism or phenomenon that cannot be studied with the traditional data and methods used in economics. The research agenda of innovation as interactive learning requires both multidisciplinary conceptualization and empirical studies of interactive and collective learning processes. The treatment of knowledge and learning requires theoretical tools from philosophy, psychology, and sociology of science and technology. Insofar as these, in turn, remain multiparadigmatic, the challenge is complex.

3.2 An optimistic view: Defining the determinants of a national innovation system

Since the introduction of the concept of NIS in the early 1990s, efforts have been made on an ongoing basis to specify its nature as a research approach and policy framework. In the following two such efforts by Charles Edquist and by Richard Nelson and his colleagues will be reviewed.

Charles Edquist is the leading developer of the NIS concept in Sweden. He collaborated in the early 1990s with Bengt-Åke Lundvall to produce a comparison of the Danish and Swedish systems of innovations (Edquist and Lundvall 1993). He introduced the NIS concept in Sweden in order to reform the Swedish industrial policy – or rather replace it by an innovation policy. In his mind the Swedish industrial policy of the early 1990s focused too exclusively on the renovation of traditional industries such as paper and pulp and engineering (Eklund 2007: 63–64). He thought that innovation studies and NIS could supply a scientific basis for innovation policy.[7]

In 1994 Edquist established with Maureen McKelvey the System of Innovation Research Programme at the University of Lindköping. It had two aims (Eklund 2007: 64): "To develop theory and clean up the innovation system concept" which he believed was too vague and "to go much more into depth on the various aspects of the Swedish national innovations system." He also coordinated the systems of innovations network, which aimed to be an international network with the task of building a more solid conceptual foundation for the study of innovations systems. Scholars from 15 countries participated, and the collaboration concluded with the publication in 1997 of a collection of papers entitled *Systems of innovation,* edited by Edquist.

In the introductory review essay of the book Edquist (1997) found that, on one level, there is an agreement of the key contents the national innovation systems. It comprises the interaction of the institutions that effect innovativeness of nation, as the definition supplied by him and Lundvall suggests (Edquist and Lundvall 1993: 267):

> The national system of innovation is constituted by the institutions and economic structures affecting the rate and direction of technological change in the society. Obviously the national system of innovation is larger than the R&D system. It must, for example, include not only the system of technology diffusion and the R&D system but also institutions and factors determining how new technology affects productivity and economic growth. At the same time, the system of technological change is, of course, less comprehensive than economy/society as a whole.

Edquist (1997: 14) reviewed the definitions of the national innovation system and observed that none of them specifies the important institutions of the system or the criteria to be used in defining them. He

---

[7] Edquist actively contacted the Ministry of Industry and the Social Democratic Party. In a letter to the minister of industry in 1994 he explained his intention (cited in Eklund 2007: 63): "I especially noted what you said about the importance of maintaining a scientific view of industry (and industrial policy). (...). This has, during the last years, become an increasingly common attitude in other countries. We who do research on the relationships between innovations, growth and employment can contribute with analyses here – of a different kind than the ones provided by traditional economists."

concludes that these definitions have remained vague and stated that there is a need to specify the important elements of the system to further develop the approach. He believes that it is possible to define all the essential factors or determinants affecting technical change and attempts to construct a systemic model of them. This constitutes a "causal" explanation of national innovative activity and a basis for the systematic planning of innovation systems (Edquist 1997: 2 and 15):

> If we want to describe, understand, explain – and perhaps influence – the process of innovation, we must take all important factors shaping and influencing innovations into account. The systems of innovations approach – in its various forms – is designed to do that (...). We will, for the time being, specify system as including all important determinants of innovation.

This comprehensive definition covers subsystems, institutions, factors, and mechanisms of diverse kinds. He further suggested that this kind of holistic approach is of "tremendous value as a tool to facilitate understanding of the dynamics of innovation" (1997: 18). In his contribution to the *Oxford Handbook of Innovation*, Edquist (2005) continued to worry about the conceptual diffuseness of NIS. It lacks the conceptual clarity, and the elements or "explanatory factors" of a system remain undefined. Instead of describing the necessary institutions, he provided a list of ten activities that are important for innovations (2005: 191).

It has been suggested that Edquist's attempt to define the determinants of innovation through which innovation becomes "causally explained" (1987: 14) reflect the optimism of a natural science aiming to work out an explanatory theory (e.g. Mjoset 2005). In my opinion (Miettinen 2002), the creation of a reasonable theory of all essential factors that influence innovations seemed to be an unrealistic project. The innovative activity of a nation is a complex, multifaceted, heterogeneous and ever-changing set of phenomena for which we do not even have satisfactory definitions.

In addition, the concept of the determinant is hardly compatible either with evolutionary theory or with the idea of interactive causality. The latter claims that novelty emerges from complex mutual interactions between entities and actors. In sociology of technology, this kind of transactive evolution has been called "co-evolution".[8] Because the interaction includes many contingent processes, the explanation is historical in nature and does not provide any basis for predicting the

---

[8] According to a pragmatist transactive view suggested by Dewey and Bentley (1949/1989: 112–115), all the entities participating in an interaction are mutually transformed or defined as a result of the interaction.

future. In dealing with the sources of the systemic unpredictability of human affairs, Alasdair MacIntyre analyses the limits of the idea of organizational effectiveness based on predictability (1984: 106–107). He finds that the inadequacy of this idea is most evident in the case of innovative adaptation. According to Bhaskar (1987), there is an asymmetry between explanation and prediction in the social sciences. Explanatory analysis cannot predict, but only "inform our understanding of the present and illuminate projects and strategies for the future" (Bhaskar 1987: 219).[9]

According to this view research can provide a perpetually self-renewing set of assumptions of the relevant mechanisms and problems that are historically necessary and locally constrained. In this view, if we propose that interactive learning and interactions between key institutions are essential mechanisms of innovation (which I consider a good hypothesis), we should focus on studying and understanding the nature and quality of these interactions in regard to some particular key technology or social practice, instead of constructing comprehensive holistic, explanatory system models.

As a policy framework, the optimistic view based on the definition of the determinants of innovation resembles what Michael Storper (1997: 283) has characterized in regional economy as "scientism and prescriptive rationality". He refers to "the tendency of the analyst to seek determinate causes of industrial performance and for policymakers to extend that via prescriptive rationality". The optimistic version of the NIS approach may be seen as an outgrowth of the idea of the "planning society" developed by the Nordic social democratic parties between the two world wars (e.g. Kettunen 2008: 148). Like the "science of science" approach delineated by Bernal (1939/1967) before the Second World War, the planning society ideology thought that rationality made possible by science and research is needed in the social and economic planning of the society.

Subsequently Edquist (2005) made it clear that a systematic approach does not imply that systems can be consciously designed and planned (2005: 191): "Even if we knew all the determinants of innovation processes in detail, (. . .) we would not be able to control them or design or 'build' SIs on the basis of this knowledge." The list of determinants is rather a placeholder for what is known about innovations. The list is provisional and will be subject to revisions as our knowledge about

---

[9] On the nature of causality and explanation in the social sciences, see e.g. MacIntyre 1984; Bhaskar (1987); Constant (1989) and; Toulmin (2001); and in economics Langlois and Everett (1994).

determinants of innovation processes increases. The determinants include complex phenomena (knowledge, learning, interaction, skill) that is hard to understand or study on the basis of rigorous definitions. Rather, they must be approached by resorting to the conceptual vocabularies and empirical results of the various research traditions from different disciplines that study on these phenomena.

Also Bengt-Åke Lundvall (1999 and 2007) has pointed out that the flexibility of the term national innovation system is important both for research and for its use as policy development tool (Lundvall 1999: 9):

> The recent models of innovation emphasize that knowledge/innovation is an interactive process in which firms interact with customers, supplies and knowledge institutions. (...) Innovation systems may be defined as regional or national, or sector- or technology-specific. The common idea is that the specificities of knowledge production reflect unique combinations of technological specialization and institutional structure. In national systems, the education and training system is among the most important for explaining national patterns and modes of innovation.

The institutional systems are historically different and different elements therefore prove to be important. Therefore, if NIS can be regarded a theory it is one in the sense of an "heuristic concept and focusing device" which "offers a broad and flexible framework for organizing and interpreting case studies and comparative analyses" (Lundvall 2004: 20). He further argues that "one of the reasons why policy makers have found the NIS-concept useful is that it combines a specific perspective on the economy with a certain flexibility in terms of what parts of the economy should be included in the analysis."

3.3 Comparing national systems for learning

Richard Nelson's contribution to the formulation of the evolutionary theory of technical change is well known (Nelson and Winter 1977; Nelson 1987). In the late 1980s he undertook a comparative study of national innovation systems. The results were published in *National Systems of Innovation. A comparative Analysis* (1993), in which the national institutions supporting innovation in 14 countries were compared. In the introduction Nelson and David Rosenberg (1993: 4) state that the book is not a theoretical enterprise: "The orientation of this project has been to carefully describe and compare, and try to understand, rather than to theorize first and then attempt to prove or calibrate the theory." Evolutionary economics is not mentioned in the introduction. The introduction and the conclusions written by Nelson include an enlightening and critical discussion of the limits of the concept of the national innovation system.

Nelson and Rosenberg place the word "system" in quotation marks to show that "rather, the 'systems' concept is that of a set of institutional actors that, together, play a major role in influencing innovative performance" (Nelson and Rosenberg 1993: 4). Their critical position rests on three main pillars. First, the authors wish to maintain distance from a strong use of NIS that would tend to develop and employ it as an explanatory concept. Second, they refrain from formulating recommendations for "a right kind of innovation system." Third, they acknowledge NIS to be a problematic concept, and they subject the three terms behind its initials – national, innovation and system – to critical scrutiny.

Nelson and Rosenberg point out that each of the three terms included in NIS can be interpreted in a variety of ways. In most of the definitions of "national innovation system" the terms "technical change" or a firm's "capacity to stay competitive" or even economic growth (through technical advance) are used along with innovative activity. In such a broad definition, it is difficult to regard innovation as something other than the overall competitiveness of national economics. The sets of intertwining terms and characterizations make a focused analytical discussion difficult (Nelson 1993: 518).

Second, no criteria have been agreed for defining the limits of a system or its essential subsystems or elements. The existing characterizations are mostly lists of different kinds of "factors" that cover not only institutions (firms, universities, education, banks) but also social qualities, cultural patterns, mechanisms and patterns of interactions.[10] Understanding the nature and quality of the key interactions between the institutions and organizations seems decisive for the approach. However, the dynamics of these interactions are poorly understood. The relationship between universities and industry can be taken as an example. In their analysis of the American system, Mowery and Rosenberg (1993: 53) state:

---

[10] In analysing the definitions of NIS in the documents of the Finnish Science and Technology Council, the distinguished Finnish sociologist Erik Allardt called them "words resembling definitions" (1995: 7): "The publications of the Science and Technology Council never clearly state what the belonging of a field or a sector to the national innovation system means. Does it mean a list of the areas that should enjoy public funding? Or is it assumed that NIS is really a functioning social system motivating individuals and groups to striving in research and development work? Or have we simply invented a kind of a new way of classifying things. The observer and reader easily start to suspect that what we find is this third alternative, that is, a new way of listing things has been invented."

There is vast array of forms of research collaboration between universities and industry, making generalizations virtually impossible. The relationship between university research and commercial technology varies considerably across industries. No single model of the constraints, advantages, and disadvantages of such collaboration is likely to be accurate for all university-industry collaboration.

Neither is there any well-articulated or verified framework linking institutional arrangements to technological and economic performance. These considerations lead one to wonder whether it might not be more fruitful to study the quality and challenges of key interactions in the nationally important or emergent industries than to construct a unitary model and standard for its outputs.

Third, Nelson and Rosenberg discuss the national aspects of NIS. Is the concept valid and useful in the context of the rapid globalization of economic activities? To what extent do the national factors explain innovative activity? Can the system be called national if the factors influencing the innovative activity increasingly transcend national boundaries? They come to the following conclusion: "Indeed, for many of the participants in this study, one of the key interests was in exploring whether, and if so, in what ways, the concept of a 'national' system makes any sense today. National governments act as if it did. However, that presumption, and the reality, may not be aligned" (1993: 5).

David Mowery and Nathan Rosenberg express their doubt about our capacity to understand – let alone master – innovation systems: "Our understanding of the management and organization of the innovation process is so imperfect that debates over (. . .) 'efficient' and 'inefficient' innovation systems will remain poorly informed for the foreseeable future" (1993: 64). Nelson and his colleagues believe that the comparison of national institutions provides an opportunity to learn from their diversity and differences (Nelson 1993: 2).

In their analysis of the structural change of the US national innovation system, Mowery and Ziedonis reflect on the practical difficulties of applying any new innovation policy intended to improve systemic performance:

> The robustness, efficiency, adaptability and the likely future path of the system are as important as the behaviour of individual parts. But here too, prescriptive advice is lacking, because of the high level of aggregation of the analysis and the absence of reliable data on which to base assessments of system-wide performance or dynamics. (Mowery and Ziedonis 1998: 105)

They study the efforts of the US technology policy to encourage inter-institutional interaction and technology commercialization, thereby creating markets for intellectual property. The measures taken to intensify the commercialization of the results of basic research took the form of two acts of Congress: the Bayh-Dole Act and the Federal Technology Transfer Act. Mowery and Ziedonis are not at all sure about the impact of this legislation on the US innovation system. There are indications that the universities are ready to accept significant restrictions regarding the publications of the results of the research undertaken with industry sponsorship. The authors conclude (1998: 114): "Delays and or restrictions on disclosure could have negative consequences for the innovative and economic performance of the US national innovation system that might outweigh the benefits derived from closer university-industry R&D relationships." Their case shows that policy measures have multiple, even contradictory effects, and that it is very difficult to show or evaluate their overall impact on innovation activity.

3.4 Further theorizing of the NIS approach in research and policy making

In their review of the concept of innovations systems, Daniele Archibugi *et al.* (1999) made two pertinent observations. First they state that the discussion of the term "system" has been strangely limited. The definitions are short and general, such as "anything not in chaos", or they state that a system is constituted by a number of elements and by the relationships between these (Archibugi *et al.* 1999: 4). However, "little reference is made to earlier work on systems theory, or to how this literature originally defined or perceived the system." Similarly Balzat and Hanusch (2004) find that the relationship between systems theory and NIS approach is barely investigated. For example, the connection to the theory of large technological systems in the history of technology (Hughes 1988) is hardly discussed at all. Second, despite attempts to measure innovative activity and the performance of different countries, they came to the conclusion that "on a more micro, firm or organizational level, (. . .) there remains a gap between theoretical developments and empirical analysis" (1999: 9). Jan Fagerberg (2005: 20) agreed in his review of innovation studies: "our understanding of how knowledge– and innovation–operates on organizational level remains fragmentary and further conceptual and applied research is needed."

Niosi *et al.* (1993) are among the few who have tried to articulate the theoretical basis of a systems concept. They refer both to von Bertalanffy's (1969) general systems theory and to Schumpeterian economics: "From systems theory and irreversible thermodynamics we borrow the concept of open system, exchanging matter, energy and information with its environment" (Niosi *et al.* 1993: 217). Saviotti finds three theoretical sources for NIS in addition to evolutionary economics. They are: 1) systems theory and non-equilibrium thermodynamics; 2) biology; and 3) organization theories that have emerged in management science and in business history (Saviotti 1994: 182–183). The cultural and social sciences are missing from Niosi's and Saviotti's attempts to find a synthesis.

Luhman's theory of a self-referential model of social systems has been suggested as a theoretical foundation for systems of innovations (Kaufmann and Tödling 2001). Luhmann's theory is based on Maturana and Varela's (1992) biological theory of knowledge. According to this theory, systems start from the organization of cells as autonomous entities, or systems that reproduce themselves continuously (autopoesis) maintaining their boundary actively vis-à-vis their environment. The specific feature of a social system is communication. Kaufmann and Tödling think that Luhmann's theory constitutes an alternative to the conceptions of NIS and regional innovation system which are "based on a rather traditional view of systems as interaction networks" (Kaufmann and Tödling 2001: 793).

In my view, extending the biological evolution and general systems concept to innovations runs the risk of slighting the cultural specificity of human activity including innovative activity. Biological theories of knowledge and general systems models (which include physical, biological and social phenomena) tend to ignore the centrality of the cultural transmission and the transformation of activities that take place through the use and development of cultural artefacts, signs, and tools (Vygotsky 1979; Burkitt 1999; Miettinen 2001). This seems true to me even in the case of Luhman's systems approach, in which communication is more an extension of the transmission of information in biological systems than something that is connected to practical human activity as mediated by symbolic and material artifacts.

Katherine and Richard Nelson (2002) have suggested that the economists of technological change could benefit from Merlin Donald's (1991, 2001) theory of human cognition. Donald is a Canadian psychologist who has studied the co-evolution of the human mind and culture. In his theory, the evolving world of material and symbolic artifacts and their use constitute a precondition of human consciousness. The world of cultural artifacts constitutes the external symbolic storage of human memory. Biological evolution is replaced by cultural evolution. As a result, using the metaphor of the biological evolution becomes problematic when applied to an analysis of the development of technology, as suggested by evolutionary biologist Stephen Gould (1987).

47

In a collection of essays on technological innovation as an evolutionary process edited by Ziman (2000), several authors suggest that, in order to understand technology as an evolutionary phenomenon, we must focus on the relationship between technological artifacts and their use (Fleck 2000; Nelson 2000; Turnbull 2000). Interactions, competencies and learning are connected to the production and use of artifacts. Systems approaches tend to abstract this substantial and material content of innovative interaction, focusing on formal and institutional structures only.

The representatives of the NIS approach identified themselves with the tradition of evolutionary economics of innovation: "Theories of interactive learning together with evolutionary theories of technical change constitute origins of the systems of innovation approach" (Edquist 1997: 7). McKelvey (1997) identifies the three principles of an evolutionary pattern of technical change: 1) retention and transmission of information, 2) generation of novelty leading to diversity, and 3) selection among alternatives. Although she argues that these three functions should exist in a system of innovation, "they will function differently, depending on the specific system of innovation" (McKelvey 1997: 201). These principles do not as such imply or presuppose a systems concept. As Niosi *et al.* (1993: 219) pointed out, "we can represent an NSI by means of a *network* of institutions, where the interactions represent links between different nodes of the network." This is the line that the study of innovation and learning networks has taken.

In the 2000s the NIS approach has been developed first of all as a framework for policy making. In this contexts the differences within the approach become visible. Lundvall made already in 1992 the distinction between the narrow and broad definition of the NIS. The former focus on institutions involved in the promotion of science and technology. The latter covers interactions of wider range of institutions including educational system, labour markets, financial system and welfare regime. The distinction between the narrow and broad views is also based on differences conceptions of knowledge and learning as well as on the economic foundations of innovation policy making.

Lundvall extends and generalizes the distinction between explicit and tacit knowledge originally suggested by philosopher Michael Polanyi – into two modes of learning and innovation: DUI mode based on learning by Doing, Using, and Interacting and STI mode (Science, Technology, and Innovation) based on the utilization of "codified" scientific knowledge. "One is experience-based and the second is science-based" (Lundvall 2007: 104). The STI mode has been suggested by the theorists of knowledge economy who think that the distribution of scientific and technological knowledge is essential for the knowledge-based economy (e.g. Cowan *et al.* 2000). In contrast, experiential "intuitive" learning is an unintended by-product or side effect of routine activities in firms such as production and marketing. They exist primarily in the form of bodily skills that cannot be fully articulated. Even fields of industry can be analysed in terms of which one of these modes is dominating.

For the DUI mode, organizational learning and the forms of work organizations that enhance experiential learning (such as teamwork, job rotation) become a key question of innovation policy instead of access to and use of developing scientific and technological knowledge. Lundvall (2006: 19) suggests that "The national differences in what people do and learn at their workplace is a major factor structuring the national innovation system and affecting its performance." Therefore, the organizational arrangements within firms (and between firms as well as with users) that influence learning become vital.

I belong to those who find the dichotomy between experiential (DUI) and science-based (STI) learning simplifying. It tends to exaggerate the tacit habitual dimension of learning and ignores the significance of reflection for the transformation of the habits (Dewey 1933/1989; Miettinen *et al.* 2012). In constructing a dichotomy it bypasses the interaction between the modalities of knowledge vital for creativity of human action and for innovation (Nonaka and Takeuchi 1995). Local experimentation and innovation is increasingly intertwined with the use of research-based field-specific scientific and professional knowledge. It is transmitted to organizations through education, training and interaction in networks and associations where local knowledge is exchanged, compared and systematized. It is not transmitted primarily in the form of "papers" but by new instruments, ideas, and practices articulated in various ways and forms. The interaction of producers with users is important but so is increasingly the collaboration between "adequately skilled employees with knowledgeable scientists" (Herrmann and Peine 2011: 699).

Another foundation for drawing the distinction between narrow and broad view is the critique of the dominating market failure justification for innovation policy. Many representatives of systems of innovations denounce it because it is based on neoliberal economic theory and find that it has much in common with the linear view of innovation. The market failure argument starts from the suggestion that scientific knowledge is a public good and its value does not suffer from the fact that others use it (it is non-rivalry). Because of these properties profit-oriented private actors lack incentives in investing in knowledge production. In classical formulation of market failure by Nelson and Arrow market failures in the innovation process emanate form three properties of R&D: uncertainty, inappropriability and indivisibility (Schröter 2009: 11). That is why the state has to invest in science and universities, support the R&D of firms and enforce intellectual property rights to provide incentives.

Critics find that the concept of market failure is based on the neoclassical notion of equilibrium and optimality and must therefore be rejected. Instead of this neoliberal justification, the NIS approach focuses on the interaction of a whole range of institutions of the systems and enhances the development of organizational skills and capabilities (Dogson *et al.* 2011: 1153): "the governments can play a crucial role coordinating and facilitating connectivity, (...) be actively engaged in facilitating a broader system than just 'market.'" The systems approach suggests the concepts of systems failure and systems instruments as a new foundation for a new innovation policy. Absence of interaction between the institutions is an example of a systems failure, providing a platform for learning and experimentation is an example of a systemic tool. Although taxonomies of systems failures have been outlined (e.g. Chaminade and Edquist 2006), empirical accounts of failures as well as policies and instruments that are used solve them is needed to show the fruitfulness of the new policy approach.

Hekkert *et al.* (2007: 414) find that the innovation system approach has two shortcomings to understand technological change: it has a quasi-static character and it focuses on macro level institutions and less on actions of entrepreneurs. Even though it is based on theories such as evolutionary economics and interactive learning it focuses on comparing the social structure of different innovation systems (actors, their relations, and institutions) and, thereby, tries to explain the difference in performance. Less emphasis is put in the dynamics of innovation system. The systems of innovation approach suffers from institutional determinism. Hekkert *et al.* develop a model of systems change by focusing on the functions of a system, such as entrepreneurial activities, knowledge diffusion through networks and market formation. Properly interacting functions lead to systems change. They outline a research approach in which key function-related events of a trajectory of a technological system are mapped and analysed to explain the dynamics of change.

Alexandra Schröter (2009) has compared the definitions of market and systemic failures as a foundation for innovation policy. Her conclusion is that the systems of innovation policy framework does not add or complement in an essential way to the neoclassical framework based on the concept of market failure (2009: 24): "the systems of innovation framework mostly describes the symptoms, rather than the underlying causes, of market imperfections that are already part of the neoclassical theory, and the framework suffers from severe shortcomings with regard to partial implementation." The systems approach uses a comparative institutional approach to detect the systemic problems. Schröter thinks it does not provide criteria to decide which problems are essential. How do we know, for example, that the lack of an internationally top-level innovation university in Finland is a real or essential system failure in the Finnish system? Schröter (2009: 21) also thinks that because of the mutual interdependency of institutions copying of a single institution will not necessarily have the desired results unless the whole institutional framework is copied.

The systems-based redefinition of foundations of innovation policy leads to a holistic policy in which all policy fields are evaluated from the point if view of their contribution to innovation. The Aalborg authors regard the NIS framework as a basis for a comprehensive, holistic policy and for new political institutions. It supplies (Lundvall *et al.* 2002: 227)

> a new perspective on a wide set of policies including social policy, labour market policy, educational policy, industrial policy, energy policy, environmental policy and science and technology policy. Specifically the concept calls for new national development strategies with co-ordination across these policy areas.

The group suggests that high-level councils for innovation and competence building should be formed transnationally, nationally and regionally. These councils should be given the authority to coordinate policies across sectors.

4

The adoption of NIS in the Finnish science and technology policy of the 1990s

4.1 The emergence of NIS in the reviews of the Science and Technology Policy Council of Finland

The main elements of the Finnish system supporting scientific and technological research were created in the 1960s and 1970s (see Figure 4.1). In the 1970s several new universities were established. The new Academy of Finland with research councils was established in 1970 as a funding organization of academic research and as a planning body for science policy under the Ministry of Education. In the 1960s it was widely recognized that science and technology are essential conditions of economic growth and international competitiveness. Consequently, the goal of increasing the GNP-share of R&D input to the level of other OECD countries was set. A dual system of science and technology policy making was adopted: Science policy was led by the Ministry of Education while technology policy and funding was under the Ministry of Trade and Industry.

Three events characterized the 1980s. First, Tekes (the Finnish Funding Agency for Technology and Innovation) was established in 1983 to support technology and product development through national technology programmes. About two thirds of the Tekes funding goes to company projects and loans and one third to university and research institute projects. Second, the public R&D funding increased in the 1980s to more than 10% annually. Third, the Science and Technology Policy Council of Finland was established in 1987 to continue the work of the former Science Policy Council. This name change was in itself an expression of the attempt to unite the thus far separate science and

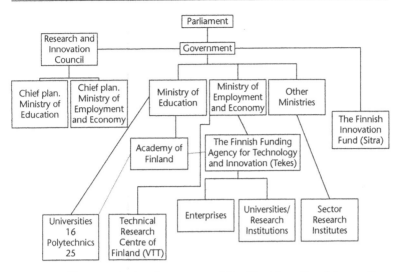

Figure 4.1. The organizational structure of the Finnish national innovation system

technology policies into an integrated innovation policy in Finland. The council introduced in the beginning 1990s the concept national innovation system and it is regarded as a key institution of the Finnish science and technology policy system.

Science and Technology Policy Council of Finland – the name of which was changed into Research and Innovation Council in 2009 – is presided over by the prime minister and has strong representation from the government, leading science and technology institutions, firms, as well as from employer and employee organizations. The Council coordinates cooperation between the Ministry of Education and of the Ministry Trade and Industry. It defines the strategy for the nation in its triannual review of Finland's science and technology policy. These documents constitute the most authoritative formulation of Finnish innovation policy. Two chief planning officers, one situated in the Ministry of Education, one in the Ministry of Trade and Industry, do the preparatory work and write the documents for the Council. Their role is also to monitor the development of science and technology policy in the international arena and make the key results available to the Council.[1]

---

[1] Also the reverse is true. Erkki Ormala, one of the chief planning officers, served first as a vice-chairman and later as the chairman of the OECD's Working Group on Technology and Innovation Policy (TIP) in the years 1994–1999.

The term "national innovation system" was adopted as an organizing concept for the 1990 Review of Science and Technology Council. This took place several years before the concept was extensively discussed and elaborated in the OECD. The Finnish Council was thus an early adopter of a new concept that had been introduced in three books published in 1987 and 1988 (Freeman 1987; Dosi *et al.* 1988; and Freeman and Lundvall 1988). The third of these, *Small Countries Facing the Technological Revolution*, edited by Freeman and Lundvall (1988), was particularly pertinent for the Finnish policy perspective. The approach of the Aalborg group (Anderson and Lundvall 1988) which reflected on the position of small, developed Scandinavian countries in the world economy and focused on interactive learning, aroused interest in Finland (Lemola 1990). Papers dealing with the concept of a national innovation system were presented by the Aalborg group in several European meetings in the late 1980s.

In 1988, the OECD initiated a three-year programme entitled "Science, Technology, Economy and Society" (TEP). This programme sponsored a conference in Tokyo in 1990 that dealt with globalization, the role of technology in economic development, and networks of enterprises. The idea of creating a viable national innovation system that would be successful in international competition was presented in the conference by Walter Zegwell. The concept was, therefore, in the air when it was used in the 1990 Review.

One of the architects of the new policy characterized the background of the adoption of the NIS concept by the Council in the following terms.[2] Already at the end of the 1980s the Council was addressing issues that transcended the confines of the traditional conception of science and technology policy. These included the use of tax incentives to stimulate R&D activity of firms, regional technology development and internationalization by improving the communication between public and private sectors.[3] At the end of the decade, the connection between science and technology issues and globalization emerged as an important theme in international discussions. The OECD Tokyo conference of 1990 was an outstanding example. All these developments imply that the "old Finnish paradigm" of science and technology policy, which focused on universities and research funding on the one hand and technology programmes

---

[2] Interview, Dr. Erkki Ormala, 13 August 2002.
[3] "The use of tax reductions in the advancement of the R&D activity of firms", Science and Technology Policy Council of Finland, Memorandum 12 February 1988. "Making international technology collaboration more effective by increasing information flows between industry and public administration." Science and Technology Policy Council of Finland, Memorandum 31 May 1988.

on the other hand, had come to an end. "National innovation system" was a conception that helped to loosen the "lock-in situation" implied by the traditional policy, address the various emerging themes under one term and make the science and technology policy discussion an important issue on the government's agenda.

NIS was taken from the sphere of research, where it had served as a framework in empirical studies, and was consciously turned into a normative conception. "It is not used as a descriptive term, as an end result, but as a prescriptive term of the ideal state of a well functioning national innovation system which is sought after by all the measures. The term was made a normative concept and it immediately became a political concept."[4] When the term was introduced in the Council, several members found it useful for the reformulation of science and technology policy and for their own interest as stakeholders. It was first introduced in a government session in 1990 and, finally, at the end of the year, accepted as a key concept in the Council's Review. The new prime minister, who became the chairman of the Council in the summer of 1991, soon adopted the term in his vocabulary, and it thereby became a strong political mainstay in the science and technology policy debate.

The three following reviews of the Council, viz *Towards an Innovative Society* (1993), *Finland: a Knowledge-Based Society* (1996), and *The Challenge of Knowledge and Know-How* (2000) further elaborated on the innovation policy. The 2000 review summarized its message by saying that "sustainable economic, social and cultural development will continue to demand comprehensive development of the innovation system" (Review 2000: 3). The language and rhetoric of the triannual reviews changed considerably at the turn of the decade. In the first review of the new Council in 1987, there was no dominant unifying concept. In the first part of the review, four members of the Council evaluated the promotion of science, Finland's educational system and industrial research activity. A descriptive review of the development of Finland's scientific research, technology, and sectoral research was presented and followed by the final recommendations. From 1990 onwards, strong catchwords were launched in each of the reviews: "national innovation system" and "innovative society" (1990, 1993), "information society" and "knowledge-based society" (1996, 2000). These permeated the discussion and the central argumentation revolved around them.

---

[4] Interview, Dr. Erkki Ormala, 13 August 2002.

4.2 Changes in the definitions and sources of legimitation of the NIS concept in the Council reviews

The definition and status of NIS changed over the years. Having begun as a tentative new conception, it became an established term in the new science and technology policy and an object of planning. I will analyse the trajectory of this reification by focusing on the following three questions: 1) In what way did the definition of NIS change? 2) How were and the foundations the status of the term substantiated? 3) What was the relationship of "national innovation system" to other organizing catchwords, such as "information society" and "knowledge-based society"? In this connection the 1993 Review requires a closer look for two reasons. First, in it the use of the term "national innovation system" was rhetorically pervasive. Second, by 1993 Finland was about to emerge from a severe economic recession, and in this review NIS was necessarily presented in the context of an economic recovery strategy. Table 4.1 summarizes the definition and status of NIS in the reviews issued by the Council.

In the 1990 review, the term was introduced in a separate chapter, where it was defined in two ways. First, it was "the totality of factors that influence development and utilization of new knowledge". Second, it was a "brief list of some integral elements of the system" including (Science and Technology Council of Finland 1990: 21–23):

1) the research system;
2) education;
3) the general atmosphere in the society;
4) interaction and cooperation;
5) internationalization; and
6) "many other elements", such as mechanisms of transfer of technology as well as regulations and statutes influencing knowledge production and diffusion.

The significance of the new concept was substantiated by an unspecific reference to the international discussion in which the term was introduced. Moreover, it was seen as an extension of traditional science and technology policy. Although the review still concentrated on the advancement of R&D, it also dealt with "the innovation system as a whole and various factors influencing its development" (1990: 23).

In the Review of 1993, NIS was introduced as the constitutive concept and developmental strategy of Finland. Instead of making any reference to the origins of the concept in the international discussion, the council

Table 4.1. Emergence of NIS as the pivotal concept of science and technology policy in the reviews of the Science Technology Policy Council of Finland in 1990–2000.

Title of review	Definition of NIS	Status and legitimation of NIS
Review of 1990. *Guidelines for Science and Technology Policy in the 1990s*	The totality of the factors that influence the development and utilization of new knowledge and expertise (p. 21)	International discussion analysing the success of various countries increasingly focuses on national systems of innovation and their effectiveness (p. 21)
Review of 1993: *Towards an Innovative Society: A developmental strategy for Finland*	A central development target in the preparation and pursuit of economic policy (p. 21) The most important single instrument in structural policy (p. 40)	Council Review of 1990; The Cabinet Economic Policy Committee defined NIS as a central developmental target in the preparation and pursuit of economic policy in 1992 (p. 21)
Review of 1996: *Finland: A knowledge-based society*	A field of interaction built on cooperation between those who produce and those who utilize new knowledge and know-how (p. 23)	In the 1990s, the development of the innovation system emerged as a pivotal line of action (...) in all industrial countries (p. 11) The development of the national innovation system as a comprehensive entity (p. 24) Continuous development of its efficiency (p. 63)
Review of 2000: *The Challenge of Knowledge and Kow-how*	A domain for interaction in the production and utilization of knowledge and know-how built on cooperation between all producers and users of new knowledge	Finland's NIS as a historically insightful policy strategy and long-term goal of its science, technology, and innovation policy (pp. 11, 14) An object of evaluation (p. 10)

referred to its own review of 1990 and to the decisions of the government and the Cabinet Economic Policy Committee in 1992, which defined the development of the national innovation system as a central objective of the Finnish economic policy. Likewise, the Ministry of Trade and Industry had defined the development of NIS as a cornerstone of the nation's industrial policy. According to the review, "these decisions created conditions for the systematic development of NIS in the future" (Science and Technology Council of Finland 1993: 7). Consequently, NIS was reified concretely as an object of planning by referring to the policy decisions made by governmental bodies and ministries.

The 1996 Review (1996: 7) defined the development of Finland's NIS as an established main pillar of the Council's policy: "During the ten years of its existence, the Science and Technology Policy Council of Finland has promoted and pursued a long-term science and technology policy line. The most important object of development is the national system of innovation and its different sectors with their internal and external interactions." The definition of NIS no longer referred to the totality of factors influencing innovation into *a field of interactions between knowledge producers and users*: NIS was "understood as a field of interaction (. . .) between those who produce and those who utilize new knowledge and know-how." Corresponding to this definition, the review underlined the significance of establishing different kinds of networks as a means of advancing the utilization of knowledge.

The Finnish national strategy for the information society was adopted in 1995. The review of 1996 added to it the conception of a national innovation system: "Finland has set it as an objective to become one of the leading information societies not only in Europe but in the whole world" (Science and Technology Council of Finland 1996: 9). The review specified the nature of the information society as "one in which the information and media industries are an important business sector, in which everyone has access to information services and has skills to use them, and in which the procedures and structures of business life and the public sector have been developed with the help of information technology." However, it went further by defining the creation of a *knowledge-based society* as a long-term developmental goal. It is a society in which "knowledge and know-how are central factors for economic, social and educational and cultural development" (1996: 9).

The 2000 Review elaborated on the themes presented in the 1996 Review. The catchword was now "knowledge-based development". A "balanced development of NIS as a whole" as well as "strengthening contacts of different policy sectors" are mentioned as prime elements of a long-term science and technology policy. The national innovation system was defined in 1996 as a "domain of interaction" between producers and utilizers of new knowledge. The review noted that the innovations system had developed partly because of regional pro- grammes (2000: 58): "The range of partners in the innovation system has changed and developed. Alongside old operators, there are new ones who contribute to the development of regional innovation processes." Among these, the expanded network of science parks as well as centres of regional expertise are mentioned. In addition, Finland's NIS was also defined as an object of evaluation (2000: 10): "the operation of the NIS is currently being evaluated by means of several studies and reviews." The special questions addressed by the review were the shortage of qualified manpower in the IT sector, the cluster programmes and the development of regionally comprehensive innovation networks.

To sum up, the use and status of NIS in the four reviews underwent two kinds of change. First, it transformed a concept taken from international discussions into a foundational term of domestic science and technology policy as well as of industrial policy. Its status was confirmed and legitimated by references to the decisions of the Council itself, government bodies and ministries. NIS was established as an object of planning whose efficiency was to be systematically developed and evaluated. Various policy programmes and measures – no matter what their origin – were dealt with as elements of the system. Finally, the concept was cemented as a long-standing and visionary strategy of the Finnish science and technology policy.

What happened can be characterized as a process of reification (cf. Moscovici 1984). The documents of the Council imply that a national system exists and that it had to be made more efficient. In the text, the national innovation system is a "natural" object, an object of systematic planning and evaluation. At the same time, many researchers disagreed how a national innovation system should be defined and what should be included in the system. The early definition of NIS by the Council well exemplifies the idea an economic imaginary which "selects a subset of economic relations as an object of calculation, management and intervention" (Jessop 2008: 16). In this way it appeals to the age-old dream of policymakers of being able to plan and control the development of complex social processes.

In the 1996 Review, a new definition of NIS emerged that underlined the interaction between the producers and the users of knowledge. This implied that in addition to planning the system as whole, it was necessary to establish various kinds of networks and interaction between public sector research activity and firms.

4.3 The arguments of the 1993 review "Toward an innovative society"

During the years 1990–1993 Finland suffered one of the worst recessions in her history. Real GPD dropped about 14% from 1990 to the 1993, and unemployment rose from 3% in 1990 to almost 20% in 1994. The recession was more severe than the depression of the 1930s in terms of many indicators, and in fact it was the most severe among the OECD countries (Honkapohja and Koskela 2001). This crisis provided the context for the 1993 Review of the Science and Technology Council. It might explain the rhetorically strong arguments for the development of the national innovation system, which was defined as a strategic choice for the nation.

The basic argument of the 1993 Review was that the development of the system was needed because knowledge and know-how constitute the key factors in international competition between firms and nations. This argument was formulated in the final section of the introductory chapter, entitled *Forward with Knowledge and Know-How*, as follows:

> The creation and application of knowledge are central success factors for individuals, enterprises, societies and state groupings. It is largely on these factors that action strategies are built. In the final analysis, it is the efficiency of our own national system of innovation that determines our place among the industrialized countries, not only now but also in the future. (...) The same applies to Finns' possibilities to achieve their individual objectives in Finland and abroad. (Science and Technology Council of Finland 1993: 9)

The passage aims at convincing its readers of the necessity of the development of Finland's NIS and of creating a national consensus on this goal. The first step was to define the creation and application of new knowledge as an indispensable and strategic asset in the international competition between nations and individuals, a familiar thesis in the knowledge society discourse. The second step was to depict the "efficiency" of NIS as being synonymous with knowledge creation and application. The third step was to postulate the system's efficiency as something that defines the place of nations and individuals in the world (of international competition). The fourth step was to postulate the comprehensive development of the national innovation system as an offer one cannot refuse.

This thesis is supported by the following six key arguments. The first three of these were related the significance of knowledge and new technology as well as research and development for the future of the nation. Two of them (4 and 5) suggested that the production and use of knowledge can be advanced by increasing the efficiency of the innovation system. According to the sixth, the interaction between parts of the system was vital, specifically the cooperation between publics sector and firms.

4.3.1 *Knowledge and know-how are the foundation of the competitive edge of the nation in modern world*

Throughout the 1993 review the argument of the significance of knowledge and know-how for the success in international competition was reiterated:

Finland has had to decide what role it is striving to attain among industrialized countries and how this goal is to be achieved. The general conclusion is that in order to develop a democratic society and an industrialized country, Finland must build its international position and competitiveness on knowledge and know-how (1993: 13).

The long-term competitive edge in the international market will primarily rest on knowledge and know-how. (1993: 39)

4.3.2 A basic policy measure is to support R&D in knowledge-intensive fields related to new generic technologies

The challenge of acquiring knowledge and know-how will be met by developing knowledge-intensive fields, centering around the new generic technologies: information, materials science and biotechnologies:

According to these studies, the longer-term growth potential is primarily found in knowledge intensive fields. (1993: 40)

Top-level research is needed to develop basic know-how and industrial applications in rapidly progressing generic technologies, which have a profound influence on the development of products and productivity, such as information technology, materials technology and biotechnology. (1993: 42)

Here, the argument that knowledge is the primary means to success in competition is used to justify the traditional goal of the Finnish technology policy, realized in the 1980s through focused funding and research programmes for strategic generic technologies – as it was in most industrialized countries.

4.3.3 Investments in R&D and education are investments for the future competitive edge

They cannot be neglected even during the economic recession.

In the face of the deep recession, the development of the national innovation system was also defined in terms of investments in R&D and in education. The review argued that immediate investments in R&D were indispensable to ensure the future of the innovation system: "Since the outcome of R&D activities shows up in a rise of productivity only after a lag of 5–10 years, while the lag for basic research and education investment is perhaps 20 years, we shall inevitably lose economic competitiveness in the future, if investment in the national system of innovation is neglected" (1993: 7).

4.3.4 *The NIS must be made more efficient*

The internal efficiency of the national innovation system needs to be improved in order to adapt to changing environments, especially to economic recession, international integration, social change, and increased individual responsibility. "Changes in the economic environment have modified the conditions for the operations of the national system of innovation and made new demands on it" (1993: 9). The means of meeting these demands is the improvement of the internal functioning and effectiveness of the NIS. "The national system of innovation is a transition which in the near future will determine the prospects for achieving an efficient system in all respects. The key tasks are to develop and intensify the internal operation of the system" (1993: 9).

4.3.5 *Systematic evaluation is needed to make Finland's NIS more efficient*

Systematic evaluation and research on the impacts of the policy measures are needed to make the system more efficient (1993: 28): "Systematic evaluation serves internal objective-setting and selection within the innovation system and improves the knowledge-base which supports decision-making on the improvement of the system." This often-repeated argument connects the tradition of rationalistic (means-end based) planning to the systems concept. Evaluation is a central means of making the systems efficient.

4.3.6 *The significance of cooperation and interaction for the system will increase*

> Cooperation and interaction are gaining more and more importance in the national system of innovation. Cooperation between the public sector and enterprises plays a decisive role in this. (1993: 46)

These basic arguments also laid the foundation for the subsequent reviews. The significance of interaction and networking increased in the 1996 and 2000 reviews.

As mentioned above, the Ministry of Trade and Industry also published its National Industrial Strategy for Finland in 1993. The Science and Technology Council used this strategy as a foundation for its NIS policy. The strategy document complemented the Council's 1993 Review. The document (Kansallinen 1993: 48) stated that "the technological development and accumulation of knowledge capital are most important explanations of the national competitive edge in the long run." It further noted that the quantity of innovations in national economics and industrial sectors is to a large extent dependent on investments in R&D. International comparisons show that the extensiveness of research activity and the developmental level of national economy are tightly interconnected: "in almost all countries with a high level of income the ratio of research input of the total production is high" (1993: 49). Therefore, investment in education and R&D not only increases productivity but also accelerates it on a permanent basis, thus creating a long-standing competitive edge.

The 1993 review presented strong arguments concerning the fate and future of the nation and her citizens by showing the necessity of the policy proposals. This also justified the removal of the whole discussion from the political arena, and that policy line was natural and inevitable.

4.4 A vehicle for national consensus: The development of the national innovation system as "an offer one cannot refuse"

The "general societal climate" was mentioned already in 1990 as one element of the national innovation system. Lemola suggests (2001: 58) that "the special task of science and technology policy has been to take care of the creation, maintenance and development of a climate favourable towards the R&D and innovation activity." The concept of a national innovation system implies that the competitive edge of a whole nation is sharpened on the whetstones of knowledge and know-how. In the global competition, only the nations whose citizens know more and are capable of learning more will succeed.[5] This leitmotif constituted the basis for a national consensus, as formulated in the 1993 Review of the Science and Technology Policy Council:

> In the final analysis, it is the efficiency of our own national innovation system that determines our place among the industrialized countries (. . .). In this sense, the comprehensive development of the system of innovation is 'an offer one cannot refuse'. (Science and Technology Council of Finland, 1993: 10)

---

[5] This imperative was recognized as the starting point of the "Green paper on innovation" of the European Union (1995: 5): "Innovation is vital. It allows individual and collective needs (. . .) to become better satisfied. (. . .) Enterprises need to innovate constantly if they are to remain competitive. The same is true of countries, which need to transform new ideas rapidly into technical and commercial success if they are to maintain growth, competitiveness and jobs."

The 1993 Review also underlined the "wide agreement in Finland" that a comprehensive development of a NIS is one of the foremost tasks of Finnish economic and social policy of the 1990s (1993: 47). Indeed, wide agreement was reached. All political forces supported the national goal of competitiveness based on knowledge and innovations. The other side of the coin was the absence of critical debate on the effects of technological advance. In Finland, interest in the evaluation of the social and ecological consequences of technology has been almost non-existent, compared to such countries as Denmark, the Netherlands, and Germany (see Miettinen *et al.* 1999; Vig and Paschen 2000).

In 1998 Erik Allardt, the distinguished Finnish sociologist and former research director of the Academy of Finland, published a paper entitled *"Technology rhetoric as a means of constructing the Finnish reality"*. In it he analysed how technology rhetoric was influencing in the description of the development of the Finnish society and in setting the goals in the society. He compared NIS to prior well-known articulations of the "national project" that refers to the successive visions of the construction of the Finnish nation.[6] Before the 1990s the goals of creating new industry by public measures and the achievement of a welfare society were the dominating images.[7] Allardt found that the term "national innovation system", along with other terms taken from technology, was a leading image in the formulation of a new project for the country. Several analyses of the change of political rhetoric followed (Kettunen 1998 and 2002; Heiskala and Luhtakallio 2006).

A group of Finnish sociologists and policy researchers (Heiskala and Luhtakallio 2006) published a collection of papers entitled *A New Division: How Finland became a competitive edge society* in which the changes in policy language were analysed. The book regarded the early 1990s as a turning point in the characterization of the national project: metaphors taken from the economy, technology, and business language replaced the language used to characterize the welfare society as a shared national goal.

In his analysis of the Finnish model of welfare state political historian Pauli Kettunen (2004) called the policy agreement of the 1990s as a "top model of consensual competiveness", a top example of consensual national response to globalization. It is continuation of the political consensus that emerged in post-war Finland. He characterized the new

---

[6] He mentions two books as examples of such articulations: President Urho Kekkonen's *Does Our Country Have The Patience to Get Rich?* (1952) and *The Social Policy of the 1960s* by Professor Pekka Kuusi (1961).

[7] Allardt referred to the speech given by Finnish President Martti Ahtisaari in 1997, in which he presented the goal of Finland being the first nation to develop into a knowledge society.

policy agreement in terms of "depoliticization", the creation of national unity and consensus by referring to external necessity. After the recession in Finland in the beginning of the 1990s, the necessity of being competitive in international markets was introduced as a matter of national survival. This was to be achieved by being innovative and by creating proper conditions for innovations (Kettunen 2002: 37):

> The concept of National innovation system demanded that the institutions related to working life, education and technology must be considered and integrated from the point of view of global competition. The "broad-based" view of NIS presented by the Science and Technology Council was as a matter of fact a new viewpoint to what is customarily called society.

The reorientation of national consensus in Finland was based on the new need for national economic competitiveness. In public discourse, politics were seen as means to meet national necessities, such as the national project for competitiveness based on knowledge and innovations. It was possible to legitimize cuts in welfare benefits and services by referring to the national primacy of this project.

Kettunen's analysis is pertinent to Finland's science and technology policy of the 1990s. The rhetoric of necessity was strong in the triannual reviews, and consensus concerning the basic "project" was strong among the political parties. Even trade union organizations did not question it. This has been explained by their participation in the formulation of technology policy (Lemola 2001). Evidently, scientific and especially technological research greatly advanced the achieving of consensus on the project for competitiveness based on knowledge and innovation. Indeed, even during the recession, it was possible to push through increases in R&D funding.

The creation of a favourable social climate for innovation implies an ideological effort to foster an entrepreneurial spirit and to oppose any competing conception, including conservative, traditional academic attitudes, and those critical of technological advances made at the expense of social justice. In his review of systemic approaches to policy making, P. Caracostas, a science adviser in the European Commission, pointed out the task of convincing "the society" of the significance of innovation:

> Science, technology and innovation have lost for their virginity for public opinion; recent crises linked to over-industrialization and technology have provoked negative reactions from the public, and researchers, industry and governments need to develop a new rationale in order to convince the society that innovation means growth, improved quality of life and more jobs. (Caracostas 1998: 309)

The consensus around the NIS in Finland was not complete. Reservations and critical comments were presented regarding the use of NIS as an organizing concept of science and technology policy. Erik Allardt published in 1995 an opinion entitled *The national innovation system as a friend of technology policy and as a foe of science policy*. He thought that since the term "innovation" refers to immediate usefulness and economic value of knowledge, cannot be used to characterize academic basic research that is committed to find new problems instead of being immediately useful. In addition he found the term "system" problematic, since it was being used without defining it or defined using "words resembling definitions" (1995: 7):

> The publications of the Science and Technology Council never clearly state what the belonging of a field or a sector to the national innovation system means. Does it mean a list of the areas that should enjoy public funding? Or is it assumed that NIS is really a functioning social system motivating individuals and groups to striving in research and development work? Or have we simply invented a kind of a new way of classifying things. The observer and reader easily start to suspect that what we find is this third alternative, that is, a new way of listing things has been invented.

Some commentators found the value commitments of the concept of a national innovation system insufficient and unilateral (Allardt 1995; Niiniluoto 1996; Alestalo 1999; Rask 2001). The activities of diverse institutions are evaluated from the point of view of their contribution to national economic competition. It is implied, without much dissent, that welfare is a more or less automatic result of a growing economy. Rask takes up, as an example of this kind of commitment, the following quote from the Academy of Finland's *Forward Look 2000* (2000: 86):

> Innovation systems have clear targets for effectiveness at the global, national and regional levels. The issue is primarily one of improving competitiveness by developing new technology. It is seen to contribute to the achievement of important economic and social goals, such as growth and employment.

The critics find that this overall commitment ignores the fact that particular policy fields and sectors of culture may wish to pursue different goals (such as environmental sustainability, equality, development of the national culture, etc.). It also tends to presume, overoptimistically, that through economic development these other values are automatically realized. The NIS perspective tends to exclude issues that many people regard as the most important challenges to humanity: ecological problems, poverty and hunger, and the constantly increasing polarization of prosperous and poor nations and people. In 2000, development aid was 0.33% of the gross national product of Finland, which is less than one half of the 0.7% targeted by the United Nations. During the 1990s, at the time when a consensus was being reached on Finland's national innovation policy and the exponential growth of R&D funding, Finland's aid to developing countries decreased.

4.5 The development of the 2000s: From social innovation to broad-based innovation strategy and centres of excellence

Reviews of 2003 and 2006 of the Science and Technology Policy Council continue to discuss the Finnish NIS as a functional system, "the efficiency, performance and productivity" of which must be increased by holistic and systemic development (Science and Technology Council of Finland 2006: 8). It was, on the other hand, regarded as a planning model that allows coordination of the activities of stakeholders of the national system. The reviews of 2008 and 2010 started also to speak about *ERI-systems*, that is *Education, Research and Innovation* systems instead of using the term national innovation system. They introduced new terms such as broad-based innovation policy, attractive innovation environment and internationally top-level competence clusters. The National innovation strategy of 2008 underlines the need of internationalization of the system speaking about the need of "global knowledge communities" and "globally networked innovation ecosystems" (National innovation Strategy 2008: 9).

Three novelties were introduced to Finnish innovation policy discourse in the 2000s: 1) the concept of social innovation; 2) an extended or broad-based definition of innovation that include technical and social innovations, improvements in public services as well as demand- and user driven innovation; and 3) the idea of the internationally top-level centres of expertise.

The 2003 Council Review mentioned the need for a social innovation strategy. It had at that time at least three meanings: 1) the extension of the concept of innovation from technical innovation (commercialized technical invention) to organizational and institutional innovations; 2) the extension of innovation to public services (and public goods), specifically to social and health-care services; 3) the inclusion a social dimension to innovation policy exemplified by such issues as welfare, social and regional equality, care of elderly people and exclusion of young people from working life. The Science and Technology Policy Council characterized the new broad policy in its 2008 review as follows

67

(Science and Technology Council of Finland 2008: 8) "horizontal innovation activities covering all the society have become the focus of policy measures. These activities are characterized by demand and user orientation, need for thoroughgoing improvement of innovativeness in the public sector and the increased importance of strong and diverse innovation environments. Innovation policy also covers the non-technological, social and various everyday occurrences of innovation."

An example of the early definition of social innovation is the opening speech of the rector of the University of Jyväskylä in 2003 entitled "Finland into a model country of social innovations".

> Largely understood, also the changes in norms as well as in cultural systems of concepts and habits can be included in social innovations. (. . .) Centers of social innovations have been established in some European countries. There the concept [of social innovation] is defined among other things as a new way of solving social problems and improving the quality of life.

The concept of social innovation was made known by a popular book *100 Hundred Social Innovations from Finland* (Taipale 2007). It was translated into English, Japanese, Russian, and Swedish. The president of Finland, Tarja Halonen wrote a preface to the book in which she found that the social innovations presented in the book "provide an insight into Finnish Society and the way it works." The editor of the book, Ilkka Taipale (2007: 2) defines social innovations as the source of societal harmony: "Gender equality, free education, universal social security and parliamentary democracy, and the consequent social stability they create, have secured Finland's welfare." The social innovations presented in the book deal with administration, social policy, health, culture, regional policy, civil society, and everyday amusement. They cover the single chamber parliament "the mother of all innovations", the status of the Romani and Sami people in Finland, bilingualism, free school meals, state alcohol monopoly, and selected civic organizations such as the Finnish Literature Society established in 1831. They stretch from historical events such as the resettlement of the Karelians after the Second World War to cultural phenomena such as Finnish tango and Santa Claus.

The book wants to show the richness of the sources of welfare and innovativeness in Finnish society. On the other hand, in this extended understanding, innovation becomes a synonym of the political, social and cultural development of society. But can any single theory or model of innovation be sufficient to make sense of this diversity? Do we not need specific expertise and understanding in dealing with the development of different spheres of society? Or more specifically, is the idea of innovation as a commercialized technical or organizational invention as proposed by innovation studies suitable for the development of public services?

A scholarly attempt to define social innovation was undertaken by the SITRA research programme called "Social innovations, renewal capacity of society and economic success: Towards a learning society" in 2002–2004. Research director Timo Hämäläinen from Sitra and professor of sociology Risto Heiskala (2004 and 2007) outlined a "theory of social innovation process".[8] They regarded social innovation as a mechanism of structural change in society. They defined structures in terms of institutions and use Richard Scott's (2008a) account of "three pillars" of institutions as a starting point. The three pillars are rules (regulative pillar), norms and values (normative pillar) and shared cultural meanings (cultural-cognitive pillar). Social innovation deals with all these dimensions of institutional order. The authors (2004: 48) defined social innovations as reforms of regulative, political and organizational structures which improve the performance of the society (for a critique, see Pol and Ville 2009).

In 2007 the Ministry of Trade and Industry of Finland adopted a broad-based concept of innovation and innovation policy. According to it, innovation is "a *utilized* [either commercially or from the point of welfare of citizens R.M.] *know-how-based advantage of competition.*[9] The National Innovation Strategy of 2008 as well as the Research and Innovation Council adopted this definition. The council review of 2010 (Research and Innovation Policy Council of Finland 2010: 16) characterized the Finnish innovation strategy as a "sustainable and balanced strategy" that "must be able to combine economic development, the improvement of environment and the increase in the welfare of the citizens."

Many observers doubt whether the idea of broad-based innovation did bring any clarity to policy making. The international evaluation of the Finnish national innovation system found that the term remains conceptually fuzzy, can be interpreted in several ways and "does not contain a clearly articulated vision, strategy and adequate measures for

---

[8] The authors characterize their theory as "a theoretical framework that synthesizes the general features of structural change processes in socioeconomic systems" (Hämäläinen and Heiskala 2007: 35). They find (2007: 33) it possible to formulate such a general theory, because of the similarity of collective learning processes in all human communities and in different levels of analysis, that is, in small groups, regions, sectors and nations. The model of institutional change developed in this book (Chapter 7) disagrees: both problems to be solved and knowledge, tools and expertise needed to resolve them are activity- and domain-specific.

[9] PowerPoint presentation by a representative of the Ministry of Trade and Industry, 3 December 2007.

the future" (Evaluation of the Finnish National Innovation System 2009: 20). It found that measures of enhancing social innovations or user involvement are not presented.

The major new policy means of the new decade was the establishment and funding of Centers of Excellence for Science, Technology, and Innovation (in Finnish the acronym SHOK). The SHOK programmes aim at high international standard and globally competitive research development and innovation in the areas that are "most important for national economy, societal development, and citizen's economic, social and cultural well-being" (Science and Technology Council of Finland 2008: 19). The objectives of the strategic centres include that "their high-level expertise and reputation attracts innovative and leading global companies and top international experts to Finland" (Research and Innovation Council 2010: 39). These centres also serve as platforms for producer-user dialogues and for collaboration between firms, universities and research institutes. They also lay a foundation for attractive innovation environments. About 20% of the TEKES funding will be funnelled to SHOKs (Research and Innovation Council 2010: 40).

The low level of internationalization of the Finnish research system was recognized already in the 1990s. It was a central concern of the innovation policy of the 2000s. For instance, in terms of publications per researcher, Finland is well below the OECD and EU averages. It was argued that although Finland's investments in R&D are propositionally high (4% of GPD), these investments are globally marginal. That is why Finland cannot maintain globally top quality research in many areas. SHOKS were also seen a solution to this problem (Research and Innovation Policy Council 2010: 39):

> One of Finland's biggest challenges is to create and maintain world-renowned clusters that can act as nodes that attract innovation actors, businesses and capital. Finns need to be proactive in their areas of strength in transnational cooperation networks. Large, multidisciplinary centres have the best capacity to become global poles of excellence and innovation, encouraging creative and open research environments, dynamic labour markets and high-quality business services.

The centres adopt the organizational form of non-profit limited company to commit the owners to long-term research programmes (with 5–10 years' time perspective). The major industrial owners of the SHOK LIMITED companies, that is, will define the research programmes of the SHOKs mainly by the established large companies. Sixty per cent of the programmes funding is public, coming mainly from TEKES. The six SHOKS selected by the Science and Technology policy Council and

Ministry of Employment and Economy and the Ministry of Education are: 1) forestry; 2) ICT; 3) metal products and mechanical engineering; 4) energy and environment; 5) health and well-being; and 6) construction. The first three areas represent the three most established areas of Finnish export industry, while following focus on areas that are anticipated be important in the future.

This new policy instrument has been criticized on two grounds. First it has been argued that because of the globalization the construction of world-class national clusters or concentrations of expertise is no more sensible. Second, it has been argued that SHOKs do nor favour the emergence of new technology firms that are regarded the key of economic growth. The evaluation of the Finnish innovation system regarded SHOKs as a tool of enhancing and renewing the knowledge base of traditional strong areas of the Finnish industry. Since the intellectual property rights are shared among the participants, SHOKS are not expected to promote start-ups, which typically in high-tech areas require exclusive intellectual property lines. That is why the evaluation concludes that SHOK is a conservative policy tool (Evaluation of the Finnish National Innovation System 2009: 31):

> Hence the SHOKs cannot be expected to be "forward looking" in the sense of being instrumental in changing Finnish production structure through the development of new sectors of production (. . .). Neither can they be expected to enhance the creation of new firms in new sectors of production. So far they can be even judged to play a conservative role in the Finnish economy and its presently strong sectors.

It is an open question whether goal of the creation of few (6–8) world-class, competitive, high-profile, and attractive innovation environments in Finland is realistic and sensible policy. An alternative view would underline local initiatives and emergence of new firms with specific high-level expertise which would allow them to find their place in international market, networks of collaboration and global value chains.

5

Policy discourse and the reality of national innovation

To what extent and how did the new innovation policy have an influence on the national innovativeness and the Finnish economic development? I will discuss this problem by analysing the development of investments in R&D and the role of innovation policy for the emergence of the Finnish ICT-sector in the 1990s. It will show that the development of R&D funding has its root in the industrial policy of the 1960s, in the science policy of the 1970s, and in the technology policy of the 1980s. It will be concluded that the rise of the Finnish ICT sector cannot be explained by the innovation policy of the 1990s. Innovation policy turned out to be a continuation and extension of the science and technology policy of the previous decades. At the end of the chapter the conclusions concerning the role of innovation policy language and buzzwords for the policy practices will be discussed.

The commitment to a permanent increase of the public investment in R&D has been a characteristic feature of the Finnish science and technology policy from the beginning of the 1980s (Lemola 2003). The share of R&D input as a percentage of GDP in Finland was 0.9%, which was then one of the lowest figures among the OECD countries. The investment in science and technology was seen already in the 1960s as a central way of modernizing of the unilateral structure of the Finnish industry which was heavily based on forest industry. The first programme for catching up the level of R&D funding of other European countries was formulated in 1973. The Science Policy Council of the Academy of Finland set a target of achieving the level of 1.7% in 1980. In the 1980s the rate of increase of public R&D funding was 10%. The funding of R&D continued to increase even during and after the severe economic recession at the beginning of the 1990s, which led to considerable budget reductions in other policy areas such as social policy and education. In 1996 the Government made a decision to substantially increase the investment in R&D. An increase of about 25% from the 1997 level in the state annual research appropriations was achieved between 1997–1999. The share of R&D input as a percentage of GDP rose from 1.8% in 1989 to 3.4% in 2004. The limit of 4% was achieved in 2009, which was the second highest share among the OECD countries after Sweden.

The increase in the investment in R&D by firms that were riding the waves generated by the information technology sector, especially by Nokia, was even more rapid in the 1990s. This achievement came essentially from the increase in the share of firms in the total R&D investments from 60% in 1993 to 73% in 2000. Nokia's share of the total R&D input of Finland was one third in 2001 and 47% of the corporate R&D costs in that year (Ali-Yrkkö and Hermans 2002). Although Nokia's share of the Finnish export, GPD, and corporate taxes declined considerably in 2008–2009 compared with 2000–2003, the investment in R&D continued to increase.[1] In 2008 its share of total business-sector R&D in Finland was 49.5% and 37% of total R&D expenditure in Finland (Ali-Yrkkö 2010:31). These figures show that the high share of R&D funding of the GPD in Finland has been to a large extent due to one firm, Nokia. Therefore, a good test for the impact of innovation policy is to evaluate to what extent it contributed to the emergence of Nokia and the Finnish ICT sector in the 1990s. This will be discussed in the following section.

The major instruments of the Finnish science and technology policy were created in the 1960s, 1970s, and 1980s (Lemola 2003). The number of universities tripled in the 1960s and 1970s from the five universities in the 1950s. The Academy of Finland and its six research councils were established in 1961 for public funding of scientific research. The Ministry of Trade and Industry began in 1968 to support the research and product development of firms. In 1983 The National Technology Agency (Tekes) was established. It became the main vehicle of technology policy. It funded both national technology programmes and the product development of the firms. In the 1980s programmes and organization associated with technology transfer diffusion and commercialization such as technology parks and centres of excellence were created, many of them on the basis of local and regional initiatives. The national technology programmes catalyzed national co-operation because firms, universities, and research institutes together prepared and implemented

---

[1] Nokia's share of the exports dropped from 25% in 2002 to 10% in 2009 and the share of GPD from 4% in 2000 to 1.5% in 2009 (Ali-Yrkkö 2010: 11).

the programmes. The funding for technological research granted by Tekes almost tripled from 1991 to 2005 being about twice as much as the funding from the Academy of Finland in 2005.

The innovation policy of the 1990s followed and further strengthened the technology policy of the 1980s. However, it did not bring any significant changes to the basic organization of the Finnish science and technology policy (Lemola 2003). The most notable institutional change in the 1990s was the increase in the role of regional policy. It took place, however, largely outside the science and technology policy. It was governed by the Ministry of Interior in charge of regional policy and its key instrument were the EU's structural funds. The first National Center of Expertise programme for the years 1994–1998 was initiated under the terms of the Regional Development Act. The second (1999–2006) and the third (2007–2013) programme period extended the programme and tried to integrate it into a national innovation policy. The programmes have been regularly evaluated. The evaluations show that programmes have served as a tool for raising awareness, learning, and capacity building for the future (e.g. Edquist *et al.* 2009: 42). It remains, however, open to what extent they have been able to stimulate the emergence of new innovative business activities. The centres of expertise programmes have contributed together with the technology programmes of Tekes to the increase the interaction between the national actors.

Table 5.1 shows that Finnish firms had the highest overall level of collaboration with universities and public research institutes, as well as other firms, clients, and suppliers among the EU countries in the

Table 5.1. Co-operation of firms in innovation activities in Finland, Sweden, Denmark Netherlands, and the United Kingdom in 15 EU countries on average 1994–1996 (European Commission 2000: 78) and in 27 EU countries 2004–2006 (Fourth Community Innovation Survey, European Commission, Press Releases, 22 February 2007).

	1994–1996		2004–2006	
	All innovation-related co-operation %	Co-operation with universities and research institutes %	All innovation-related co-operation %	Co-operation With universities %
Finland	67	43	44	33
Sweden	54	24	43	17
Denmark	61	20	43	14
Netherlands	29	9	39	12
UK	30	17	31	10
EU-15, EU-27	25	13	26	9

Eurostat 2000 statistics. It was almost threefold compared with the average of the 15 EU countries. The OECD scorebook figures for the years 2004–2006 confirm the high level of co-operation of the Finnish firms (OECD 2009: 125). It is, however, unclear whether this increased national interaction is sufficient for the emergence of new firms that are able to operate in the international market. The rapid internationalization of the activities of Finnish firms underscores the increasing significance of non-proximate relations (e.g. Ylä-Anttila 1996). The integration of geographically restricted and global networks of production may be the key challenge in fostering the regional innovativeness.

5.1 Did the NIS policy contribute to the rise of the Finnish ICT industry in the 1990s?

Some international commentators (Hart 2006; Sharif 2006) have suggested that there is a connection between the adoption of the national innovation system approach in the Finnish policy and the rapid development of the Finnish economy in the 1990s. According to Sharif (2006: 752), "the policies that respond to the NIS and helped to haul Finland out of recession included developing Finland's competitiveness (...) by developing knowledge intensive fields that centre around technologies such as information technology, material science and biotech (...)." Hart found that (2006: 2) "The Finnish political economy, riding the success of Nokia, generated nearly from scratch what seems to be an extraordinarily competitive innovation system (using the systems of innovation framework as a guide, no less!)." On the other hand, the success of the Finnish economy from the 1990s onward has led some observers to speak of "the Finnish model" as an attempt to define characteristics of the innovation system, and more largely the features of the economy and society that explain the economic and success of the nation (Castells and Himanen 2002; Oinas 2005; Gerlils 2006).

The attempts to find a strong connection between the economic development of a country and the quality of its innovation policy might be analysed as what social psychologists call the attribution error (e.g. Hewstone 1989) or in terms of the phenomenon psychologists and management researchers call "the halo effect" (Rosenzweig 2007). The attribution error refers to the systematic tendency of people to attribute behaviour to an actor's dispositions or features and to neglect the contextual and situational factors. The halo effect in turn refers to the tendency to evaluate all features of a person, group, or organization on the basis of an overall impression. One special form of this effect relevant in economic life is the attribution of positive qualities to a social entity on the basis of good performance.[2] On occasion this phenomenon seems sometimes to assume a special form in innovations policy: if the economic development of one country is more rapid than in others, its innovation system also must be excellent and can therefore be benchmarked as a model for success. As in attribution error, the explanation is not found in the intertwining contingent developments and, as in the halo effect, one expects to find a unique combination of interacting institutions and policies that constitute a success model.

The story of the rise of the Finnish information and communication technology sector and particularly of Nokia is a good case for studying the alleged connection between innovation policy and economic development. It has been suggested that the story of the Nokia model "mirrors that of Finland's own transition from the industrial to the information society" (Castells and Himanen 2002: 28) and Nokia is regarded as a model of a new global business management culture in Finland (Tainio and Lilja 2003). In 2000 it constituted half of the Finnish IT sector, its share of the exports of the sector was 70%, and it accounted for almost 25% of Finland's total exports.

The Finnish science and technology policy did play a role in the rise of Nokia, but surely not the adoption of the NIS concept in the early 1990s. Its possible fruits are being harvested today and will be enjoyed in the decades to come. The Finnish science and technology policy of the 1970s and 1980s did create conditions for the rise of the Finnish IT sector in the 1990s. However, the essential reasons for the development of Nokia and the IT sector are to be found elsewhere. The historian Martti Häikiö, who wrote the history of Nokia Corporation (see Häikiö 2001 and 2002), came to the following conclusion:

> I have come to the conclusion that the fierce development of Finland cannot be explained by an "innovation policy", that is, by public or private additional investment in research and development. The phenomenon must be studied from the point of view of the interaction between new inventions and public regulation. The explanation for this new developmental phase is to be found in the liberation of competition, i.e. deregulation, which occurred simultaneously with an unprecedented "quantum leap" in technology, i.e. the transition to digital technology. It was characteristic of this phenomenon that these two developments were chronologically simultaneous but not at all necessarily

---

[2] Rosenzweig (2007: 64) regards the halo effect as "the most fundamental delusion that distorts our thinking about business." He presents several illuminating examples (Cisco, AGG, among others) in which the same features (values, customer orientation, etc.) of the firm that were regarded as explanations of success during its growth were evaluated as its weaknesses when the firm's performance was falling.

interconnected. Such coincidences have happened in prior history maybe once in a century. (...) The role of the public policy is limited to the regulation of competition. Instead of speaking of an innovation policy it might be better to speak of the removal of the barriers to competition and development.[3]

Other researchers have presented more moderate interpretations, typically suggesting that Nokia's success was a combination of skilful corporate management, effective technology policy and good luck (e.g. Koski *et al.* 2002). I find the evaluation of Hyytinen *et al.* (2006) of the background of the rise of the Finnish ICT-sector quite balanced (2006: 74): "There was no systematic plan to restructure the Finnish economy or to build a globally competitive ICT-sector. Rather, a number of private initiatives, processes and policy measures were working simultaneously."

The reasons for the success of Nokia and the Finnish ICT sector include at least the deregulation of financial market, the formation of competitive Nordic markets for mobile phones via the NMT standard in the 1980s, and the decision by Nokia management to concentrate on digital wireless mobile phone technology shortly before the rapid development of the global mobile communication market in the mid-1990s. The global success of the European GMS standard played an important role. In addition, the transformation of the Nokia's management practices contributed to its development into a global player in the telecommunication sector.

I will analyse below how Finland's science and technology policy contributed to the development of Nokia and the Finnish ICT sector (for more complete accounts, see Häikiö 2002: Ali-Yrkkö and Hermans 2004; Palmberg and Martikainen 2005; Hyytinen *et al.* 2006). In 1973, the Science Policy Council of Finland recommended that Finland's R&D expenditure should be raised from 1% to 1.7% of GDP by 1980, that is, to the level prevailing in the developed European industrial countries. This was not achieved in the 1970s (Lemola 2004: 275). In the 1980s the growth averaged 10% annually, which was the most rapid growth rate in the OECD area. After the economic recession in the early 1990s the growth rate again rose to 10%. The rate of 3.4% of GNP achieved in early 2000s was one of the highest shares among OECD countries. From the point of view of the telecommunication sector, it was important how this funding was directed.

After the economic crisis and the devaluation of the Finnish mark in 1967, Finnish politicians concluded that the future of the Finnish economy could no longer be based on the wood and paper industry alone.

---

[3] Martti Häikiö, Helsingin Sanomat, 23 January 2006.

The industrial policy was reoriented toward the establishment of an electronics industry. It was done in the form of Valco, a state-owned company that started to produce television tubes in 1978. The enterprise was a failure and the heavily unprofitable production was stopped in 1980. The Technology Development Center (Tekes), established in 1983, directed public funding to telecommunication projects with the participation of universities, research institutes and telecom firms. This funding was without doubt important in creating the critical mass of expertise in key telecommunications of technologies that could be channelled to Nokia when the decision was made to focus on mobile technology (Lovio 1989 and 1993). The public funding of the GMS technology programmes was particularly important, although the benefits from it were only realized years later (Ali-Yrkkö and Hermans 2004: 111). In addition, the Tekes funding was important for Nokia's R&D during its critical years at the beginning of the 1990s, although this funding did not exceed 5% of the total R&D funding for Nokia (Ali-Yrkkö and Hermans 2004).

In late 1990s the share of Tekes funding was about 1.5% and in the 2000s from 0.2% to 0.4% of Nokia's total R&D expenditure (Ali-Yrkkö 2010: 26). These measures, however, can be characterized as traditional technology policy measures. A corresponding success so far has not been achieved, for instance, from the investments in the biotechnology sector.

Important factors for Nokia's success were the active role of the public telecom operator (Palmberg 2002) and the government's participation in the creation of the Nordic Mobile Telephone System in 1981 (Lehenkari and Miettinen 2002) and in the Pan European GSM (Global System for Mobile Communication), which was adopted in 1988.[4] As a result of the joint creation of the NMT standard, the Nordic countries in the 1980s constituted the first transnational mobile communication market in which individual consumers could freely buy their mobile phones. Competition in this market and feedback from the consumers contributed to Nokia's preparedness to meet the challenges of a rapidly expanding new business area.[5]

[4] According to Hyytinen et al. (2006: 68): "Telecommunication standardization in the Nordic and European contexts may be the single biggest explanatory factor behind the Finnish ICT success."
[5] The significance of the NMT and the European GMS standards for the success of Nokia and Eriksson in the international telecommunication market is widely acknowledged (e.g. Bresnahan et al. 2001: 857): "The GMS standard was critical for the growth of a continental wireless market in Europe that benefited the Scandinavian firms first (...) The formation of a European standard, was, however, key for creating a sizable demand [for them R.M.]"

In addition the public telecommunication operator also helped the industry by procurements and by collaborating with them in product development. In 1987 the Finnish Post and Telegraph Office even urged the Finnish producers (Mobira and Telenokia) to start the production of network equipment to curb the market power of the Swedish Eriksson and equipment prices more generally. This collaboration took place outside the official technology policy through horizontal collaboration between professionals in the telecommunication sector.

In 1985 Mobira (a joint venture of Nokia and Salora) had a 26% market share of the Nordic NMT handset markets compared with 17% for Eriksson and 6% each for Siemens and Motorola. The first GMS call in the world was made in Finland in June 1991. Nokia was well equipped to meet the challenge of expansion when GMS mobile technology became almost universally accepted during the 1990s.

Recent literature (Castells and Himanen 2002; Oinas 2005) has recognized at least three features in Nokia's strategy and decision-making that were important for its development and success. At the beginning of the 1990s Nokia was a diversified conglomerate. In 1986 it had ten divisions, 45 business units, and 180 lines of business. It produced televisions, portable computers, cables, rubber boots, and toilet paper. In 1992 the new management made the decision to focus exclusively on communication technology, more specifically on the as yet unproven digital GMS technology. The decision proved to be wise. Nokia became the leading mobile phone producer in the world, with a 39% share of the global mobile phone market in summer 2007. Second, in 1994 Nokia was listed on the New York Stock Exchange and the financing based on Finnish bank groups were replaced by money from global financial markets. This was a precondition for the international expansion of the firm in the late 1990s. The governance structure of the firm changed accordingly to conform to the practices of Anglo-American global stock market corporations.

Third, Nokia established a network of hundreds of suppliers all over the world and an extensive network of research that was able to ensure the company's ability to increase production without a considerable decrease in quality. In the 2000s Nokia has moved both product development and production closer to its markets by establishing plants in Romania, Hungary, and England in Europe, as well as in India, China, South Korea, Mexico, and Brazil. Nokia exemplifies a type of global firm that was unthinkable in Finland in the 1980s and has served as a model for the Finnish firms in other sectors as well.

Consequently, I am inclined to think the success of the Finnish ICT sector and the Finnish economic miracle of the 1990s cannot be explained by the Finnish model of innovation policy. Rather the opposite is the case: the "exemplary model" owes its existence to the success of the Finnish ICT sector. Or it may be said that the success of Nokia and the telecommunication sector has influenced the Finnish business system and the policy making institutions. Nokia's management practices have been a model for other firms, and national policy making has also reacted to its needs and expectations (Tainio and Lilja 2003).

When a national economy develops exceptionally rapidly, there is a tendency to believe that its economic and innovation policies constitute an exemplary model that can be used as a "benchmark." This rationale, however, is problematic in at least two respects. First, contingent historical factors or unique developmental processes might explain the success better than the policy pursued or the make-up of the policy-making institutions. Second, the factors that were responsible for success under one set of circumstances will not necessarily bring success in the future. Those who are looking for exemplary models will too easily focus their attention on the patterns and practices of the recent past, and this may keep them from exploring the novel approaches that are needed in times of rapid change. The history of national innovation systems supplies an example of this. Freeman (1987) introduced the concept to explain the institutional factors of Japan's superior technological and economical development. While these institutions were novel and impressive, they did not ultimately enable Japan to maintain its competitive edge.

One more factor contributing to the success of Nokia needs to be discussed. The 1970s and 1980s witnessed a radical increase in the level of education of the young generations in Finland. In 1970, 13.6% of the age cohort 20–24 attended universities. In 1990, this share was 39.7%. This dramatic rise in educational level and the quality of the school system was without doubt a central precondition for the structural changes in Finland and for the emergence of the telecommunication industry. A young, well-educated, and hard-working workforce became available, one that was looking for new opportunities. The number of R&D personnel in Nokia increased from roughly 4000 in 1993 to 18,000 in 2002. Almost two-thirds of this personnel in 2002 were Finns (Ali-Yrkkö and Hermans 2004: 110).[6]

In addition to the deregulation and the development of telecommunication technology and its markets, also other societal developments contributed to the Finnish industrial transformation in the 1990s. A broader analysis of the institutional conditions of this transformation

---

[6] An important reason for that is the low salary level of engineers in Finland. The salary of a Finnish engineer is two-thirds of the salary of her/his colleague in Germany.

is needed. The development of the Finnish educational system laid the groundwork for the rise of the ICT sector in the 1990s. This corresponds with what Freeman (1987 and 2002) found in his studies of Japan and Singapore. The development of the Finnish unitary school system was not inspired by the NIS policy, but rather by a national welfare project that underlined the importance of providing equal opportunities to the population and access to education regardless of social background. This project increased opportunities for upward social and economic mobility through education and it has been thought to have contributed to economic growth. Paradoxically, although the values of equal opportunity, welfare and becoming a civilized member of culture were dropped from the NIS language, they inspired the reforms of the educational system that constituted a major precondition for the transformation of the Finnish economy in the 1990s.

5.2 Redistribution of power and democracy in the age of innovation policy

The adoption of the NIS vocabulary was connected to the policy of structural transformation formulated by the government led by Prime Minister Harri Holkeri in 1987. Holkeri was the chairman of the conservative Coalition Party. This government programme formulated the goal of a "governed structural transformation" from a closed, national factory-based economy into a global, open, knowledge-based economy. The liberalization of financial markets in the 1980s was a tangible step in this direction. The programme of the Holkeri government also underlined the key significance of knowledge and expertise for securing the competitive edge of the nation. The concepts of NIS and knowledge-based society can be seen as the means by which the policy of structural transformation by the Holkeri government was further elaborated.

A history of the Finnish parliamentary science and technology policy (Tiitta 2007) finds that an important turn in the policy took place in the late 1980s and in the 1990s. It is characterized by three developments. First, power in science and technology policy making was removed from the parliament to ministries, specialists of different funding organizations, institutions, and firms, and, ultimately, to the Ministry of Finance. "When the control of policy simultaneously became more holistic than before, the significance of the preparatory work done in the ministries increased at the cost of the value debates [in the parliament and in society at large R.M.]" (Tiitta 2007: 230).

Second, the power of the Ministry of Trade and Industry, which became responsible for the Innovation policy, increased on the costs of the Ministry of Education. Tiitta also finds that (2007: 280): "The Ministry of Finance has become the most important ministry in controlling of the funding for science and research. Simultaneously science and technology policy slid ever more tightly into a part of the general economic policy." He presents an example of this (2007). The Committee for Education and Culture of the parliament – composed of the representatives of all parties – unanimously suggested increases in the basic funding of the universities in 2000 following the suggestion of the Ministry of Education. Because the Ministry of Finance opposed the suggestion, the increase was dropped from the final budget book.

Third – as already shown – the funding for applied technical research and product development increased steadily in the 1990s, and its share grew in relation to basic "academic" research. The funding for Tekes increased in the first half of the 1990s in spite of the cuts in other areas of public administration, including universities. In 1990–2000 the share of Tekes of the total R&D funding in the state budget rose from 16.8% to 30%. In 1997 the number of staff of Tekes (265) was twice as big as the staff of the Finnish Academy (Pernaa and Tiitta 2007). In the 2000s, Tekes has allocated annually about twice as much money to research as the Academy of Finland.

Some observers find that a technological political elite developed in the 1990s. In a survey (Kuitunen and Lähteenmäki-Smith 2006) addressed to those involved in technology policy, the respondents were asked to evaluate which organizations they find influential in political decision-making with regard to technology. Almost all the respondents were agreed that Tekes (96%), the Ministry of Industry and Commerce (95%) and big companies (93%) were the most influential actors in decision-making when compared for example with universities (71%), the parliament (67%), the Ministry of Social Affairs and Health (28%) or civil organizations (20%). The authors conclude: (ibid.: 99) "The politicians have remained notably absent from the core decision-making in Finnish technology policy."

To explore the relationship between democracy and the participation of citizens and the innovation policy, two phenomena are discussed below: strategic foresight and the way in which the key reforms of the research and university system are prepared and realized. One of the achievements of the last two decades in Finland has been the normalization of parliamentary democracy after the post-war strong period, characterized by a strong presidential power. At the same time, however, the parliament and the civil society have been increasingly left in the margin in the preparation of many important reforms.

Foresight is a key activity in the Finnish innovation policy as expressed by the Science and Technology Policy Council (2006: 37): "Wide-ranging development of foresight from the perspective of research and innovation should be continued. (...) Close connection between foresight and decision making is essential." Sitra, the Finnish Innovation Fund, the "libero of innovation system" (Evaluation of the Finnish National Innovation System 2009: 11) has by the far largest resources to organize innovation policy-related research and development programmes and foresight exercises. It has been able to hire well-known foreign scholars to analyse the Finnish system and present their vision of its future (e.g. Castells and Himanen 2002; Sabel and Saxenian 2008). Sitra characterizes its role as a think tank on its website as follows:

> We predict, analyse and evaluate the key drivers of change and their impact on Finland. We develop and implement new operating models through practical implementation and experimentation. Sitra identifies the needs for changes in society and enables them.

In two books that emerged out of a Sitra project, Hämäläinen and Heiskala (2004 and 2007) found that innovation policy calls for "strategic policy intelligence" or "a strategic system of foresight and evaluation" (2004: 122). The methods of such intelligence are technology forecasting, assessment, and foresight. Strategic visioning takes place at national, sectoral, and regional levels. The organizational locus of this intelligence are various interaction forums in which researchers and decision makers learn from each others and develop shared language and understanding of key policy issues. Hämäläinen and Heiskala (2004: 138) think that think-thank organizations can take the role of bridge builder between the cultures of research and policy making. "They interpret, condense and package the results of academic research in a way that makes it easy to approach and utilize them." They suggested the establishment of a centre that was in charge of the coordination of visioning and of the accumulation of knowledge on forecasting and evaluation. Subsequently the Science and Technology Policy Council (2008: 26) was planned to have a central role in creating "a transparent, extensively interactive process capitalizing on the results of foresight for the preparation and maintenance of national focus area choices." In practice, numerous national actors have organized foresight exercises. Examples of national foresight projects organized in Finland between 2004 and 2010 are presented in Table 5.2.

Table 5.2. Examples of foresight exercises done in Finland in the 2000s

(1) *A Caring, Encouraging and Creative Finland.* Review to the deep challenges of knowledge society (2004). Report made by Pekka Himanen to the Future Committee of the Parliament of Finland.

(2) *Finland to Become the Leading Country of the Innovation Activity* (2005). A report of the competitive innovation environment (SITRA).

(3) *A Renewing, Human-centric and Competitive Finland.* The National Knowledge Society Strategy 2007–2015. (2006) Prime Minister's Office.

(4) *Towards a Wellbeing and Competitive Society* (2006). Views of the national foresight network of the future of Finland. SITRA.

(5) *Finnsight 2015. Science and Technology in the Finland of the 2010s.* (2006). Foresight exercise organized by TEKES and the Academy of Finland.

(6) *From Efficiency to Sharing; A new phase of knowledge society* (2009). The Knowledge Society Academy of the Future Committee of the Finnish Parliament. Reported by DEMOS think thank.

(7) *The Script for Splendour.* An account of the ingredients of the material and spiritual wellbeing of Finland in the 2010s. (2010) Pekka Himanen commissioned by the Government of Finland.

(8) *Wellsprings of Finnish Vitality* (2010). Report of SITRA's wellsprings of Finnish vitality development project.

In addition to the foresight projects organized by Sitra (2, 4, and 8 in Table 5.1), Tekes, in collaboration with the Academy of Finland, also organized a foresight of the future of the Finnish science and technology policy in the years 2005–2006 (5). The first knowledge society strategy (3) organized by the prime minister's office very closely resembles foresight exercises. The future committee of the parliament, the Technology Industry of Finland, and the Finnish government have ordered visions of the future of Finland from philosopher Pekka Himanen (1 and 7). Himanen wrote together with Manuel Castells the book *The Information Society and the Welfare State; The Finnish Model* (Castells and Himanen 2002), funded by Sitra. In the new visions Himanen developed further the idea of combining competitiveness or the "absolute leadership" in the world in specific areas (Himanen 2007: 133) with welfare and care of fellow citizens. In his view, the SHOKs are the means of achieving the world leadership.

In spite of their differences, these foresight exercises and documents have many common features. All the foresights wishfully want to combine welfare, caring, and competitiveness, as can be seen from the titles of the foresight documents listed in Table 5.1. The documents are mostly anonymous consensus documents, except the visions written by Pekka Himanen. Alternatives visions are not presented. The method of foresight has been more or less organized discussions of working groups or panels. The final document has been written either by a secretary (representative of organizing body such as Sitra or a consultant) or a chairman of the working group, often a university researcher. Methods based on systematic utilization of different views and expertise such as Delfoi have not been used and the differences of opinion in the groups are not visible in the final documents.

Half of the foresight reports in Table 5.2 present suggestions for measures with a list of the actors or types of actors in charge of their implementation. However, these measures remained general and did not include the means and instruments by which they are to be put in practice. Examples of suggestions are: "We need to reintroduce the principle of reasonableness into working life (firms)" (Himanen 2004: 26) and "efficient innovation systems will be created for each urban region, overlaps will be eliminated and interaction will be developed by substantial areas on a national level (Ministry of Trade and Industry, Ministry of Interior, cities, Finnish Science Park Association TEKEL)" (Suomi 2005: 29). Often the measure was to launch a new development programme (A renewing 2006: 20): "Initiation of an innovation programme aimed at developing social and health care services (Ministry of Social Affairs and Health, Ministry of Trade and Industry, Sitra, Tekes, actors of the field)."

As indicated by Table 5.3 the majority of the participants in the foresight exercises were representatives of ministries and state agencies, technology funders and firms. They constitute 70% of the participants of the three foresight projects (2, 3, and 4) included in Table 5.2. The participation of unions, professional communities and civil society organizations is non-existing. A professor from university Helsinki who participated in

Table 5.3. The participants of the two foresight exercises organized by Sitra (2005 and 2006) and of the participants of the preparation of the national knowledge society strategy (2008).

	Sitra 2005	Sitra 2006	National KS strategy	Total and share (%)	
Sitra and Tekes	3	12	1	16	10.5
Academy of Finland	1	1	–	2	1.5
Ministries and state central agencies	4	18	20	42	27.4
Firms, employer organizations, and firm associations	11	24	14	49	32.0
Unions	–	–	1	1	0.7
Universities	6	9	2	17	11.1
Research Institutes	2	9	1	12	7.8
Civil society organizations and associations	–	7	2	9	5.9
Others (municipalities)	–	5	–	5	3.3
Total	27	85	41	153	100.0

two of the exercises (4 and 5 in Table 5.1) found that in them "the results of the foresight projects has already been written when the task has been defined and the participants selected. (...) They have been selected because they have already adopted this vision of the Finnish future."[7]

The repeating consensual talk of primacy of innovation and competitiveness in the programmes has, however, been also increasingly interpreted as ritualistic language. A distinguished member of the Finnish academic community, Chancellor of the University of Helsinki Kari Raivio, for example, argues that the words "top university" and "innovation" may be "the most futile terms" without any proper meaning when speaking about science policy and universities.[8] Innovation is about commercialized products and services. Universities are funded to do research. Firms innovate by making money out of the research results, he thinks. A cosmologist Syksy Räsänen who has worked in several international universities thinks that the term "huipputukimus" (top research) is an inadequate term in the characterization of how science develops and how scientific communities work.[9] He found it a purely political term used in funding: "I have never heard anybody speak about top research in scientific communities. I don't even know what it is in English." The Academician and internationally known molecular biologist Leena Palotie found in 2007 that "we are soaking in the pool of our complacency, since we are on the top in many international league-lists. We purport to have the best school and innovation system in the world, although everybody inside them knows that this is not the case."[10]

In 2009 Sitra launched the wellsprings of Finnish vitality development programme that was to use broad-based discussions to create a common understanding of the future of Finland. "The development project included three leadership forums that brought together some 200 opinion leaders and decision-makers from various fields of Finnish society to seek pathways towards vitality. Between the forums some 30 experts (...) met in workshops to process the themes that emerged in the forums" (Nurmio and Turkki 2010: 2). The programme extended the participation to unions, members of parliament, and civil associations. The workshop activity and reporting followed the traditional model: the results of discussion are presented as a consensus report.

The report – like its predecessors – made many kinds of recommendations. For instance, the report finds that "early childhood education is a universal service that constitutes the broadest, most comprehensive and perhaps most far-reaching tool for prevention of social and health care

---

[7] Heikki Patomäki HS 3.3.2006. [8] Kari Raivio HS 22.12.2010.
[9] Syksy Räsänen HS 10.11.2010. [10] Leena Palotie HS 14.2.2007.

problems" (Nurmio and Turkki 2010: 45). It suggests that "all children over the age 3 must have the right to receive early childhood education teaching services for 3 or 4 hours if the parents so wish (. . .) Pre-primary teaching should be made obligatory by law, ensuring that every child participates." This recommendation was made without participation of the specialists in early childhood development, pre-school pedagogy, or the practitioners in the field. Had they been involved the, risks of accelerating the cognitive development of small children by these arrangements would surely have been seriously discussed.

The welfare and educational reforms of the 1960s and 1970s were prepared by appointing a committee with a broad-based participation of the stakeholders. The goal of the committee work was to create legislation that received as wide an acceptance by citizens as possible and to avoid lapses relating to legislative techniques. Different opinions and minority reports are an important part of Committee work. The reform of secondary education realized in the 1980s can be taken as an example. The degrees and curricula of vocational schools and colleges were unified in the reform. In a massive planning and development project in the years 1975–1977, some 777 different curricula of vocational schools were unified into 20 basic study lines (Pernaa 2007: 85). Fourteen committees with 2300 specialists participated in the planning process (2007: 86). The extensive participation of the professionals and practitioners of the field in the planning process greatly advanced the implementation of the reform.

The use of committees had already decreased in the 1980s. The important reforms of the 2000s were prepared by either by rapporteurs or small preparatory work groups without the participation of stakeholders. The suggestion for the reform of the sectoral research system was given in 2007 by a work group appointed by the government and chaired by Yrjö Neuvo from Nokia Corporation. Two liquidators, Yrjö Rantanen and Niilo Jääskinen, made the suggestion for the "structural change of the economic and administrative status of universities".[11] Professor Paavo Uusitalo criticized this procedure, suggesting that a broad-based committee should be formed to plan the university reform[12]:

> A rapporteur named by a minister is an advancer of the goals of the minister and her/his trend of political ideology. The knowledge base of the reports is

---

[11] Prof. Jorma Rantanen is a doctor of medicine and functioned as general director of a Finnish sectoral research institute, the Finnish Institute of Occupational Health, between 1974 and 2003. Niilo Jääskinen is an attorney, a member of the Supreme Administrative Court of Finland and a specialist in legal issues related to the EU.

[12] Paavo Uusitalo HS 2.3.2009.

selective. The rapporteur can be compared with a solicitor who in a civil case collects data that is favorable from the point of view of his client but disregard the knowledge that is unfavorable for the client.

The suggestion included a structural reform of the Finnish university system by merging smaller universities. Work groups denominated by the ministry of education prepared the three merges. The most ambitious of the merges was the establishment of the so-called "innovation university" by merging Helsinki University of Technology, Helsinki Business School, University of Arts and Design. The initiative came from the rector of the University of Arts and Science and it was strongly supported by the industry.[13] The ministry of education set up a group of 10 persons chaired by State Secretary Raimo Sailas from the Ministry of Finance. It included the rectors of the three universities, one secretary from each, a secretary-general, and two representatives of business sector. The group listened to a group of 12 specialists (mainly CEOs of big Finnish corporations) from the business sector. The report (Opetusministeriö 2007) speaks about the establishment of "a world-class top university" using the international ranking lists of universities as a reference point.[14] To start a development towards this end the working group suggested that the state funding of the new university should be doubled in a few years.

Matti Vanhanen's second cabinet decided to establish the innovation university in 2007 and grant 500 million euros for its operations. The technology industry promised to contribute 80 million euros. The parliament, the academic community and the personnel of the universities were largely excluded from the planning process. The academic community criticized the reform on three bases. First, it did not find the idea of establishing a top innovation university that should climb up in the international league lists sensible or well founded but rather an expression of wishful thinking or a "state of will" characteristic of the innovation policy elite. Second, it did not find it justifiable to channel the public funding to just one university without any competition or regard for the

---

[13] Research director Hannu Toivonen from Kemira Inc wrote (HS 9.5.2008): "To be able to produce top expertise in Finland, we need a top university. In spite of the counterarguments of the academic people business life generally thinks that we don't have a world-class top university in Finland. (...) The reforms needed to maintain high-quality basic research require much money that they naturally cannot be realized in the whole wide university network. Choices must be made. Why do we not invest in an innovation university?"

[14] The ranking lists of world universities were used as a reference, in spite of the fact that each of the universities at the top of the lists (such as Harvard and Stanford universities) alone have a budget and teaching personnel comparable to those of the whole university system of Finland and that the number of students in the Finnish system is seven-fold compared to these universities.

quality of research. Third, it doubted whether a top university could be established by an administrative decision and by combining existing universities that traditionally are not strongly oriented to research. Both the practice of making strategic foresight and the way in which university reforms were prepared support the analyses of the empowering of the "innovation party". The idea of strategic intelligence seems to suggest that an elite comprised of selected researchers, decision makers, and opinion leaders, supported by think tanks, is able to form a vision of the future for the nation and realize it by managing the innovation system. Some critics find this idea as an heir of the idea of a centrally planned society (e.g. Julkunen 2007). This way of policy making has not extended democracy or the participation of the citizens, associations, or the subject-area specialists or professional groups that in practice are in charge of innovating and developing services in the different sectors of society. Since the ideas of broad-based innovation and user involvement were included in the innovation policy in the 2000s, this exclusion can be seen as one of the paradoxes of the Finnish innovation policy.

5.3 The epistemology of transdiscursive terms

It is time to return on a more theoretical level to the question of what makes a term, such as NIS, cluster, or knowledge economy so powerful in organizing discourse within the research community and in policy making. Chapter 2 reviewed the concepts that clarify different dimensions of policy buzzwords. The term *director of attention* (Godin 2006) suggests that a buzzword underlines the importance of a set of phenomena for policy making without providing explanations or deeper understanding of these phenomena. The concept of *boundary concept* (Löwy 1992) suggests that the conceptual fuzziness of a buzzword allows it to function as an interdisciplinary organizer, heuristic device, and to facilitate communication between different social groups. *Diagnosis of an era* (Noro 2000) suggests that visions concerning the nature and challenges of the present society provided by social scientist are not theories but rather performative messages to public discourse that generate new questions. The concept *economic imaginary* (Jessop 2008) underlines the selective and constructed nature of models of economy and, on the other hand, studies the mechanisms through which they are distributed and struggle to become a hegemonic policy paradigm.

The concept of *transdiscursive term* (Miettinen 2002) refers to the fact that these terms develop in interaction between research and policy making.[15] This interaction takes place in more or less stable hybrid social arenas and institutions with representation from research, policy making, and public administration. In spite of their development in these hybrid arenas, transdiscursive terms continue to have divergent meanings and uses in research and policy making. That is why transdiscursive terms not only constitute a means of communication across boundaries but also a source of tension, inducing constant debate and reflection on their value and relevance.

Jari Jääskeläinen's study (2001) of the uses of the concept of the *cluster* supplies an excellent example of the versatile functions of a transdiscursive term in research and policy. Jääskeläinen first reviews how Porter's theory was brought to Finland. A cluster research project was established in 1993 at the initiative of ETLA (The Research Institute of the Finnish Economy), and the ideas and results of the project were used in the redefinition of Finnish industrial policy. Later on it was adopted by other ministries and, in 1996, eight cluster programmes were formed under six ministries. In this process the concept served "as a framework for research and method, as a description of economy, as a means of policy making, as a means of strengthening the role and influence of an organization and as an expression of modernist attitude" (Jääskeläinen 2002: 67). One Finnish senior economist, who was a central figure in introducing the cluster concept to Finland, described the relationship between cluster research and the reformulation of the industrial policy by the Ministry of Trade and Industry in 1993 as follows:

> The important thing for the new industrial strategy was that there was a recession in the country. There was a consensus of opinion that we could not survive by the old means. Visions were needed of how to survive in the long run. It was largely understood that the economy of Europe and the whole world was changing. There was also a need to state things in fresh and clear ways to induce action. Porter's model of competitive advantage just happened to be the framework within which different stakeholders could be included in the discussion. It was a language that was largely understood. Porter's model was not the purpose in itself and the framework could also have been some other. But since we had a large on-going research project

---

[15] I do not use the term "boundary concept", suggested by Löwy (1992) because it refers to the crossing of the disciplinary boundaries alone, and it underlines unilaterally the constructive boundary-crossing capability of this concept. The term "transdiscursive" has a connection to Karin Knorr-Cetina's (1983) concept transepsitemic arena, which refers to arenas where researchers collaborate with various other kinds of actors, such as users, clients, funding agencies, and representatives of public administration. However, I prefer "transdiscursive" instead of "transepistemic" since, in policy use, the epistemic dimension of terms is subsumed to other purposes, such as consensus creation and empowering.

based on it, it was natural to adopt its framework and results as a starting point.[16]

Several interesting points are included in this statement. First, the model did not, as Jääskeläinen concluded, provide content or direction for the new policy, as such. Instead, it served as a vehicle with which the various stakeholders could speak about it. It seems that there was no necessary or direct connection between Porter's model of competitive advantage as a representation of the world (or of sources of the competitive edge of the nation) and the actual industrial policy measures. The transition from direct sectoral and firm subsidies to indirect forms of support, such as R&D funding, did not originate in the model. The epistemic dimension relevant for the use of the concept in research seems to be different from its function as a vehicle of organizing discourses in policy making.

In Table 5.4, I present six socio-epistemic functions that transdiscursive terms have in the borderland between science and policy making. I call them social-epistemic because social aspects, including the pursuit of power, and the epistemic or cognitive aspects are intertwined in their use. On the other hand, the relationship between them varies. Scientific credibility gives cultural authority to transdiscursive terms in policy making. Social scientists produce diagnoses of an era for public and political debate. Policymakers ask researchers to clarify terms that have already been adopted in policy discourse. All of the functions have been either discussed by the theoretical literature and they appear in the policy documents or in the utterances of the participants in innovation policy making.

Table 5.4. Six social-epistemic functions of transdiscursive terms in and between research and policy making (Miettinen 2002: 137; Jessop 2008: 24).

1.	They must have a minimal epistemic function of providing a representation or empirically grounded account of aspects of reality
2.	They function as epistemic-organizers or umbrella terms able to organize in a new way and integrate various themes that were formerly separate
3.	They supply a world view or a diagnosis of an era
4.	They serve as boundary concepts or boundary crossers by engaging various social groups in a shared discussion
5.	They serve an ideological consensus-creating function
6.	They help in mobilizing various actors and in empowering the proponents

[16] Interview of Pekka Ylä-Anttila, the Managing Director of ETLA (The Research Institute of the Finnish Economy), made by Jari Jääskeläinen, 14 January 1999 (Jääskeläinen 2001: 128).

5.3.1 *An epistemic funtion of providing a representation of reality*

The epistemic function has traditionally been dominant in scientific research. Science is about producing knowledge that is as objective as possible. Scientific communities have created institutional practices (such as peer review) as well as methodological rules and norms in an effort to reach this goal. Accordingly, such virtues as conceptual coherence, empirical accountability, and theoretical foundations are emphasized. Albert and Laberge found that the reliance on science supplied the foundation for the cultural authority of the OECD recommendations. As one of the civil servants they interviewed put it: "we were quick to accept recommendations of the OECD because we feel that they come from committed professionals who base their findings on studies from leading scientists" (Albert and Laberge 2007: 229).

There is, however, a major tension between the epistemic and reality-representing function of such terms, on one hand, and their future-orienting and discourse-organizing functions, on the other. These terms are criticized by the representatives of the scientific communities as premature or inadequate in making sense of the phenomena they are trying to characterize. The French philosopher and historian of science Georges Canguilhem (1988: 57–58) has developed the concept of a *scientific ideology* to describe how science-inspired visions are extended to social life and used as foundations of policy making:

> By scientific ideology I mean a discourse that parallels the development of science and that, under the pressure of pragmatic needs, makes statements that go beyond what has actually been proved by research. In relation to science itself, it is both presumptuous and misplaced. Presumptuous because it believes that the end has been reached when research in fact stands at the beginning. Misplaced because when the achievements of science actually do come, they are not in the areas where the ideology thought they would be, nor are they achieved in the manner predicted by the ideology.

The tension between epistemic and political functions of the transdiscursive terms is expressed in the scientific critique of the foundations and uses of these terms. "New production of knowledge" and "Mode two of knowledge production" are among the best-known new conceptions in the science and technology policy of the 1990s. Several scholars have questioned their foundations (e.g. Weingart 1997; Godin 1998; Shinn 1999; Krücken 2002; Tuunainen 2002). Terry Shinn (1999) cannot find any empirical foundation for the extensive emergence of "hybrid institutions" proposed by the model two. In the same vein, Peter Weingart (1997) points out that the authors of models of the radical transmutation of knowledge production grossly exaggerate the features of some sectors of research systems and then make them into a normative model of future knowledge production. He also thinks that the empirical evidence of a fundamental change in knowledge production is almost entirely lacking (Weingart 1997: 608).

5.3.2 *An epistemic organizer able to connect previously separate themes*

The epistemic organizing function of transdiscursive terms refers to their ability to draw together, subsume or connect in new ways knowledge and things that were previously regarded as separate or that were previously addressed in separate research programmes or traditions. Löwy's reference to "the strength of loose concepts" implies this idea. In being able to connect previously separate issues in new ways, transdiscursive terms facilitate movement across the boundaries of traditional, specialized disciplines. In Löwy's account this takes place between scientific and clinical communities. The idea can be extended to include transdisciplinary or hybrid communities (e.g. OECD policy-making bodies) through the participation of researchers, civil servants and politicians.

The term "national innovation system". The early definition of NIS, also adopted by the Science and Technology Policy Council of Finland, encompassed all the elements and processes (determinants) that influenced the emergence and use of new knowledge and innovations. According to many NIS researchers it was and remains important to keep the definition open and flexible (see Edquist 1997: 27).[17] Whenever a new "determinant", i.e. a relevant institution or a social process, is discovered, it can be added to the sphere of the term.

In his study of the adaptation of the concept "knowledge-based economy" as an umbrella term in OECD policy making, Godin (2006) found the term not only integrated the newest terms from the literature. It also served as a new label for indicators: Godin thinks that the "knowledge-based economy" is an umbrella concept: "it allows to gather existing ideas and concepts of science and technology, and any indicators, into a conceptual framework, i.e. all under one roof" (Godin 2006: 24). Indicators that had been used for years or even decades by the OECD were "subsumed under the concept of knowledge-based economy" (2006: 22).

---

[17] Edquist (1997: 27) thinks that "the conceptual ambiguity of the systems of innovations approach is a strength in providing openness and flexibility that makes room for comparing perspectives and solutions (. . .) At the same time, a hundred flowers cannot bloom forever."

5.3.3 *Provide a diagnosis of era and a world view*

The notion of a national innovation system incorporates an apparent analysis of our time. It is a thesis of sources of success and survival in the changing world. As argued above, one of the goals of the NIS theorists was to provide policymakers with "a world view and basic principles of policymaking" in a new context. Because of this diagnosis and world view it has the power to attract supporters.

5.3.4 *Function as a boundary concept able to engage various social groups in a shared discussion*

Many of the transdiscursive terms mentioned above have functioned as boundary objects, that is, as verbal vehicles that make it possible for people with different backgrounds and from different institutions to talk about the same issue and still maintain their own world view and intentions. This is an important function of transdiscursive terms, for they help to reorganize political discourses by crossing boundaries, that is, by enabling various traditionally non-collaborating stakeholders to talk to each other about a common topic.

Löwy (1992: 374) defined boundary concepts as "loosely defined concepts which, precisely because of their vagueness, are adaptable to local sites and may facilitate communication and cooperation". All the actors can see their own peculiar concerns, concepts, and interests as part of the new conception. In research and politics, the term "national innovation system" brought various previously unrelated issues and phenomena together under the same rubric and programme. A term that functions as a transdiscursive, organizing term is necessarily an open term, that is, as a term that is compatible with a variety of uses and interpretations.

A former civil servant from Finland in science and technology administration who was involved in the advancement of the Finnish NIS policy describes this use of the term as follows:

> NIS as an indeterminate concept worked well in the context in which it was meant to work. Our discussions with the unions included unemployment and salary payment capacity: Innovations create jobs and capacity for salary payments. When regional development was discussed, it was possible to speak about the regional innovation system and balanced regional development. With industry, the discussions covered e.g., the issue of productivity gains. In this way, NIS provided a means of discussing with these stakeholder groups using their terminologies and agendas (. . .). A loose term was extremely useful since it was not necessary to argue about definitions, because it was possible to

adopt freely and flexibly the definition which each one of the stake holders wanted to give to it from the perspective of his own context.[18]

5.3.5 A function of mobilizing actors and empowering the proponents

An analysis of the reviews of the Finnish Science and technology Policy Council showed that the NIS vocabulary was used to create national consensus on what is important and what had to be done. Arguments were presented by the proponents of the new term to convince citizens and different social groups of the necessity of a vision and to create an atmosphere and attitudes favourable to it (e.g. Billig 1991). Its use encouraged various stakeholders to think of the vision and world view implied by the concept. It made the acceptance and realization of its world view an issue of moral duty: "The systematic development of NIS is an offer one cannot refuse." The consensus built by the terms "national innovation system" and "cluster" can specifically be seen as a part and continuation of a national project to create and maintain a nation.

5.3.6 A function of mobilizing actors and empowering the proponents

The function of the term "national innovation system" in redistributing power is implicit in classical rhetoric. The term is used by a proponent not only to convince audiences, but simultaneously to increase his or her influence and to get others to discuss matters of shared interest on the terms laid out by the proponent. Jääskeläinen has shown how, by introducing the cluster concept, the Ministry of Trade and Industry extended the concerns of industrial policy to the spheres of science and technology and social policy, and was thereby able to mobilize other ministries to join it. Without doubt, the success in implementing the national programme helped secure funding for R&D in negotiations in which other actors (such as the Ministry for Social Affairs and Health and the Ministry of Labour) were attempting to push through their own agendas. Section 5.2 reported the redistribution of power from parliament to ministries and specialists of funding organizations and the increased power of the Ministry of Trade and Industry (from the year 2008 the Ministry of Employment and Economy) and the Ministry of Finance on the cost of the Ministry of Education in which process the idea of national innovation system played a role.

Research work and policy making are interdependent in various ways. The concept of a national innovation system emerged in an attempt to

---

[18] Interview, Dr. Erkki Ormala, 13 August 2002.

explain differences in economic growth rates between nations. Its development as a term, as a possible a scientific concept, and as a research programme was dependent on its reception in the field of policy making. Its credibility as an organizing concept depended on its status in scientific communities. An academically marginal concept is not likely to achieve such a status. On the other hand, political acceptance and success help a research programme obtain funding and strengthen its position in academic discourse. The epistemic, social, and political arenas are interwoven through the links between scientific and political activities. In the case of NIS, communities such as the OECD and EU policy-language-producing institutions were vital venues for this sort of interaction.

The introduction of the concept of social innovation and of the broad-based concept of innovation in 2007 in Finland is an example of how political terms become layered. From the point of view of policy making, it may, however, be decisive, to investigate what kind of policy instruments and means are developed and implemented with the change of the vocabulary. In my analysis (Miettinen 2002) the introduction of the term national innovation systems did not substantially change the policy instruments used in Finland in the 1990s. Neither was the most important new policy instrument of the 2000s, the centre of expertise (SHOK), derived from the concept of broad-based innovation that was introduced at the same time.

5.4 From policy discourse to practice: Performativity through instruments and multi-voiced expertise

Many proponents of the NIS approach have suggested that it is above all a conceptual framework for constructing reality. They find that a traditional epistemic critique of it, i.e. a discussion of whether NIS is a good explanation or representation of the conditions of innovation, is misguided (e.g. Eriksson 2005). This constructivist position has been recently discussed in terms of performativity of language.

The term "performativity" comes from J. Austin's (1976: 3) linguistic philosophy. He introduced the concept of performative speech acts to overcome what he called the "descriptive fallacy" in the study of language. Performatives, in contrast to "constatives" or descriptive utterances, cause a change in social life. Paradigmatic examples of such performative or operative speech acts are (1976: 5) "I do" (uttered in a marriage ceremony) or "I name this ship". Consequently, language use and practice are not separate: "When saying what I do, I actually perform an action" (Austin 1979: 235). Several authors have criticized Austin's view of giving "magic force" to words. Austin analyses conditions under which performatives may be successfully realized in terms of "conditions of felicity". Bourdieu (1991: 73) points out that these conditions are social conditions that must be analysed to understand whether a performative is successful or not in inducing change.[19]

The concept of performativity was introduced to the economics sociology by Michel Callon. He (1998) suggested that a discourse is performative if it contributes to the construction of the reality that it describes. In 2006 he analysed the performativity of economy by extending Austin's idea to include economics and scientific discourses more generally (2006: 10): "Scientific theories, models and statements are not constative; they are performative, that is, actively engaged in the constitution of the reality that they describe." Donald MacKenzie's (2006) study of option markets and option theory is a major attempt to test and develop the theory of performativity in economics. In the beginnings of the 1970s the Black-Scholes-Merton Model of option prices was developed simultaneously by three economists.

Mackenzie asks whether this theory affected the option markets. His answer is instructive in many ways. First, he shows that the theory could not be applied to markets directly. The theory's core is a differential equation that would have been opaque to anyone without college-level training in mathematics. It would take too much time to use it to calculate prices manually or to use calculators in trading situations (MacKenzie 2006: 35). But, several parties developed sheets of option prices based on the model that could be used by trading companies and individual traders on the open-cry trading floors of Chicago and on other option exchanges. These sheets were "material mediators between option pricing models and floor traders" (2006: 40). The sheets were practicable, cognitively simple enough to use, and they were made easily available at a reasonable price. In addition to this they enjoyed the cognitive authority of financial economics. They were in wide use and supplied a language that facilitated communications between traders, exchange officials, and regulators.

On the basis of interview material, Mackenzie shows that the sheets did influence pricing. The estimates of the model and the sheets were used in trading and in setting prices in the 1980s. As a consequence, the option prices fitted the Black-Scholes-Merton Model better in the 1980s than in

---

[19] According to Austin (1976: 14), the first condition for "a happy functioning of a performative" is: "There must be accepted conventional procedure having a certain conventional effect, that procedure to include the uttering of certain words by certain persons in certain circumstances . . . ." All of Austin's examples of performatives are about using words in well established and ritualized social institutions. His optimism about the power of words may derive from this framing. His idea of the strength of the performatives may be more problematic when applied to the transformation of social practices i.e. when new institutions are created. There are neither accepted conventional procedures nor "powerful" words related to them.

the early 1970s. Mackenzie therefore concludes that performativity in the sense that the model – through material mediators – had an effect on the phenomenon it described. However, after the dramatic fall of the US stock market on 19 October 1987, it lost its power: the prices ceased to fit the model. Mackenzie calls this *counterperformativity*.

Mackenzie's case provides a key to the limits of the performativity of language use. As suggested by cultural-historical activity theory, pragmatism and constructivist sociology of science human activity is mediated both by language (and other sign-systems) and by material tools. That is why language alone cannot without material mediators transform social-material reality. An absence of relevant tools and instruments often makes understandable why visions of foresights often remain dreams and the goals of developmental projects are not achieved. Austin's account of "how to do things with words" and his examples concern institutionalized ways of acting and using language. When we orient ourselves to the future and try to create new social realities, the situation is evidently different.

Pragmatist philosopher John Dewey criticized the rationality based on aim-means distinction. Goals and aims are not independent of means. Intelligent means allow wise redefinition and transformation of aims. And vice versa "the principle of magic is found whenever it is hoped to get results without intelligent control of means" (1922/1988: 22). Instead of ready-made aims the development and novelty is realized through working hypothesis and in practical experimentation. In experimentation unanticipated problems and contingency plays a role, requiring constantly new solutions and tools, and therefore learning. The systems of means needed for innovations are domain-specific and historically developed: they are totally different in the music education of children, in nanotechnology, and in the construction industry. Innovation in each domain or community requires both knowledge and expertise of the tradition of the domain and dialogue across boundaries.

When Lev Vygotsky, the founder of the cultural historical tradition in psychology, formulated the concept of mediated action in the 1920s (Vygotsky 1979), he suggested that two main types of means, namely signs and tools, that play different role in activity. Signs (models and concepts) are used as "internal tools" to control the activity whereas tools are used to transform the material environment. As a matter of fact, a whole arsenal of mediating artefacts is needed in activity and even more so in changing an activity (Miettinen and Virkkunen 2005). Consequently an understanding of the relationship between language use and the actual use of different means (mediating artefacts, material mediators) and related skills are essential for understanding a practice. Vygotsky and

Dewey agreed in this. The study of the semiotic mediation of the use of tools was the starting point for Vygotsky's theory.[20] In a letter written to Arthur Bentley in 1951, Dewey characterized how he intended to continue his philosophical project (cited by Sleeper 2001: 16):

> If I ever get the needed strength, I want to write on *knowing* as the way of behaving in which linguistic artifacts transact business with physical artifacts, tools, implements, apparatus, both kind of being planned for the purpose and rendering inquiry of necessity an *experimental* transaction.

The principle of mediation both by language and material tools can be applied to analyse the relationship between innovation policy language and policy instruments. It turned out that because of the "conceptual fuzziness" of such terms as NIS, the specific policy means cannot be drawn from them. Because of their fuzziness and openness, different – even contradictory – interpretations and policy measures can be reconciled with them. Additional knowledge and foundations are needed to find and develop relevant policy instruments that are able to take steps to turn the policy ideas into reality. An example of this problem is the contested nature of the policy instruments of Finnish innovation policy in the 2000s, such as regional policy of expertise and SHOKS, Centres of Excellence for Science, Technology, and Innovation.

On the other hand, the limitation of prevailing innovation policy instruments developed by the OECD and EU need to be regarded. During the 1990s and 2000s the measurement and comparison of innovative performance of countries or "efficiency" of national innovation systems became a fundamental tool of making innovation policy (Balzat 2006: 63–65). Quantitative comparisons of countries are based on indicators that measure different dimensions of innovation. The central output of these measurements is a league list, in which the countries are ranked according to their scores. Both the OECD and European Commission have developed indicator-based performance evaluations: OECD Science, Technology and Industry Scorebook. These can be characterized as NIS benchmarking. Many analysts have pointed out that it is very difficult to find good indicators of knowledge transfer and use and the indicators used suffer from conceptual and technical weaknesses (Godin 2002; Grupp and Schubert 2010). What is even more important is that it is not possible without a thorough historical and contextual analysis to derive concrete policy advice or policy instruments from

---

[20] "The practical intelligence and sign use can operate independently of each other in young children, the dialectical unity of these systems in the human adult is the very essence of complex human behavior. Our analysis accords symbolic activity a specific organizing function that penetrates the process of tool use and produces fundamentally new forms of behavior" (Vygotsky 1979: 24).

these comparisons. In an overview of national innovation approach literature Luc Soete *et al.* (2010: 1117): make the following final conclusion:

> Innovation system has become a phenomenon that is most often analyzed in a qualitative way, or using an indicators scorebook approach. (...) It is also clear that this approach has its limitations in terms of being able to reach concrete conclusions and concrete policy advice. It is one thing to reach the conclusion that institutions matter, but it is quite another to be able to suggest a concrete assessment of how institutional arrangements influence in innovation performance, and by how much. In order for the innovation systems approach to remain influential, it needs to address these concrete issues.

NIS benchmarking provides a good example of how a policy tool influences the policy making and its aims. It shares a lot with other benchmarking tools that were developed as a part of Lisbon strategy and the so-called Open Coordination Method (OCM) to evaluate and develop both competitiveness and social inclusion in European countries (De la Porte and Nanz 2004; Room 2005; Bruno 2009). Indicator-based comparisons provide valuable information about differences between countries but they constitute only a starting point for learning from the experience of other countries. Sabel and Zeitlin (2010) see OCM as a promise for a new experimentalist governance in the EU. In the model, the national lower level units (ministries) can advance as they see fit the framework goals established by joint action of member states and EU institutions. In return for this autonomy "they must report regularly on performance, especially as measured by agreed indicators, and participate in a peer-review in which their own results are compared with those pursuing other means to the same general ends." (2010: 3). Finally, framework goals, metrics, and procedures themselves are periodically revised.

Several researchers, however, have also observed the contradictions or paradoxes related to the indicator-based benchmarking. First, since evolutionary thinking (and the NIS approach) underlines complexity, historical specificity, and heterogeneity of national systems, it avoids the idea of an optimal system and regards the idea of measurable best practice as problematic (e.g. Balzat 2006: 93). Second, the indicator-based comparisons do not provide knowledge of the contingent and multidimensional reasons that explain the differences (Arrowsmith *et al.* 2004: 32). To learn from the comparisons the historical and institutional reasons should be studied and understood (Grupp and Schubert 2010:78). Without such contextual learning neither the means of improving the situation nor alternative patterns for socio-political development can be defined (Room 2005: 144).

According to Graham Room (2005: 124) the comparison of league lists tend to lead to a particular way of thinking: "The language used is that of laggards catching up with the leaders, with the assumption that those leaders hold out the future to which the laggards must adjust." This way of thinking tends to make European nations more performing and competing bodies instead of collaborative members of a union (Bruno 2009: 278). In the absence of a deeper study of the practices, the implementation of a best practice remains uncoupled from the performance measurement phase in NIS benchmarking (Balzat 2006: 96).

Room (2005: 22) thinks that the benchmarking practice that emerged from the EU Lisbon strategy suffers from what can be called basic ambiguity or a democracy deficit. Benchmarking should serve as a tool of policy learning, but it does it only in a limited way. It is a top-down system where goals are posed by the Commission and benchmarkings are prepared by expert committees without the contribution of parliaments, civil society organizations, or practitioners of the activities that are being benchmarked (de la Porte and Nanz 2004). Room (2005) thinks that a more bottom-up system is needed in which citizens and their organizations, professionals, and practitioners at the local level learn from each other across national boundaries.

Indicator-based performance benchmarking in the form of league lists as a policy instrument influence policy thought and practice. The obsession with placing in league lists – that gain its authority from the OECD and the EU – directs attention away from historical and local conditions and may degrade the quality of decision-making. This happened in my mind when an innovation university was established in Finland by strongly basing itself on international league lists of universities and framing the decision in terms of "climbing up to the top in the lists".

Since 2000 Finland's 15-year-old students have been top three times in the OECD PISA comparisons. This outcome has been a surprise for the Finns themselves. A large body of literature looking for explanations for the success emerged (reviewed in Chapter 6). Among the reasons presented are the quality of teachers and the high esteem of the teaching profession, decentralized governance of comprehensive schools that gives much responsibility to municipalities and school communities as well as a unique special education system. No one of these alleged "reasons" is easy to imitate because they are each a result of the development of decades and are composed of a complexity of practices and instruments. The expertise on special education, for example, is based on a long-term research-based development of diagnostic and pedagogical tools, that is, tests, learning materials, remedial methods, and games. The analysis in the next chapter clarifies in which way the indicator-based comparisons can be complemented by historical and qualitative inquiry that has been done together with the experts and practitioners of the field.

6

Institutional change and learning: The case of Finnish basic education

6.1 Production of capabilities and innovativeness

Reformation of the educational system has been seen as a central condition for modernization and the rapid growth of a national economy (e.g. Freeman 2002). The school system and adult training institutions play a key role in the production of a capable workforce. In a knowledge society, the level and quality of the workforce's capabilities becomes an ever more important issue. It is no wonder that the concept of national innovation systems has been renamed by innovation researchers as systems of competence building (Lorenz and Lundvall 2009) or systems of learning (Edquist 2005). However, the mechanisms by which education and other capacity-building institutions contribute to innovation have not been systematically analysed. The PISA (Programme for International Student Assessment) studies that have been issued by the OECD since 2000 are constructed to provide information on the production of such capabilities in basic education. PISA evaluates the key competencies of 15-year-old students in member countries in three domains: reading, mathematics, and scientific literacy. The idea of competence in the PISA studies is defined as follows (OECD 2001a: 14):

> PISA focuses on things that 15-year-olds will need in their future lives and seeks to assess what they can do with what they have learned...PISA does assess students' knowledge, but it also examines their ability to reflect on the knowledge and experience, and to apply that knowledge and experience to real life issues.

Items testing reading proficiency in the assessment are constructed to correspond to situations in which written information is assumed to be used in civil society and working life. To do well in the reading test, the students are supposed to draw conclusions and reflect on the consequences of the information provided in the printed and digital texts. To what extent the test results measure real life capabilities and predict success in further studies or in working life is still debated (e.g. Hopmann *et al.* 2007; Schleicher 2007). Critics have pointed out that there is no research-based evidence that what PISA measures is important for the future of the students nor that there is a connection between the test's scores and economic development (Hopmann 2008).

Since the PISA studies only started in 2000, longitudinal studies of the results are still few. A Canadian study (Brink 2010) found that the results of the PISA in 2000 predicted both access to further education and success in working life. Many sociologists of welfare as well as economists of education have concluded that cognitive capabilities significantly influence both school success and remain crucial throughout a person's career (Warren *et al.* 2002; Esping-Andersen 2009). A well-known researcher of the welfare state Gösta Esping-Andersen (2009: 115) concludes: "Since cognitive (and non-cognitive) abilities influence school success and, subsequently, adult's life chances, the polity challenge is to ensure a strong start for all children. Investing well in our children will yield very large returns both for individuals' life chances and for society at large." The PISA studies provide information for the evaluation and further development of the hypothesis presented by welfare researchers.

PISA was established to meet the need of governments to obtain information with which to develop educational policy. The comparison of student achievements was meant to lead to comparison ("benchmarking") of school systems and to stimulate policy reforms. In this sense the PISA studies realize – although on the level of only one key institution – the goal that inspired the comparison of national innovation systems: the need to find explanations for differences in educational achievement. And for the time being, PISA is the most extensive enterprise in comparative education. The publications of each study have gained unparalleled public and governmental attention in European countries and in other OECD counties. They have caused speculation about the reasons for the differences and have led to the benchmarking of the school systems of countries that performed best in the study and to changes in educational policies (e.g. Hopmann 2008).

In PISA the students are divided into six levels of achievement according to the scores they receive on the tests. Countries are compared in relation to the level of the overall score as well as in relation to the

Table 6.1. The percentage distribution of students according to levels of expertise in reading in some OECD countries in 2009 (OECD 2010a: 194).

Proficiency in Reading	Finland	United Kindom	Greece	Bulgaria	OECD average
5 and 6 excellent	14.5	8.0	5.6	2.8	7.6
4 good	30.6	19.8	18.2	11.0	20.7
3 satisfactory	30.1	28.8	29.3	21.8	28.9
2 passable	16.7	24.9	25.6	23.4	24.0
1 weak	8.3	18.5	21.3	41.0	18.8
Total	100.0	100.0	100.0	100.0	100.0

distribution of students on different levels. Table 6.1 shows the PISA results of four European countries in 2009 in reading proficiency.

The OECD report (2010) defined "groups" of countries whose scores did not differ statistically significantly from each other. Finland (536 points) belongs – the only European country represented – to the group of countries with highest scores, together with Korea and Hong Kong, China. In this group of countries more than two thirds of students have achieved level 3 in reading proficiency and the proportion of weak readers is less than 10%. The United Kingdom (494 points) belongs to a group of European countries whose results did not differ from the OECD average and in which the proportion of high achievers is significantly lower and the proportion of weak readers considerably higher than in the first group. The United States, Germany and France belong to this group. Greece (483 points) belongs, along with Italy and Spain, to the group performing slightly under the OECD average. Bulgaria (429 points) is a European country that is on an equal level with such developing countries as Mexico and Thailand. The proportion of weak readers is considerably high, more than 40%.

The OECD has regarded the achievement of level 3 in PISA reading capabilities as a "minimum indicator" for the capacity for lifelong learning (Istance 2003: 88). Functional literacy in a knowledge society demands the capacity to read demanding (political, professional, and scientific) texts and to understand and interpret their contents to be able utilize them in one's own activity. This level of literacy is a basic condition for the capacity of following and utilizing the development of new knowledge in the domains of knowledge and expertise, a capacity increasingly needed in professional work. In addition, it constitutes a foundation for the capability of firms and other organizations to adapt to the development in a knowledge society.

In their theory of firms Cohen and Levinthal (1990) discuss the individual and organizational conditions of the absorptive capacity which they regard as a key condition of the innovativess of firms or service providers in a knowledge economy. A person who can follow the development of knowledge in the area of her expertise will be able to utilize it for the good of her organization. Although the absorptive capacity is not reduced to the individual capabilities of the personnel, it is dependent on them. Particularly important is the role of individuals in the interface between an organization and its environment. Individual "gatekeepers" (Allen 1977) or "boundary spanners" (Conway 1995) are able to follow the development in a knowledge domain outside the organization and translate its results into an understandable form for the rest of the personnel of an organization that represents other domains of expertise. The concept of literacy in a knowledge society as outlined by PISA has an evident affinity with this kind of capacity: it underlines the capacity to interpret, draw conclusions from, utilize, and communicate to others the contents of written and electronic texts.

In Table 6.2 the figures from Table 6.1 have been reorganized by indicating a) the share of the students that have achieved a good or excellent reading and knowledge utilization capability, b) those who have achieved at least level three in reading skills, and c) the share of the weak achievers. The first group may be regarded as a group that will be able to follow the development of their respective domains of knowledge in working life, a group that, therefore, might become an active contributor to innovations in their organizations. Following Istance (2003), a group that has achieved at least level 3 may be regarded as lifelong learners and active citizens of the knowledge society. The group of low achievers is at risk of becoming excluded from further education and from knowledge activities. Esping-Andersen finds (2009: 116) that "falling behind the PISA minimum means that respondents have difficulty in understanding even basic information; this is accordingly a measure of cognitive dysfunction."

Table 6.2. The proportions of students that have achieved levels 5 and 6, and level 3 in reading and the proportion of the low achievers in some OECD countries in the PISA 2009 study (OECD 2010a: 194).

	Finland	United Kingdom	Greece	Bulgaria	OECD average
4 to 6: good and excellent	45	29	24	14	28
Over 3	75	59	53	36	57
Weak 1	8	18	23	41	19

6.2 Explanations for the success of Finnish students in PISA tests

Finnish students have been ranked high – first, second, or third – in all PISA studies. In addition, the variation among schools and across students has been exceptionally low in Finland. Various explanations have been suggested to answer the question of why Finland has been at the top in all the assessments (e.g. Välijärvi *et al.* 2002; Kupiainen *et al.* 2009; Sahlberg 2011). In this section six partly interrelated sets of explanations suggested in the Finnish and international discussion are reviewed. I start from the explanations related to the Finnish language and population and to the history of the nation. I then proceed to the explanations related to the characteristics of the Finnish comprehensive school, its governance as well as to teacher training and the special education systems. These "factors" of success are the result of partly independent developments and decisions. On the other hand, these factors uncover the diversity of mutually interacting reasons contributing to the state of the art of Finnish education.

6.2.1 *The Finnish language and population*

The Finnish language is a phonetic language. Words are written as they are pronounced, which makes spelling easier for Finnish students compared to some other languages, such as English. Consequently, two thirds of Finnish children have basic decoding skills and one third of them can read meaningless words before they begin school. In addition, the programmes presented on Finnish public television are not dubbed. Foreign programmes have text translations in Finnish on the screen. Following the programmes calls for quick reading. It has also been suggested that the cultural uniformity of the student population has an influence on the results. Finland has fewer immigrants than most other European countries. The share of non-native students in the PISA 2001 study was in Finland one fifth of the OECD average. Although the share is increasing and constitutes a major challenge for Finnish schools, it is still low by European standards. Since these conditions, however, prevail in many other countries, they may be regarded as a weak explanation of the results. Many other small or culturally unified countries (Denmark, Norway, or Hungary) have different PISA results compared to Finland. There are other countries that have a phonetic native language (such as Spanish) which have not succeeded in the PISA comparisons.

6.2.2 The political history of Finland

An explanation often suggested for the Finnish PISA success is that the school system has played a central role in the creation of the national independence, identity, and culture of a country caught between two strong neighbours, Sweden and Russia. This is why, it is argued, the school system and teachers instrumental in the construction of a national culture have enjoyed an exceptionally strong position in Finland.

For several centuries Finland was a part of the Swedish kingdom, and the Swedish-speaking nobility ruled it. When the Swedish army was defeated by the Russians during the Napoleonic Wars, Finland became an autonomous part of the Russian Empire in 1809. Within its autonomy, Finland was allowed to develop its own national institutions, including a currency, an administration, and a school system. In the mid-1800s, 85% of the Finnish population spoke different dialects of the Finnish language, while Swedish was the language used in administration, science, literature, and the school system. In the 1850s a nationalist movement led by the Swedish-speaking educated classes emerged. It considered the creation of a cultural identity and civilization based on one's own mother tongue as the basic precondition for the emergence of an independent nation. The slogan of the leading figure of the nationalist movement, Johan Wilhelm Snellman (1831–1881), was "one nation, one language". A radical nationalist movement, the so-called Fennoman movement, worked on making Finnish the official language, advancing Finnish literature and ultimately making Finnish the language of public life.

Finland's declaration of independence occurred in the context of the Russian Revolution. In the spring of 1918 a three-month civil war was waged in Finland. By European standards it was a bloody conflict: 1% of the population died and 80,000 members of the Red Guard were imprisoned. The war polarized the Finnish population into two opposite camps. Finally, the Finnish and Swedish languages became official languages of the country after Finland became independent in 1917 and compulsory school attendance was enacted in the law in 1921.

The independent Finnish school system and especially the university were seen as the central means for the creation of the cultural foundations of the nation. For this reason they also played an important role in the agendas of most of the political parties. The necessity of a strong education and culture for the survival of a small and linguistically solitary nation was a recurrent theme in policy discourse. Although there were disagreements of how education should be organized, its value for the nation was not questioned. For instance, when the comprehensive school reform was discussed in parliament in 1967 a representative of the opposition who resisted the reform because of its high costs, agreed that "the strength of culture and education is the only safety of a small nation" (Pernaa 2007: 21). This heroic story of a "struggle for survival" and the creation of a nation is important to the national self-identity of Finns. However, it may also be seen as a typical case of the nation building that took place in European countries in the late 1800s and early 1900s.

6.2.3 *The late economic transformation of the country and the need to integrate the population*

In both the Winter War (1939) between Finland and the Soviet Union and the Second World War (1941–1944) Finland managed to maintain its national independence. After the Second World War the nation faced huge challenges, including the resettlement of 430,000 refugees from southeastern Finland, which was ceded to the Soviet Union, the reconstruction of the country, and the payment of war reparations to the Soviet Union. In the 1960s Finland underwent a rapid and late transformation from an agrarian society into an industrial society with a massive migration of the population from agrarian regions to cities.[1]

The comprehensive school reform created opportunities for upward social mobility while educating the workforce for the emerging industries and services. This combination may explain the esteem that education enjoys in Finland and also the commitment of students to work hard in school. This may be comparable to other, now developing countries in which economic transformation, modernization, and reform of the school system are related to each other. This hypothesis is supported by Strang's study on class-based inequalities of education. He (2005: 495) concludes that the weak effect of socio-economic background on student achievements is best explained in terms of modernization and characteristics of national school systems and not by economic development or overall inequality.[2] Critics (e.g. Sabel *et al.* 2011) have pointed out that

---

[1] In the 1960s the integration of the extreme left became a central goal of leading politicians, above all of President Urho Kekkonen (Smolander 2004). The creation of a welfare state contributed to this integration.

[2] Strang (2005: 494) specifies the connection between the characteristics of the school system and the influence of socio-economic background on the student achievement measured by the PISA 2000 reading scores: "The greater the number of school tracks, the stronger the effects for class background. Similarly, the greater the difference between schools in student performance, the stronger the effects of class background." In Strang's study the strongest relationships between class background and student achievement were in Germany, Portugal, and the UK, and the weakest in Iceland, Korea, Latvia, Canada, Finland, and Norway.

historical explanations alone are not sufficient since the Finnish students did not succeed particularly well in international comparisons before the PISA studies of the 2000s. In the international mathematics and science studies instituted by International Education Association (IEA) in the 1960s and 1980s Finnish students ranked average (Sahlberg 2011: 60) although they performed well in the Reading Literacy Study of the 1980s. The reasons for the success must, therefore, be sought from the teacher education reform and from the organization and features of the comprehensive school system.

6.2.4 The popularity and esteem enjoyed by the teaching profession as well as the university-level education of teachers

Among the most frequently mentioned explanations for the high scores of the Finnish pupils are the high quality of teacher education, the trust that the teachers enjoy, as well as the freedom and responsibility that are given to them. Finnish parents and the general public appreciate schooling, teachers' work, and the equal educational opportunities provided by the Finnish school system. The high image of schooling may be seen in the popularity of the teaching profession among Finnish students: it consistently ranks the highest of the most popular careers among university entrance examinees, competing with such traditional favourite professions as physician, lawyer, engineer, or journalist. In his review Simola (2005: 459) concludes that "Finnish teachers apparently enjoy the trust of the general public and also of the political and even of the economic elite, which is rare in many countries."

The law on teacher education issued in 1971 required that all teacher education be provided at the university level. Teachers earn a Master of Science degree at a teacher education institute (or Department of Applied Education) at one of seven Finnish universities. The training is closely connected to educational research, and the students become familiar with research work through their Master's thesis. Special education training was also established in the 1970s. These reforms improved both the quality and the status of teacher education and educational research in Finland. Finnish teachers today view themselves as part of a wider community of professional educators and researchers. They are able to move from schoolwork to research projects and to positions outside the school that require expertise in training and education. It took time, however, before the teacher education reform made its influence felt in school activity. It was not until the 1990s that teachers who had been through the reformed education became a majority in the profession as a whole.

6.2.5 The decentralized, trust-based governance of the comprehensive school system

Both the university-level education and a decentralized governance that grants much responsibility to schools and teachers together contribute to the attraction of the teaching profession. The president of the Finnish teacher union comments on this as follows (OECD 2010b: 124):

> Teachers in Finland are very independent. They can decide almost everything: how they will teach, what they will select from the basic (national) curriculum, when they will teach each particular topic. The fact that teachers have so much independence and respect influences young people as they are deciding what programme they will follow in the university. If they choose teacher education they know they will be entering a profession that enjoys broad trust and respect in the society, one that plays an important role in shaping the country's future.

The governance of the Finnish comprehensive school developed from strict state control towards an increased autonomy of the schools. The first core curriculum for comprehensive school in 1970 was very detailed and its implementation was controlled strictly with several inspection mechanisms. This was found to be necessary to ensure that educational equality would be realized in all parts of the country after decades of a parallel school system. After the 1980s the curriculum became less detailed, and municipalities and schools were required to make their own curricula within the national frame supplied by the core curriculum. In the 1990s the evaluation of student performance was defined as a task of schools. It was seen as an essential part of the development of schools and teaching. All forms of inspection were eliminated in the 1990s. No national tests are issued in Finland to compare schools or control educational activity. This gradual change in the mechanisms of governance in the 1980s and 1990s has been characterized as a transition from a culture of control to a culture of trust (Aho *et al.* 2006). The foundation for such a transition is that the schools have developed into strong multiprofessional communities which are able to analyse the problems and challenges of teaching and find the solutions to solve them.

6.2.6 Special education systems based on the early recognition of learning difficulties and the immediate provision of support for them

It is widely agreed that an important reason for the success of Finnish students and for the homogeneity of their learning achievements is the special education system (Sabel *et al.* 2011). Its core principle is the early identification of learning difficulties and the immediate provision of sufficient support to meet the school's learning objectives while allowing the student to remain in class with his/her peers. Intervention in early grades prevents the accumulation of learning difficulties over the school career. In 2010 approximately 30% of all Finnish comprehensive school students had participated in special education, most of them in part-time special education in small groups to improve reading, writing, and maths skills. This is the highest figure among OECD countries (Kivirauma and Ruoho 2007).

Within each school a multiprofessional peer-evaluation organ, a student welfare group, supports the work of teachers. It regularly evaluates the situation in classes and discusses measures for supporting the students and evaluating their progress. It is composed of the principal, the school psychologist, the school nurse, the special education teacher, the classroom teacher whose class is being evaluated, the social worker, and a student advisor. It is this infrastructure that makes school communities able to identify problems in a timely fashion and use the evaluation results to help the pupils. Hosoya and Ushida (2006) compared the PISA scores of Finnish students with those of another culturally homogeneous and industrially developed country, Japan. In trying to explain the higher scores of the Finnish students, they (2006: 89) conclude that this was "due to the good support systems for low achievers and the systems are attended by qualified teachers and small class size."

Without a doubt, additional explanations could be found. Finland has a well-developed maternity and child health care system. Many of the potential developmental and cognitive problems are recognized in the regular check-ups for toddlers and young children. This constitutes an important foundation for the policy of early recognition of the learning difficulties. Second, the students who participated in the first PISA test in 2000 were children whose parents had passed through the new comprehensive school system. The cumulative effects of education might be visible in the results. Third, it has been suggested that the Finnish students are used to having as a part their of daily schoolwork the types of tasks that constitute the PISA test. To confirm such a hypothesis, extensive comparisons of the national curricula, teaching materials, and classroom work would be needed.

The explanations supplied are interdependent: the esteem and popularity of the teaching profession evidently has its roots in the history of the country, in teacher education reform, in the increasing decentralization of school governance that allows autonomy as well as in the development of strong multiprofessional school communities. However, in order to learn from Finnish school practices or "benchmark" the good results, it is important to understand in more detail how the school governance, school activity, and special education have been developed, how they work today, how they interact, and what kind of problems they face. An account of institutional change and learning is needed. Such an account may provide a realistic understanding of the possibilities of benchmarking the good practices of different countries.

6.3 How to study institutional change and learning

In the last two decades institutional approaches have been strengthened in sociology and organizational studies (for recent reviews, see Greenwood *et al.* 2008; Scott 2008a and 2008b; Djelic 2010). Organizations are "embedded" into an institutional context or an organizational field. A multi-organizational field has become the primary unit of institutional analysis. It constitutes a level of analysis that allows the study of the interplay between the local organizational actions and macrostructures of the society. DiMaggio and Powell defined an organizational field as follows (1983: 148):

> Those organizations, that in the aggregate, constitute a recognized area of institutional life: key supplies, resource and product consumers, regulatory agencies, and other organizations that together produce similar services and products.

They further suggest (1983: 148) that the virtue of this unit of analysis is that it does not direct attention only to competing firms or to networks of organizations that actually interact but to the totality of relevant actors.

In the 1990s a transition took place in institutional studies from studying isomorphism – that is, why organizations of a field tend to become homogeneous – to institutional change, institutional entrepreneurship, the mechanisms of the distribution of locally emerged practices from one place to other places, as well as to power in institutions. Both neoinstitutional theory and the economics of innovations (Hodgson 2004) used to regard continuity and "taken for grantedness" as basic features of institutions. The explanations for this were sought from the standards and norms given by state agents, international bodies, or by industrial and vocational associations as well as from the regularities of human behaviour (e.g. Jeppeson 1991; Powell and Colyvas 2008; Meyer 2010).

The neoinstitutional theory of institutions tends to explain the stability and continuity of institutions through the preconscious habitualized patterns of behaviour characterized by the concepts of *habit* (Veblen 1914/1990; Dewey 1922/1988), *habitus* (Bourdieu 1977) and *organizational routine* (Nelson and Winter 1982). Rule following and habits are often complemented with the phenomenological concept of "practical understanding" (e.g. Schatzki 2002) and Polanyi's concept tacit knowledge, which both also refer to preconscious embodied skills or forms of behaviour (e.g. Hodgson 1997). In addition to behavioural patterns the isomorphism of institutions is also explained by the shared meanings or cultural symbol systems that are taken for granted by the individuals socialized in the organizations of the field.

These behavioural foundations of institutional theory have been criticized on two grounds. While they provide an explanation of the habitualized dimension of behaviour, they are weak at explaining how habits are changed. This explanation does not help in understanding individual and collective agency, that is, people's active orientation to alternative futures and commitment to transformative projects (e.g. Eminbayer and Miche 1998; Knorr-Certina 2001; Miettinen *et al.* 2012). Agency has been dealt with in organizational studies in terms of entrepreneurship. According to the critics, this concept focuses too much on the role of strong individuals in order to make sense of collective change processes. In recent studies this problem has been addressed by the concept of distributed agency, in which the contributions of different types of agents as well as their collaboration is studied (e.g. Garud and Karnoe 2003; Battilina and D'Aunno 2009).

Second, the psychological and social explanations – such as intentionality, shared systems of beliefs, scripts of interaction and norms – do not take sufficiently into account material objects and objectification in explaining institutionalization and institutional change (e.g. Hasselbladh and Kallinikos 2000). Without cultural artifacts it is very difficult to explain collective activity and learning, the accumulation and transfer of knowledge, or the transmission of knowledge and practices from one place to another. The concept of artifact mediation introduced by cultural-historical activity theory clarifies the decisive role of objects and artifacts in the development and change of human activities. It is instrumental in making sense of distributed agency. Consequently, I will analyse the change of institutions using cultural-historical activity theory (Engeström *et al.* 1999b) and the Deweyan pragmatism, which share many similarities in their analysis of the transformation of human practices (e.g. Miettinen 2006). It also has much in common with pragmatic constructivism within institutional studies, which underlines the significance of constant reconstruction of institutions, local experimentation, and learning from other actors (Berk and Schneiberg 2005; Sabel and Zeitlin 2008; Thelen 2010). To include power and politics insights from historical institutionalism, the study of policy and public governance will be included (e.g. Rose and Miller 2010). My approach can be characterized by four methodological principles.

First, the unit of analysis is an object-oriented multiorganizational field. Independent and partly interdependent organizations are organized around the production of an object, that is, of a service, product, or technology. Activity theory finds a field as a network of activity systems. A field is a multi-level, heterogeneous, and constantly changing entity (e.g. Clemens and Cook 1999: 461). Although the establishment of shared rules and the standardization of means and instrumentalities takes place constantly, they are variously interpreted and used on the local level. The different expertise of professional groups and organizations in the field are needed for the production of a product or a service. Local experimentation and forms of spontaneous horizontal collaboration play an increasingly important role in the development and change of a field. To understand the change of a field, examining the development of the forms or governance and the forms of interaction between the organizations on different levels (state, region, municipality, and local) of the field is needed.

Second, a field develops by solving contradictions and major problems that emerge in its activities. This understanding of the sources of change is the central thesis of the dialectical tradition in cultural psychology, social sciences, and organizational studies (e.g. Hargrave and Van de Ven 2009). In the pragmatist theory of problem solving, a crisis of the established habits calls for reflection and experimentation (Dewey 1938/1991). For example the economic transformations from an agrarian to industrial and then from industrial into a knowledge-based economy call for redefinition of the nature of capabilities needed as well the organization of the educational system. Also policy making has been analysed as a process oriented to solve key social and economic problems by formulating policy programmes (e.g. Campbell 1998; Rose and Miller 2010). However, policy programmes need proper means and instruments to be realized and are transformed as a result of the development of these means (Lascoumes and Le Gales 2007). Typically contribution, expertise, and collaboration of various organizations and professions are needed to accomplish this. Policy measures also have unintended consequences that give rise to new problems and contradictions. In this chapter the system of streaming in the Finnish comprehensive school will be analysed as such an institutional contradiction.

Third, objectification and cultural artifacts are essential in explaining the development of knowledge, the accumulation of expertise and institutional learning. Mediation by cultural artifacts is the basic concept of cultural-historical activity theory (Vygotsky 1979). "All forms of activity (active faculties) are passed on only in the form of objects created by man for man" (Ilyenkov 1977: 277). The forms of activity are objectified into cultural artifacts (systems of signs and tools) that can the transferred across organizational boundaries. Learning is organized around remediation e.g. the adoption, development, and use of new relevant means and instrumentalities.

In his theory of the evolution of human consciousness, psychologist Merlin Donald has convincingly suggested that modern human consciousness cannot be explained as a result of biological evolution alone. Instead, the key is external memory or the externalization of memory (Donald 2001: 262): "modern humans can employ a huge number of powerful external symbolic devices to store and retrieve cultural knowledge." Bruno Latour, a theorist of the science of technology, has analysed the ways in which man (humanity) "delegates" tasks and norms to artifacts (Latour 1992). As a result, technical artifacts have a script, an affordance, a function, or a programme of action and goals (Latour 1994). Empirical studies on distributed cognition have shown that human agency is distributed between men and artifacts (e.g. Goodwin 1995; Hutchins 1995). The philosophers John Dewey and Vladislav Lektorsky characterize the intentional and normative nature of artifacts as follows:

> A tool...is also a mode of language. For it *says* something, to those who understand it, about the operations of use and their consequences.... In the present cultural setting, these objects are so intimately bound up with interests, occupations and purposes that they have an eloquent voice. (Dewey 1938/1991: 52)

> The instrumental man-made objects function as objective forms of expression of cognitive norms, standards and object-hypotheses existing outside the individual. (Lektorsky 1980: 137)

In these approaches, instead of working via cognitive processes in the head or in bodily schemes, human capabilities are preserved and transmitted, first of all through artifacts and the ways in which they are used. Consequently we need to study the functions of both epistemic (concepts) and practical (tools, methods) artifacts in the dynamics of a change in practices. In activity theory the adoption or development of new mediating artifacts in order to meet the requirements of change in conditions, or remediation, is a key mechanism for change and learning.

Fourth, the creation of a new artifact or a practice is a collective process as has convincingly been shown by science and technology studies (Fleck 1979; Latour and Woolgar 1979) and has beautifully been captured by Mary Douglas in her book *How Institutions Think* (1981). This is why the forms of distributed agency as well as horizontal and vertical interaction meant to develop and transmit knowledge and instrumentalities within a multiorganizational field need to be analysed. Lundvall's theory of national innovation systems regards interactive learning as the most in important process of the system. In this approach learning is seen primarily as a by-product of production, innovation and interaction (e.g. Johnson 2010).

An activity-theoretical approach finds that the development of organizational forms specifically meant to enhance learning, separate from forms of production or networks of innovation, to be vital. Innovation studies suggest that knowledge and expertise need to be combined in interaction to achieve something new. Interaction, however, can take place in various ways and does not always require that all the participants learn.[3] We need to include the object and contents in the analysis of interactive learning and find out concretely who learns and what is learned, what "solutions", new means or models are produced and transmitted in the interaction and how their use contributes to the change and development of the field. Finally, an analysis is needed of whether the forms of governance enhance and inhibit experimentation, collaboration and learning in a field.

6.4 The emergence of the Finnish comprehensive school and the challenge of student diversity

Finland underwent a rapid and late economic transformation from an agrarian society into an industrial and service society in the 1960s and 1970s. The percentage of labour force employed in the agricultural sector was 46% in 1950. This percentage more than halved in twenty years, reaching 20% in 1970. The need for a better educated workforce

---

[3] Subcontractor networks can either be a relationship of the submission of the subcontractor to the economic requirements and specifications of the principal or a process of mutual learning. Teamwork may be more a waste of time than a vehicle of creation. A multidisciplinary project with contributions of expertise from several organizations can be organized effectively based on a division of labour without significant mutual learning between the partners. Collaborative product development may serve the sharing of information about the use activity without stimulating mutual learning. Consequently, forms of organization alone are poor indicators of learning or the creation of new capabilities.

became pressing. At the same time the development of the dual track education system accentuated the problem of regional and social inequality. At the end of the 1960s half of each age cohort in the countryside, and in cities 70–90% of each cohort – continued to the grammar or middle school, and the shares were rapidly increasing. The students who failed to enter grammar school had no opportunities to continue to higher levels of education. In addition, grammar schools were concentrated in cities, and two thirds of them were private and charged tuition fees creating regional and social barriers for attending school. The system divided the students into two groups at the age of 11. Both the contradiction of the quality of workforce and that of the dual track system needed to be resolved.

In 1968 the government brought to parliament a suggestion for a comprehensive reform of the school system. Its key argument was that in order to enhance social equality, equal opportunities for all students to study according to their capabilities must be provided (Pernaa 2007: 20). The plan to replace primary and grammar schools with a unified public school common to all children had already been presented by two committees already in the late 1940s and in the 1950s. Because of resistance from advocates of the private school system, the idea was not accepted by parliament until 1963. The School System Act of 1968 initiated the establishment of a 9-year comprehensive school. The reform was realized in the years 1972–1981.[4] The government coalition of the leftist parties, the Social Democratic Party, the People's Democratic League (which included the Communist Party), and the Agrarian Party introduced the School System Act to the parliament in 1968. The political initiative had come from the leftist parties, and the Agrarian party raised regional equality and the maintenance of the vitality of sparsely populated agrarian regions as central aims in supporting the reform. The school reform started in northern Finland in 1972 and gradually spread to the south, finally its implementation in the capital district was started in 1976. The conservative party supported the reform after the operational conditions of the private schools were secured and the implementation of a streaming system in comprehensive school was included in the reform. It found the new school to be useful in "the mobilization of talent reserves" and the creation of the human capital necessary for economic growth.

---

[4] Comprehensive school consists of six years of primary school for children aged 7–12 and three years of lower secondary school for children aged 13–15. In primary school the same teacher (a "class teacher") teaches all subjects. In the lower secondary schools the various subjects are taught by specialized subject teachers.

The significance of the reform as a major social political reform and a key institution of a welfare society was underlined by the left-centre majority coalition. The chairperson of the Committee for Education and Culture of the Finnish parliament, Anna-Liisa Tiekso, characterized the significance of the new law as follows in the parliament discussion of 27 April 1967 (Pernaa and Tiitta 2007: 27):

> The proposal given to the parliament . . . is a starting point for legislative work for which it is hard to find a point of comparison. The transition to the comprehensive school system has been compared, among others, to the suffrage reform and such a comparison is not exaggerated. It is an expansion and development of democracy, provision of equal and current basic education to every child. After this reform, the wealth or domicile of the parents will not determine which direction knowledge will take in its early stages.
>
> The government's proposal can be characterized as a significant social-political reform. It relieves the parents of middle school fees and other costs of schooling by providing free of charge education, school meals, accommodation and transportation. In this sense it can be compared to significant social-political reforms such as the National Health Insurance or survivor's pension. The school reform signifies an increase in the level of civilization of the whole population. Since the comprehensive school is opposed to, even to date, on the basis that the reform in the proposed form/shape/state would lead to a decline in the quality of learning, one must ask: Doesn't the elevated level of education of the whole population also enhance the discovery/ detection of exceptional talents and open up possibilities to those youngsters whose capabilities would otherwise remain unrealized?

At the end of her speech she refers to the most important ideological debate related to the reform, the problem of the diversity of the capabilities of children. The representatives of conservative parties regarded the foundations of the reform as unrealistic, that is, the belief that every student in an age cohort would be able to complete the curriculum of nine-year comprehensive schooling. They argued that the talented students should be taken into better account in the reform and that it may lead to the lowering of the quality of education in the school system. To mitigate this, they demanded that a streaming system be included in the comprehensive school reform.

The comprehensive school reform can be regarded as a strong egalitarian political programme. However, no one had a clear picture in advance of whether and by what means every student would be able to complete the studies at the new school. The experiences of the comprehensive school reforms in other Nordic countries – which were used as models for the Finnish reform – were not yet fully available. In that sense, the reform can be regarded as an extensive social experiment and a project of developing the means and pedagogy of taking into account the diversity of students.

Behind the debate was the perennial question of the nature of human capability, which still persists in debates about education and which has become ever more important because of the development of the "knowledge society". The elitist views continuously underline the importance of special arrangements for talented students and suggest that an egalitarian policy of helping the weak jeopardizes the production of excellence. The conservative position in the 1960s was without doubt based on the then still dominant concept of capabilities, the idea of intelligence as a general inherited prospensity that is unevenly distributed in the population. This was the conception suggested by Sir Francis Galton in his book *Hereditary Genius* (1869/2009). This was also the concept of intelligence that was adopted in the so-called differential psychology that developed tests for measuring intelligence and its different attributes (for reviews, see Kamin 1974; Gould 1988; Hauser 2010).

One of the key discussions in developmental psychology in the 1900s was the problem of the relationship between cultural learning and natural development. The two most distinguished theorists of the field, Jean Piaget (1950/1971) and Lev Vygotsky, had different interpretations of this relationship. Piaget thought that learning could not influence the natural development of thought and intelligence. His theory is a naturalistic, non-historical theory of human development. Vygotsky (1934/1987), the founder of the cultural-historical approach in psychology, had a more historical and interactive view of learning. An individual mind emerges from social interaction. Thought develops through the internalization of spoken language and shared ways of acting.[5] Also, pragmatist scholars such as Mead and Dewey agreed with the concept of the interactive and historical origins of self and human capabilities (Dewey 1927/1988: 331–332): "Everything that is distinctively human is learned, not native, even though it could not be learned without native structures which mark man off of other animals. (. . .) To learn to be human is to develop through the give-and-take of communication an effective sense of being an individually distinctive member of a community."

Vygotsky (1979: 86) proposed the concept "zone of proximal development" to characterize the interaction between learning and the development of a child's capabilities. It refers to the zone in which a child

---

[5] Chapter 2 of Vygotsky's main work *Thought and Language* (1934/1987) provides a classical, still powerful critique of Piaget's understanding of individual development. The book develops a viable and increasingly recognized theory of the social and cultural origins of thinking and individual consciousness (see e.g. Wertsch 1985).

cannot solve problems independently but can do so under adult guidance or in collaboration with more capable peers. This zone is a historically changing territory of pedagogical possibilities. The mercantilist economists thought in the 1600s and 1700s that a majority of the population would never be able to learn to read and write. In the 1950s the same type of argument was presented in many countries concerning the possibility of the majority of an age cohort to go to secondary school. Today, an increasing understanding of learning problems (such as dyslexia) as well as new remedial tools supplied by special education have removed obstacles of language learning and "extended" the boundaries of learning and the development of capabilities.[6]

The challenge of a comprehensive school and the development of the special education related to it had led to a redefinition of the idea of individual differences and their meaning. As knowledge about learning difficulties deepened, it became evident that students learn basic capabilities in different ways and in different rhythms and that individualized pedagogical strategies are needed. Second, it is understood that specific learning difficulties in reading and writing might lead to cumulative problems in learning and attending school and lowered self-confidence, and might impede the development of an individual's capabilities. Finally, studies on learning problems have shown that in spite of specific problems in learning, pupils may be strong in other ways, i.e. have special talents and interests which when realized would allow a full and constructive participation in society. The recognition and nurturing of these talents is an essential part of teachers' work and the provision of individually tailored capacitating services is an important task of schools. It is now known that people with severe dyslexia (e.g. such historical figures as Leonardo Da Vinci or Edison) might be exceptionally talented innovators and entrepreneurs (Wolf 2008: 209):

> The single most important implication of research in dyslexia is not ensuring that we don't derail the development of the future Leonardo or Edison; it is making sure that we do not miss the potential of any child. Not all children with dyslexia have extraordinary talents, but every one of them has a unique potential that all too often goes unrealized because we don't know how to tap it.

The transition from the idea of capabilities as measurable, inherited general intelligence or talent to the concept of different learners who

---

[6] The potential of an individual to develop is based on the extremely flexible machinery of human brain which allows the construction of a variety of functional organs and skills (e.g. Luria 1973; Wolf 2008). The genetic makeup of an individual does influence the formation of these organs and skills but does not determine their direction nor quality as was supposed by the traditional view of intelligence.

can contribute to society in various ways is still in its beginnings. So is the investigation of its pedagogical implications, although the special education system in the comprehensive school has taken important steps to understand how to deal with diversity.

6.5 The crisis of the streaming system and the development of the part-time special education system

To tackle the problem of the diversity of the student population, a streaming system was included in the first curriculum for comprehensive school implemented in 1970. The crisis of this system and how it was solved is an example of an endogenous institutional contradiction as a source of development. In the streaming system the students were grouped into two or three levels in mathematics, the second national language (Swedish), and foreign languages in grades 5–9. The students and their parents had to make the decision about to which group the students will be placed in the age of 11 or 12. In the mid-1970s, during the implementation of the comprehensive school, there were already signals that the system led to the reproduction of a dual track school system and, therefore, worked against the cornerstone of Finnish educational reform, the ideal of educational equality. The popularity of upper secondary school as a preparatory school for university increased very rapidly in the 1970s. Vocational colleges were filled with upper secondary school graduates who were not accepted into a university. As a result, the students who only had a diploma from comprehensive school were in a weaker position when applying to vocational colleagues. Especially those students who had selected lower streams in comprehensive school had difficulties in entering secondary education. This problem and the growing "student flood" catalyzed the establishment of committees that started to prepare the reform of vocational education in Finland in 1974.

The committee that was in charge of planning the interface between comprehensive school and secondary education found in its inquiries that 30% of students in the 9th grade had selected combinations of streams that did not allow access either to upper secondary schools or to vocational college. In the school year 1974–1975, 46% of the boys had selected streams that enabled them to enter secondary education. The goal that comprehensive school should prepare all students to be eligible for all secondary education was reasserted in the school legislation issued in 1985. This legislation closed down the streaming system and completed the policy of a unitary school system. A speech given by prime minister Kalevi Sorsa connected the reform to the ongoing technological and economic change (Pernaa 2007: 41):

> Human knowledge and skills are the motor of the development of new technology. (...) Even a small country can find, in addition to securing its traditional industries, new...possibilities if it has an internationally competitive, that is, a better educated population and work force than other countries have.

With the reform the streaming system ceased to be a legitimate means of dealing with student diversity. Diversity was planned to be addressed by forming different teaching groups within classes so that every students could achieve the goals of the curriculum and be eligible to secondary education. Again there was no plan or means by which this would be achieved. However, an alternative pedagogy of dealing with diversity developed from the student care and special education system. In the 1950s and 1960s it focused on the rehabilitation of handicapped children. In the 1970s and 1980s special education was transformed and became a more general institution for addressing the diversity of children.

The special education system developed from the rehabilitation of handicapped and exceptional children and was seen in the 1950s as a part of social policy. The Central Union for Child Welfare in Finland has published every fourth year starting in 1954 a handbook called *Care and Education of Exceptional Children in Finland*. In the first handbooks (Lasten 1954) each chapter dealt with one type of disability, from cerebral-palsied and mentally subnormal children to visually, acoustically, and orthopaedically handicapped children. Reading and writing difficulties were not mentioned at all before the year 1962 and remained marginal in the handbook until the late 1980s. The 1966 handbook estimated that 1% of students need special education of reading and writing difficulties. The evaluation of this need changed rapidly. In the 1970 handbook the percentage became 5–10% and in the 1979 handbook 15–20%. While the attendance given to "children who show special reading and writing difficulties" remained marginal in the handbooks, developmental psychologists started to study these difficulties in the 1960s. The first Finnish tests for diagnosing reading difficulties were published in 1968 (Ruoppila *et al.* 1968). The first studies on part-time special education focused on reading and writing difficulties were done in the mid-1970s, and the first textbook devoted exclusively to these difficulties was published in 1977 (Ahvenainen *et al.* 1977).

The establishment of comprehensive schools meant a rapid increase in part-time special education, which mainly focused on reading,

writing, and speech difficulties. The number of part-time special education teachers hired in basic education in Finland increased twenty-fold
over the years 1967–1977. In 1968 there were only 4682 students – fewer
than 1% of those enrolled in comprehensive schools in Finland – who
received part-time special education for reading and writing difficulties.
By 1979 that number had increased ten-fold to 46,150 (Kivirauma 1989:
120). The increase of the part-time special education went on in the
following decades. While some 5% of students received special education in 1970, by 2010 approximately 30% of all Finnish comprehensive
school students received at least some special education. A majority
receives part-time assistance for minor learning difficulties, while the
remaining 8% receive full-time special education in segregated class-
rooms. It could be said that the Finnish school has developed two
parallel special education systems: a traditional one based on special
schools and classes and a new one based on part-time special education
dealing primarily with less severe language and maths learning problems (Kivirauma and Ruoho 2007: 298).

Remedial teaching[7] and part-time special education gradually became
core elements in the comprehensive schools in Finland, allowing a
growing proportion of children to stay in the regular classroom and to
gain a basic education even though they encountered periodic learning
difficulties. According to the 2004 national core curriculum:

> Remedial teaching is a form of differentiation characterized by individualized
> tasks, individualized use of time, and guidance and counseling. Remedial
> teaching is to be commenced as soon as learning difficulties are observed, so
> that the pupil does not lag behind in his or her studies. (. . .) Remedial
> teaching is to be provided as often and as broadly as is appropriate from
> the standpoint of the pupil's academic success.

The comprehensive schools, in partnership with local social service
professionals, have assumed responsibility for tailoring teaching and
other learning-related services to individual students' needs. The obliga-
tion to give remedial teaching to a pupil "who has temporarily been left
behind or who otherwise needs special support" and special needs
education "to a pupil with moderate learning and adjustment difficulties" is included in the Basic Education Act.

During the 1990s the aim of the Finnish special education system
became articulated: the early identification of learning difficulties and

---

[7] Remedial teaching is extra teaching given by the class teacher or subject teacher outside
the class to one or a few pupils who have learning difficulties. Teachers are paid for this extra
work.

the immediate provision of sufficient support to meet the school's learning objectives while allowing the student to remain in class with his/her peers. The key feature of the part-time education system was the principle of early intervention, which means that special support resources are concentrated on the first few years of the comprehensive school. In addition, in the first and second grades almost 90% of the part-time special education teaching is used to treat language problems (Kivirauma and Ruoho 2007: 295). This might be based on the strong position of language studies in Finnish education and, on the other hand, on the increased psychological understanding of the role of language in the development of individual abilities. Gradually it became evident that the solving of language-related problems in the early years creates a foundation for continuous learning in school.

The system of part-time special education developed in the 1970s because of the educational policy goals, the principles of equality and integration, as well as the "principle of overcoming the learning problems". These ideas became even more important in the mid-1970s as an alternative pedagogical strategy to streaming. On the other hand, the new special education was influenced by the development of socio-cognitive student care in the 1970s. The Student Care Committee of 1973 suggested that municipalities should establish school psychologists and social workers in the schools. Special education teacher training focused in the 1960s on the training of special school and class teachers. From 1972 the growth took place in the training of the "classless" teachers, that is, part-time special education teachers who primarily worked with reading and writing difficulties.

To coordinate the agents involved in student care within the school, a multi-professional institution of collaboration called the Student Welfare Group (SWG) developed in the late 1970s. These groups were formed locally in many municipalities to coordinate the work of service providers.[8] In 1981 the National Board of Education gave instructions in which the establishment of SWGs in schools, especially lower secondary schools (grades 7–9), was recommended. The group was to be responsible for ensuring the physical and psychological well-being of students, for overseeing their progress, and for the overall environment for learning in the school. Although there was no legal mandate establishing or

---

[8] For instance, a report from the municipality of Siilinjärvi states that a student welfare group was formed in 1976 (Ahvenainen 1983: 136): "The collaboration of the school with other service providers were crystallized into the SWG meetings held twice a month. Also the parents have a possibility to participate." In Siilinjärvi the special education teacher called and lead the meetings and kept the minutes.

requiring a SWG or prescribing membership in it or its recommendations, in the beginning of the 2000s 70% of schools had an active SWG. In most schools the SWG includes the principal or head teacher, the school psychologist, the school nurse, and the special education teacher – and depending upon the issue being discussed, it might also include the classroom teacher, the social worker, and a student advisor. Other professionals, such as the school doctor, also participate when needed. The meetings are used to gather information about the school and students from different sources, to discuss school-wide challenges and to plan. Typically, the SWG reviews every class in the school and often the situation of each student at least once a year.

The new part-time special education system developed gradually from the psycho-social student care system and developed into an important means for the individualization of teaching. It also has contributed to a new understanding of learning and capabilities. The programme has contributed to the understanding of language capabilities as a foundation for further learning and development. It contributed to the recognition of the potential of individuals with specific learning difficulties and in this way widened our understanding of the complexity of human capabilities. At the same time a transition took place from the psycho-medical concept of special education to the pedagogical concept of learning difficulties that pupils experience in achieving curriculum goals (Graham and Jahnukainen 2011: 276). The pedagogical principle of "beating the learning difficulties" was based on the aim of keeping every student in the same school system. It included the idea that a "considerable part of the learning difficulties are related to the inappropriate learning process itself" (Vuoden 1971: 105). They, therefore, can be solved by a cleverer organization of teaching and with better learning materials and methods. The terms "deviant", "exceptional", and "subnormal" – characteristic of the psycho-medical conception of special education – were gradually replaced by the term "different learner". The tools developed to label students diagnostically and to make the decision to remove them to special classes were increasingly used as tools for recognizing learning difficulties in order to provide immediate support for the students.

6.6 Constructing the foundations of professional expertise: The development of diagnostic tools, remedial materials, and pedagogical solutions

As suggested by the concept of mediation, the core principle of Finnish part-time special education – the early recognition of learning difficulties and immediate support for learning difficulties – would be futile unless relevant means of recognizing learning problems and means of intervening were not made available. As a matter of fact, diagnostic tools are essential in recognizing and defining learning problems. They also suggest the direction for the remedial teaching and special education. These tools constitute the backbone of the expertise of the special education teachers and teacher training. The development of screening methods for learning problems made part-time special education possible: pupils with learning difficulties must be recognized in order to arrange support for them. The work done by school psychologists and researchers to develop the screening tests in the 1960s and 1970s was therefore key to the development of the new part-time special education.

A study on the work of special education teachers in the city of Espoo in the capital district (Thuneberg 2004) showed that the teachers use 19 different screening tests or intervention packages, including both tests and remedial materials.[9] Some of the tests were clearly limited diagnostic tests, others more indefinite packages of tests and teaching materials. Many of them specified a certain purpose, age level, and type of education, constituting a set of tools or a product family. The special education teachers selected and combined these tools according to their needs and the problem to be addressed.

Table 6.3 shows the actors involved in the provision of relevant tools for special education in Espoo. Almost all the actors in the table arrange courses on the background and use of tools for special education teachers. The special education teacher training units of the universities also develop tools, follow, and evaluate tool development and contribute to their implementation through the education and small-scale surveys.

The table of actors involved in the provision of tools allows an analysis of what the recent institutional literature has characterized as a distributed and multi-level concept of agency, "distributed across different kinds of actors" (Garud and Kornoe 2003: 277). In institutional change, "different types of forces and agents are involved, including individual agents" (Battalina and D'Aunno 2009: 47). Agency needs to be analysed on the field level, organizational level, and individual level. In addition, agency is a temporal phenomenon: different actors contribute to the development of the field in different moments or phases of a developmental process. To clarify this, I will take three examples that

---

[9] Espoo is one of the three cities of the capital district. It has 244,930 inhabitants and 97 comprehensive schools. It is the second biggest city in Finland.

Table 6.3. The developers and suppliers of screening and diagnostic tests and special education teaching materials and software used by the special education teachers in the city of Espoo

Type of Organization	N	Name of Organization
University Research Institutes	2	Niilo Mäki Institute (NMI), University of Jyväskylä and Centre for Learning Research (CLR), University of Turku
Small firms specialized in tools of special education	3	CognAid, Scribeo, Opperi
Professional and civic associations and the firms owned by these	3	The Finnish Union of Speech Therapists (owns Early Learning), The Finnish Reading Association, The Finnish Psychological Association (owns Psykologien Kustannus Oy)
Publishing houses	3	Otava, WSOY, W&G, PS-kustannus
Hybrids	1	Mathland – "Mathland", municipalities in collaboration with Opperi

clarify further the agency of the development of tools and provisions for the field of special education.

The most widely used test in the 1980s and 1990s for the screening of maths problems in Finnish schools, MAKEKO, was developed by an experienced special education teacher, Hannele Ikäheimo, in collaboration with university lecturers from the Department of Teacher Education at the University of Helsinki. In order to effectively distribute and meet the demand of tests and materials Hannele Ikäheimo established a firm Opperi. Opperi sells MAKEKO tests and other tests related to the learning of mathematics. It also organises courses related to the learning of mathematics. Another innovation by Hannele Ikäheimo, together with other special education teachers from the schools of the capital district in 2000, was the suggestion to establish a maths learning and resource centre, Mathland for city municipalities. The teachers had an idea for a space in which the existing know-how and the teaching and learning of maths is gathered in one place. The departments of education of the cities of Espoo and Helsinki gave a positive response, space and funding, and in the autumn of 2000 three part-time teachers started to develop Mathland. A group of Mathland's developers explain the idea (Järvinen *et al.* 2003: 48):

> Mathland is both a physical place and an idea for an activity. Mathland is a resource centre for teachers, which provides ideas, means and education for the development of teaching of mathematics from preschool to upper secondary and vocational school. In Mathland concrete means are sought with which learning can be supported in the problematic points of special education. Mathland also supports developmental projects in schools.

The activities of Mathland in Helsinki include a resource centre, training, consultation, the development of materials and pedagogical solutions as well as the coordination of experimentation in schools. A large variety of teaching and learning materials, e.g. hands-on materials, literature, research reports, computer programs and videos, is available and can be borrowed. There are open afternoons for consultation with teachers and for working with children.

Another example is the development and implementation of an Internet-based diagnostic and remedial software program called Graphogame by the Niilo Mäki Institute (NMI) located in the University of Jyväskylä. The Niilo Mäki Institute is named for Niilo Mäki, a neuropsychologist, who was a pioneer of special education in Finland and held the first professorship in special education in the University of Jyväskylä from 1948. Mäki received inspiration from the Yale Clinic of Child Development and Child Guidance, which was directed by Arnold Gesell, where Mäki worked in the 1930s. The NMI was established in 1990. It has a personnel consisting of approximately 50 people, 35 of whom are researchers. The aim of the institute is to recognize and understand neuro-cognitive dysfunctions and the learning difficulties based on them and to find means of teaching, intervention and rehabilitation. In addition to research projects and the development of diagnostic tests, learning games, materials, and books, the NMI maintains a place for consultation, the Child Research Clinic together with the Child and Family Counselling unit of the City of Jyväskylä. The NMI holds about 50 courses a year for teachers, special education teachers, and psychologists in 13 different localities around Finland. It sells tests, learning games, and materials as well as literature directed at special education teachers and psychologists. It also publishes *NMI Bulletin*, a peer-reviewed journal on learning difficulties.

The development of the Graphogame software is an example of research-based tool design and of the societal impact of basic research. In the Jyväskylä Longitudinal Study of Dyslexia, headed by Professor Heikki Lyytinen, the goal was to understand dyslexia by defining its precursors and to develop preventative training tools to overcome or at least minimize the consequences of dyslexia. One hundred and seven children with a familial risk for dyslexia were followed for 13 years. The central cognitive bottleneck proved to be connected to speech perception, especially the perception of phonemes and the connection between sounds and letters. Low letter recognition at the age of 4 proved to be a strong predictor of dyslexia. The research groups therefore decided to focus on phonetic differentiation in designing a preventative training tool,

Graphogame. The research group characterised Graphogame as follows (Lyytinen *et al.* 2009: 672):

> The game is available via the Internet to children who have parental permission. (...) We believe that children with familial risk and/or low letter knowledge during the few months preceding school entry benefit from preventive playing in terms of avoiding unwanted failure experiences during the early months of school instruction. Therefore, we have recommended that kindergartens where all children in Finland have their pre-school year just before school that the game should be used during the last two months (April-May) and preferably with massed practice. This means short 5–15 minute periods several times per day for as long as children require to learn the letter-sound connections (...). Today, more than 50,000 children in Finland have tried the game, and very few have failed to benefit.

Teachers and special education teachers received a free prototype of the game on the condition that they send the results (the points achieved) of the pupils who played the game to the researchers. This data was used to develop the game further.

Graphogame richly illuminates the principle of mediation. First, Graphogame is a tool that helps children to learn a particular skill of reading and writing in a culture based on the Greek alphabet: the construction of the connection between letters and sounds. Second, as a software tool it can be distributed extremely rapidly in the field of special education and was immediately and freely available to children, parents, and teachers all over Finland. It shows the efficiency of the Internet-based open source model of innovation. Third, it was also immediately integrated into the Finnish special education policy of early recognition and intervention by recommending that it be used in Finnish kindergartens. Graphogame functions as a mediating artifact on individual, family, organizational, and field levels, and is also an instrument of special education policy making in contributing to the realization of the principle of early recognition and immediate intervention.

The adoption and further development of the Varga-Neményi (V-N) method of teaching mathematics provides another example of collaborative and distributed agency. Four teachers of mathematics visited Hungary in 1999 in order to learn why Hungarian children did so well in international mathematical Olympiads (Lampinen and Korhonen 2010). They concluded that one reason was due to the method of teaching maths developed by Tamás Vargas and Eszter Neményin in the 1970s and 1980s. Independently of the teachers, Dr. Marjatta Nää-tänen from the Department of Mathematics at the University of

Helsinki had made the same discovery. She arranged for the translation of the first learning materials of the method into Finnish, and field experiments on their use were organized in several schools around Finland.

The Finnish Varga-Neményi Association was established in 2005. It organizes annual summer seminars in which teachers involved in experimentation with the method meet, exchange experiences and develop new solutions. A dissertation on the method was defended in 2008 in the Department of Education at the University of Jyväskylä (Tikkanen 2008). In 2008, the association had 130 members, and it publishes literature and materials related to the V-N method. A horizontal, transnational, and local network of learning and development related to maths teaching and learning was born.

In each of the three examples of the development of instruments of special education, individual and collaborative agency are intertwined in different ways. The examples also contain instances of transcending the boundaries between professional groups, producers and users, the theoretical and practical, and individual, local, and national levels. Special education teacher Hannele Ikäheimo became an "entrepreneur" by establishing the firm Opperi but she developed its main product MAKEKO together with partners from the University of Helsinki. The firm was a method of distributing their tests and a platform for developing new ones. She was also included in developing the idea of Mathland, which grew into a regional instrument when the municipalities provided space, resources, and funding for the centres.

The Niilo Mäki Institute works at the forefront in the scientific study of dyslexia. It is an example of a multidisciplinary "epistemic community" in which various projects and enterprises are realized in research groups. Of course the role of the research leader, Prof Lyytinen, is central but the papers published by the research group are typically written by a collaboration of three to six authors. The institute also has a conscious policy of combining research, clinical work, the development of test and remedial materials as well as training. It is an example of epistemic agency that Donald Stokes (1997) has aptly characterized as "use-inspired basic research". The social motive of helping children with learning problems is intertwined with the motive of understanding their nature, neurological background and the early symptoms of the problems through scientific research.

A group of teachers and a mathematician comprised a core group that started the implementation of the Varga-Neményi method in Finland and the translation of teaching materials. Mathland centres in different cities and researchers were involved. Finally, the establishment of the association transformed experimentation with and development of the method into a transregional and field-wide enterprise.

Division of labour, complementarity of expertise, and collaboration between different professional groups – and the development towards multiprofessionality – are essential parts of distributed agency. Psychologists, logopedians, special education teachers, and subject teachers have different starting points in developing the tools. Tests and materials are meant for different situations, age groups, and learning problems. Psychological tests typically diagnose individual cognitive or social development, and the tests designed by teachers typically evaluate the learning of students in relation to the goals in the curriculum. Both are needed and used and both complement each other. Since the object of special education, problems of learning, is complex, developing and constantly opening new challenges, a variety of expertise and tools is needed. Variety is not only a starting point for selection and standardization, as suggested by evolutionary theory. It is also a source for complementarity and the creative hybridization of practices.

6.7 The change in the governance of school: From a culture of control to a culture of trust

In Finnish primary schools teachers have traditionally been allowed to select the contents of teaching and decide how to teach. National tests have never been implemented in the Finnish school system except for the matriculation examination. The curriculum instituted in 1970 for the new nine-year comprehensive school system was rather detailed, but no national testing system was established. Evaluation was left to the schools and the teachers. The core curriculum of the year 1985 took the first important steps towards the decentralization of curriculum making. The idea of replacing normative control with management by results was appropriated in the Finnish public administration in the late 1970s. The municipalities and schools were required to write their own curricula in which they specify their own goals corresponding to the local circumstances (minority languages, religion, cultural traditions, etc.) (Peruskoulun Opetussuunnitelman Perusteet 1985: 18).

> The new school legislation underlines the right and responsibility of the municipalities and schools in the development of the curriculum and school activity and provides new opportunities for this activity. (. . .) The passing of authority to a place where the actual school work is being done was carried out to make the possible remedial measures easier.

A system that specifies the hours to be taught for each subject was established to give room for local planning. The municipalities and schools were to use 10% of the hours as they preferred.

The core curriculum of 1985 recognized that neither the problem of content nor the selection of teaching methods can be solved in the national curriculum. Local planning is needed to avoid overburdening of the study programmes (Peruskoulun Opetussuunnitelman Perusteet 1985: 59):

> The amount of knowledge included in the content of the different school subjects is essentially almost unlimited. It is not possible (...) to define the amount of knowledge in the national syllabuses nor even in the curriculum of the municipality. That is why the selection of content by a teacher or teachers through collaborative planning is important for the implementation of the syllabus. The final interpretation of the goals always takes place in the school, and the connection between the curriculum and the teaching work is realized through teachers.

The core curriculum of the year 1994 strengthened the responsibility of the municipalities and individual schools in curriculum planning and evaluation. The core curriculum, a booklet of 113 pages, explained its curriculum philosophy as follows (Peruskoulun 1994: 9):

> Research results show that the personal participation of teachers in designing the curriculum is a precondition for real change in the internal life of a school. Teachers feel that curricula designed by others are extraneous and they are not committed to implementing them.

Self-evaluation became part of each school's curriculum development (1994: 23): "The self-evaluation of schools is part of the conscious development of the curriculum. It is a necessary means of creating a productive school that is conscious of its objectives." The residual forms of inspection were discontinued during the 1990s. Schools undertook evaluation as a means of developing instruction and in order to help individual pupils with learning problems. In grades 1–5 no grades are given to avoid comparison and rivalry. Qualitative characterizations of student progress are written to motivate and help students and to inform parents.

The transition in comprehensive school governance in Finland between the 1970s and the 1990s has been characterized as a shift from a culture of control to a culture of trust. Aho and his colleagues (Aho *et al.* 2006: 131) describe the significance of this shift as follows: "Decentralization and increased local autonomy have not only enabled schools to have more freedom to establish optimal teaching methods and learning environments. They have also given them true leadership and responsibility in education development and school improvement." The headmaster and director of the mathematics-natural science track at Olari School in the city of Espoo came to a similar conclusion:[10]

A great deal of confidence is placed in teachers [in Finland]. A great deal of power, responsibility and freedom is given to them, and they deserve it. No ponderous control mechanisms are needed. In many countries inspections and constant testing form a barrier to creativity and misdirect the teacher's energy. In Finland the teachers plan their teaching, from the curriculum design to the individual lessons. (...) Subject teachers in Finland follow the same curriculum as university students who are majoring in the subject. The teacher's network therefore includes people who are active in their areas of research, and new achievements in science trickle down to schools through unofficial channels.

When the teachers speak of the "ponderous system of control" and constant testing they refer to the fact that in many countries the achievement of students and the schools are monitored and controlled by standardized tests (e.g. Apple 2006; Lowe 2007). Since the 1980s, curriculum and control systems based on predefined goals and standardized tests have been implemented in many countries and regions (e.g. Scoppio 2002). The new generation of standards-based governance combines the ideas of high standards, accountability trough standardized tests and the formation of educational markets (Levin and Fullan 2008; Hargreaves and Shirley 2009). Test-based information was used to oversee the learning results and to provide a necessary knowledge base for the choice of school and the formation of an educational market. For instance, according to the No Child is Left Behind Act (NCLB) of 2002 in the US, the states are required to set standards for skills in reading and mathematics and a timeline by which students will achieve active proficiency in these skills. The "adequate yearly progress" is monitored by testing.

The implementation of the NCLB Act led to debate about the impact of "high-stakes testing" on curricula and the quality of education (e.g. Au 2007; Nichols and Berlinger 2007; Madaus *et al.* 2009; Ravitch 2010). Tests drive the curriculum and influence teaching and learning. In her metasynthesis of 49 studies on how high-stakes testing affects curriculum contents, Au concludes (2007: 258): "The primary effect of high-stakes testing is that curricular content is narrowed to tested subjects, subject area knowledge is fragmented into test-related pieces, and teachers increase the use of teacher-centred pedagogies." Madaus *et al.*

---

[10] Tapio Erma and Maija Finkman, Helsingin Sanomat 2.12.2007.

133

(2007) found three unintended consequences of high-stakes testing: an increase in dropout rates, an impact on student motivation, and effects on students and their families. Although a test-based system may pressure schools and students to improve, it also causes stress and loss of self-confidence and an instrumental motivation oriented to test taking.

Doubt over whether the NCLB Act is able to reach its goals is increasing in the US. There is a constant discrepancy between state test scores reporting success and NEA (National Educational Assessment) scores (Ravich 2010: 161). It is not clear at all whether the differences between pupils from well-to-do and disadvantaged backgrounds have decreased, and differences between the schools seem to persist. These reflections have raised a more fundamental question of whether the use of centrally defined standards and evaluation based on tests is a viable model of improving the quality of education. This doubt materializes when the measures that state/regional administrations are able to take if a school fails to improve are evaluated. As Diane Ravitch (2010: 100) has recently pointed out, the measures provided by the NCLB Act to solve the problem – transferring pupils to better schools, establishing charter schools or using external after-school tutoring – have proved to be inefficient and do not help the schools improve their teaching.

This critical discussion has extended to the debate about the functionality of tests and standards as a means of governing of innovations. Public statistics and reports on learning outcomes based on aggregated test scores covering schools, subjects, and class levels influence all participants in the educational system: students, parents, teachers, testing specialists, and school administrators. They produce a highly decontextualized and technical way of speaking about schools and school activity (Graham and Neu 2004: 310): "No matter how much heat a debate of a particular test result may generate, the debate in the end is about testing and not about education." I think this critique is relevant in analysing any accountability system based on indicators and scores. There is a tendency to create a particular kind of language and discourse that is insensitive to or detached from the contents and concrete problems of the activities evaluated.

Charles Leadbeater (2002) evaluated the consequences of the implementation of management by targets (or results) in public administration in the UK. He concluded that target-driven management does help in making administration more efficient and transparent, and even more reliable, but it simultaneously works against innovativeness: "the target culture is becoming the enemy of change" (2002: 24). In his view (2002: 18–19), the introduction of management by targets in public administration has spawned centralized and controlled state machinery, leaving less room for creativity, innovation and initiative.

6.8 The multiorganizational field of special education and the forms of interactive learning

The fourth principle of an activity theoretical approach to institutional change and learning was the need to analyse the developing forms and forums of interactive learning between organizations in the field. In Figure 6.1 one of the organizations or types of organizations that contribute to the development of special education in Finland is presented.

Figure 6.1 does not uncover the frequent and multifaceted interactions between the organizations that are both on regional and national level. Typically, important development projects in research institutes are funded both by municipalities, the board of education, and funding organizations, such as the Academy of Finland or Finland's Slot Machine Association. Interest groups and civil organizations bring people together from various organizations.

Early institutionalist literature discussed the role of professional associations as standard setters and regulatory agents that legitimatize by "theorizing" new solutions for an institutional field (Greenwood *et al.* 2002). The view of the field of the Finnish special education system underlines the multiplicity of associations and their contribution to the

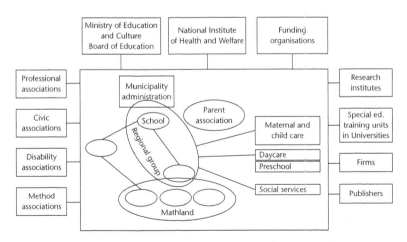

Figure 6.1. A structural description of the multiorganizational field of Finnish special education

development of the field. Figure 6.1 makes a distinction between four kinds of associations in the field: 1) *Professional associations* (such as the Finnish Union of Speech Therapists, the Finnish Union of Special Education, the Finnish Psychological Association, and unions for class and subject teachers), constitute the first group. 2) The Finnish Reading Society and the Finnish Association of Different Learners are examples of *civic associations*. 3) *Disability associations* are the most numerous group of associations.[11] All of them provide some kind of tools, education and peer support. 4) *Methods associations* are organized around a method, such as the Instrumental Enrichment method and the Varga-Neményi method of teaching mathematics.

The vocational associations give norms and help support professional knowledge trough training and by publishing books, tests, and learning materials. In the field of Finnish special education, one of the disability organizations, the *Central Union of Child Welfare in Finland*, has played an important role in the early development of the field and in the accumulation of theoretical and practical knowledge. In 1954 it began to publish a handbook called *Care and Education of Exceptional Children in Finland*, which was meant for social service, heath care, and education professionals. Written by leading specialists in the country, it included a summary of information about the different types of handicaps and problems in development, their care, the national regulations related to care as well as a full list of capacitating services available in the country. The handbook was published every four years until the 2000s. The eleventh revised edition was published in 2002. The book has been an authoritative handbook and a basic textbook in the field.

The civic associations can be regarded as social movements that try to influence both policy making and public opinion. The "Right to learn" campaign organized by the Finnish Diverse Learners' Association in collaboration with the Finnish National UNESCO Committee inspired by the United Nations Literacy Decade (2003–2012) is a good example of how a civic initiative can bring people together from various organizations, professional groups, and positions. The Finnish Diverse Learners' Association is an interest group of adults with learning and reading difficulties who found that the school was not able help them properly. The consultative committee of the campaign was presided by the director

---

[11] To these associations belong: 1) The Finnish Diverse Learner's Association (dyslectics); 2) the Finnish Association for Autism and Asperger's Syndrome; 3) The Finnish Association on Intellectual and Developmental Disabilities (FAIDD); 4) The ADHD-Association; 5) The Finnish Tourette's Association; as well as 6) various associations related to blindness and deafness.

general of the National Board of Education and the National Institute For Health and Welfare as well as the president of the association. The campaign composed of a series of seminars in different regions where researchers, politicians, civil servants and special education teachers were invited as speakers and discussants. The aim of the campaign was to show that persons with dyslexia are often talented individuals and successful in working life, even in science. The campaign managed to "normalize" reading and writing difficulties, showed that they can be successfully addressed and encouraged politicians, municipalities, parents, and schools to recognize and address learning difficulties.

In addition to underlining the diversity of actors and their contributions to the field, it is essential to analyse their interaction. In Table 6.4 examples are presented of the forms of interaction between the agents in the field, which take place on different levels. The table makes an artificial distinction between these levels. In reality many of the activities transcend the boundaries between local, regional, and national. The national Right to learn campaign was realized in the form of local events. In the yearly national seminars of the Finnish Varga-Neményi association, the results of using of the method in local schools are compared.

In the previous section there was a description of the decentralization of school governance. One aspect of this decentralization is the way in which the Board of Education implements reforms and prepares suggestions for the parliament for changes in education acts. These are prepared in collaboration with local actors in the field. For example, the implementation of the 2007 strategy of special education and the preparation of the changes to the basic Education Act issued by the parliament in 2011 were realized by a four-year developmental project (2008–2011) funded and headed by the National Board of Education with a participation of 233 municipalities geographically covering the whole country. The project was aided by two university institutes which provided training and feedback on the plans for student care written by the municipalities as a part of the project. The plans "experimented" with the ideas and concepts (inclusion, intensified support, learning plan, etc.) that were planned to be included in the act. Preparing the changes in this way enables previously developed and shared "promising practices" to be included in the act to be standardized. On the other hand, the large-scale participation of municipalities and schools in preparatory work enhances the implementation of practices outlined by the new act. The preparation of the changes to the act can therefore be regarded as a form of interactive learning and co-construction, although the civil servants of the Board formulate the regulations and the parliament may change them.

Table 6.4. Forms and forums of collaboration between the organizations and people on different levels within the field of special education in Finland

1. *Local*
   (a) Regular unofficial collaboration between teachers and special education teachers
   (b) The multiprofessional student welfare group (SWG)
   (c) "Transfer meetings" of the teachers of the comprehensive schools and kindergartens of a neighbourhood to share information about the children entering primary school

2. *Municipal*
   (a) *Regional special education teacher groups within municipalities*; exchange of information, tools and experiences; connection administration of the municipality
   (b) *Mathland*, a resource centre and working space for teaching and learning mathematics
   (c) Hundreds of *further education courses* organized by municipality: transmission of new knowledge and tools and the sharing of experiences with fellow teachers
   (d) *Study visits* to other schools

3. *Regional*
   (a) Regional non-commercial *Good-practices-expositions* in the capital district. The schools exhibit and share their pedagogical innovations and practices. Administrations, research groups and teacher training units present recent developments of the field, new tools, plans and services
   (b) *Regional associations* of unions and associations

4. *National/*field level
   (a) Further education and training: (1) *Yearly National days of Special Education Development* organized by the Board of Education; (2) *Summer Days of Special Education* organized by The University of Jyväskylä, which deal with topical issues in the field in the form of lectures and discussions; (3) obligatory *VESO further training days* organized by the municipalities and *training courses* organized by the research institutes (NMI, CLR) and special education teacher training units; (4) courses and conferences organized by the associations (e.g., the Varga-Neményi Association)
   (b) The Yearly *EDUCA-expedition* organized by the Trade Union of Education in Finland and the Finnish Fair Corporation. All the organization of field are represented and exhibit their topical issues and products
   (c) *Campaigns*: the Finnish Diverse Learners' Association's *Right to learn* campaign
   (d) Large-scale programmes of developing and experimenting with practices related to the changes in the school regulation organized by the National Board of Education

The continual melding of inputs from actors in different domains in the development of an institutional field blurs boundaries between design and production, planning and execution (Garud and Karnoe 2003: 295). The political programmes (universalism, equality, the principle of overcoming the learning difficulties) and laws are essential conditions for the establishment of the field. On the other hand, there are gradually built professional competencies and a variety of tools and technologies, which have been developed without any unified plan. The expertise of special education is a distributed expertise – or to use John

Dewey's term, it is associated intelligence. It is based on or mediated by sets of cultural artifacts produced by multiple professional groups and agents. Special education teachers makes sense of learning problems and try to help students with a developing arsenal of diagnostic and pedagogic tests, methods and materials. These instrumentalities constitute a shared cultural, objectified foundation of the expertise in special education. They are the instruments of realization of the special education policy of the early recognition of learning difficulties and the immediate provision of support for them.

The richness of distributed agency and initiative to form new associations within the field is possible because of the autonomy of the agents in the field. A strict national control from above based on standards and inspection procedures would have directed the efforts of the field in predetermined directions and would not have stimulated the emergence of new associations, experiments, sets of tools, and complementary expertise within the field. In this sense the change in the form of governance from centralized control to decentralization and the stimulation of initiative and interaction between the various actors have been important conditions for the development of a viable field. In terms of the evolutionary theory of innovation, centralized control based on standards inhibits the emergence of variation, which constitutes a constitutive foundation for development.

6.9 The nature of institutional development and the limits of emulation

In this chapter the institutional explanations for the success of Finnish students in the PISA studies were reviewed. The key explanations, the popularity of the teaching profession and a university-level teacher education, decentralized governance, and the special education system are not a result of a conscious plan or an attempt to create educational excellence. The comprehensive school reform was strongly inspired by the idea of educational equality. But the practices and parts of the system developed partly in a contingent way. The decision to transfer teacher training to universities and make it masters degree was as much a part of the reform of the degrees of the third level education than quality of the teacher training. The masters studies as a part of teacher training were strongly opposed by the planners of teacher education until the late 1970s (Simola and Rinne 2010). Only later was it considered to be a cornerstone of excellence in the school system. The decentralization of school governance was a result of many developments and intentions. There was a crisis of the detailed centralized governance in many agencies and the delegation was seen as a general solution. The curriculum ideology developed in the 1980s and 1990s towards increasing the responsibility of schools and teachers. On the other hand, budgeting cuts caused by the economic slump of the 1990s significantly reduced the resources of the National Board of Education and limited the possibilities of constructing a system for overall evaluation and oversight. The law on municipal self-governance issued in 1995 did not allow direct state control (by directives or by rules) of the service provision in the municipalities. This stimulated an increase of new forms in interaction between the hierarchical levels of administration.

Swedish economist and theorist of Nordic welfare and planning society, Gunnar Myrdal, suggested that this is how the coordination and welfare institutions were created. It was not a result of a plan or political ideas of the majority of those who held power (Myrdal 1961: 58–59):

> It happened in a very much more accidental, less direct and less purposive way: by an unending sequence of acts of intervention by the state and many other collective bodies, in the play of market forces. (...) These sets of interventions were mostly motivated ad hoc, and regularly had the much more limited – and often, from the point of view of the now accomplished Welfare State, obstructionist or even subversive – objectives, directed by special interests. That in the end the accumulated result of all this intervention by public, semi-public and private organizations, and the gradual, planned coordination which they necessitate came nearer and nearer to the "created harmony" of the welfare state.

Myrdal's account characterizes well the emergence and contribution of the distributed agency in the field. This development could also have been different. While Finland can be proud of its comprehensive school it is afflicted – like many other countries – by an exclusion problem. A considerable minority of students – especially boys – does not continue their studies in the secondary education after the comprehensive school nor is recruited to working life. The suggested numbers of alienated young people range from 30,000 to 50,000. It was recently (2012) discovered that there are 110,000 young people under the age of 30 in Finland without secondary education. It is widely agreed that the present services over several administrative bodies are unable to find and help these young persons. This phenomenon is a new societal contradiction that requires consequent measures to be taken in order to be resolved.

The situation might be different, had the suggestion of the Education Committee in 1971 (Vuoden 1971, 1973) been realized. The committee suggested a 12-year unitary school in which a three-year secondary school would be integrated into a nine-year comprehensive school. In its plan vocational education and key parts of general civic education – characteristic to upper secondary school which prepares students for university – would have been integrated into secondary school, and all students would have access to tertiary education. The reform proposal did not gain sufficient political support and was not realized.

How can the Finnish model of comprehensive school be emulated or benchmarked? In March 2000 the special summit of the European Council in Lisbon declared that Europe was to become "the most competitive and dynamic knowledge-based economy in the world, capable of sustainable economic growth with more and better jobs and greater social cohesion" (European Council 2000, §5). As a part of this goal it introduced a new governance strategy, the Open Method of Co-ordination (OMC). The idea of benchmarking, originally developed as a part of Total Quality Management in industry, played a central role in the OMC. Benchmarking consists of comparing one's performance with one's competitors and using objective criteria as a way to gain a competitive edge (Bruno 2009: 270). This idea was adopted in the EU to enhance policy learning and to solve the governance problems of the EU. It was meant to spread best practices and to achieve convergence towards the main EU goals without top-down standardization. The key measures were the creation of a system of indicators which make the differences between the countries visible and allow analysis of the development in relation to the selected goals (benchmarks) (see e.g. Room et al. 2005; Braadbaart and Yusnandarshah 2008; Bruno 2009). In addition, periodic monitoring, evaluation, and peer review between the member countries were suggested as a method of mutual learning. It is suggested that countries start to take measures to achieve the level of those countries that rank high in the scorebooks and comparisons.

The OECD PISA studies can be regarded as a part of this evaluation and accountancy regime. In this logic, the success of the Finnish students in the PISA studies sets the Finnish school system as a best practice to be emulated. The focus in the development of benchmarking has thus far primarily been in the creation of a system of indicators that allow the comparisons to be made. Only few studies have been carried out of the actual learning from the practices that have ranked high in the comparisons.

The institutional and historical embeddedness of schools may make the emulation difficult. Among the explanations provided for the success of the Finnish students were decentralized trust-based school governance, the high esteem of the teaching profession, the early recognition and immediate remedial measures for learning difficulties, and the activity of student care groups in schools. These factors are all historically developed institutional facts that are not easily observable in a single school or by observing school activity. It is a paradox that Finland ranks high in international comparisons by not allowing – against the mainstream educational policy – comparisons between students and schools on the national level.

It is questionable whether the popularity and esteem for the teaching profession can be emulated. It is based both on the university-based teacher education and the autonomy of the teachers due to the decentralized system of school governance. Equally difficult would be to emulate the principles and practices of the early recognition of learning difficulties and immediate remedial measures for learning difficulties without the resources and multiprofessional expertise that were developed over several decades in Finland.

Can the student welfare groups in Finnish schools be transferred to other places? Its existence as a multiprofessional group was based on the need to coordinate the activities of the professions involved in student care: teachers, school nurses, special education teachers, school psychologists, study counsellors as well as other service providers (child, social, and health care). The creation of these professional groups through training and funding their activities within schools was an achievement of the welfare state. Evidently, the key practices of schools are deeply embedded in the multi-organizational field and the forms of collaboration within it. This embeddedness and interdependency between organizations make the emulation of separate practices within a field difficult.

7

Capability-cultivating services as a foundation for welfare and innovation policies

7.1 The welfare state as a developer of capability-cultivating services

The discourse of the welfare state and welfare policy complements the debate on innovations policy in two ways. First, it takes welfare of the citizens as a starting point for national policy making instead of focusing primarily on economic development. Second, it studies the interdependency between social policy, economic development and democracy. In the last few decades it has focused on the problem of how the instruments of social policy and risk sharing should be adapted to the demand of the flexibility of labour markets caused by techno-logical development and globalization. It has not, however, discussed systematically the relationship between economic development and the capability-cultivating services such as education, the public library system, day care, and the child and family clinics created by the welfare society. I will argue that the further development of these universal capability-cultivating institutions are vital for meeting the demands of welfare, for knowledge society development, and for international com-petitiveness of the country.

These services constitute the heart of the new enabling welfare state. They cultivate and provide the human capabilities that are the founda-tion of the absorptive capacities of firms and other organizations. They contribute to development of trust and social capital that stimulate creative collaboration across boundaries of organization and fields. They make possible flexible transitions to new areas of production. If the message of the old welfare state was that social policy is economic policy, the message of the new welfare state will be that education and development of human capabilities is economic policy.

It restates the central ideal of the old welfare state, namely the virtuous circle of equality, welfare, and economic growth in new circumstances. This is also included in Manuel Castells' and Pekka Himanen's (2002: 158) idea of the Finnish model of the information society: "Only by defending the combination of information society and welfare state in the EU, and by addressing the rise of new sources of inequality can the Finnish welfare state continue as a genuinely inclusive society."

The traditional view of the welfare state gave only marginal attention to education and other capability-creating, civilizing institutions. This focus on social insurance and the redistribution of resources has continued until recently. Comparative welfare state scholars have had a tendency to exclude education from their analyses, although education and skills are evidently at the core of the welfare state (Iversen and Stephens 2008: 621). From the point of view of innovation policy and the knowledge society, the educational system and other institutions of capability building are lasting achievements of the welfare state. This can be seen by reviewing the emergence and development of the public library system, the institutions of adult education, the music school system, day care as well as the child welfare clinic system in Finland. All these institutions were established in the 1960s and 1970s through legislation, substantial state funding and support for the training of professionals.

The public library system contributes to the development of functional reading capabilities as well as to the knowledge of society, culture and science. There is one or several (main and branch) public libraries in the 311 municipalities in Finland.[1] In 2001, 46% of Finns were registered library users, while the number in the EU was 27%. The approximate number of loans per inhabitant in Finland is 20, which is by far the highest figure in the world. There was a fairly dense network of municipal libraries in Finland already after the Second World War. The library system was consolidated by the Library Act passed in 1962, which granted state support both for the construction of library buildings and for the maintenance of libraries. The agrarian municipalities received two thirds and cities one third of operating costs. Poor and remote municipalities received extra support of 10–25%. The library inspectors of the National Board of Education consulted and directed

---

[1] The cities have a main library and branch libraries in each main suburb. The city of Helsinki, for instance, has a central library and 40 branch libraries. In the countryside, library buses are extensively used.

the establishment of services. Loans from public libraries rose tenfold between the 1960s and the 1990s. An international library statistics comparison commissioned by the European Commission and UNESCO ranked the library services of 40 countries according to eight indicators (Fuegi and Jennings 2004). Finland was ranked the first, followed by Denmark, Estonia, Iceland, the UK, Sweden, Norway, and Slovenia. The public library system has been on the cutting edge of digitalization in Finland and has provided free of charge access to computer use and Internet connections for citizens.

The Finnish institutions of adult education emerged from the strong tradition of civic associations that at the end of the nineteenth century stated to organize study circles as well as cultural activities such as music (choirs and orchestras) and theatre. Christian, social democratic, and agrarian-nationalistic adult education national associations were established in the first decades of the 1900s. The Finnish system of adult education developed out of the centres and activities created by these associations. Today the system comprises adult education centres, study circles, vocational adult education, folk high schools, and summer universities. The first laws on state support for the civic and workers' institutes – later called adult education centres – were passed in the 1920s. The further development of these institutions was established by legislation in the 1960s and 1970s when they were granted state support.

In 2009 there were 206 adult education centres in Finland, and 780,000 (about 15% of the population) citizens participated in their courses. The most extensive areas of studies in the centres include craft, visual arts, and music. In certain areas of craft the centres have become the primary carriers of skill and tradition. In recent decades, courses in foreign languages and the use of information technology have rapidly increased in number. An important element of the centres is their public lectures on history, culture, and politics. Since the 1990s these adult education centres have played a growing role in dealing with unemployment by organizing vocational education for the unemployed. According to Eurostat statistics, 55% of Finnish adults participated in adult education in 2005–2007 which was the second highest figure in Europe after Sweden.

After the economic slump of the 1990s, the amount of state funded labour market training meant to enhance the employability of unemployed persons rapidly increased. It was organized mostly by vocational adult education centres established in the 1970s and was the most important means of the active labour market policy of the 1990s. The number of the people who started training increased from 36,000 in 1990 to 90,000 in 1995. The quality and effectiveness of this training were called into questioned both the researchers and by the participants. The need for a more intensive regular collaboration between vocational schools, adult education centres, public service providers, and firms was called for. Evidently, much could be learned from the Danish flexicurity and German craft training systems in accomplishing this.

A "success story" comparable to that of the Finnish comprehensive school is Finnish music education. The international music world has registered how from the 1980s young Finnish composers, directors, and opera singers have staffed music houses all over the world. An example is Andrew Clark who writes in the *Financial Times* (27 October 2001):

> The flowering of Finnish creativity these past three decades is not just a freak development on the fringe of Europe, indulged in by a minority of foreign enthusiasts. There is a perfectly good reason for this. It boils down to the huge investment the Finns have made in their musical education (. . .). How else can you explain why since the 1960s – with a population not greater than London's – Finland has produced more leading musicians than any other country in Europe?

The present Finnish music education system is an outcome of the interaction between initiatives of private citizens, civil associations and state policy. When the Finnish Association of Music Schools was established in 1956, there were 14 music schools for children in major cities. The goal of the association was the institutionalization of the music school system. It created a labelling and qualification system for schools, and began the training of music school teachers and the planning of a unified curriculum for music schools (Ritaluoto 1996). The preparation of the curriculum took place in collaboration with the music university Sibelius Academy. The music school system was, therefore, planned from the beginning to be compatible with the higher musical studies in the Academy.

An act providing state support for music schools was accepted by Parliament in 1969. A school that met the conditions defined by law received funding from the state budget of about half of its operating costs.[2] In 2001 a total of 88 music schools enjoyed state support. In addition, the conservatories, which are the schools that train music school teachers, receive additional support. The often-heard anecdote told by teachers at the Sibelius Academy is that from the late 1970s the

---

[2] At the beginning of the 2000s the state budget covered 49% of the costs, municipalities 34%, and student fees 17%.

students who entered the academy were better musically educated than the students who had already left it.

The oldest universal service in Finland is the maternity and child heath care clinic system. The act that initiated these clinics came into effect in 1944, and the system's functions were updated in the National Public Health Act of 1972. Today there are 860 child clinics, which are mostly part of municipal health centres. Virtually every mother and child in Finland uses their services. The check-ups for toddlers and young children are regular and today increasingly include the neurological evaluation of pre-school children, in which potential learning or developmental problems can be recognized.

The Child Day Care Act was passed in 1973. The guidance and support from the state was instrumental in the establishment of day care centres, especially in the countryside (Kröger 1995). In 1973 there were 52,000 municipal day care posts, and in 1985 the number was 150,000 (Välimäki and Rauhala 2000: 397). A change in the law in 1985 provided a subjective right to day care to children under the age of 3. In 2001 the law required the municipalities to organize pre-primary education for all 6-year-old children. Day care became partly integrated into the educational system. The five-year wellness check by the maternity and child health care clinics is regarded as an important step in the diagnosis of learning difficulties. It is often done together with the teachers from day care centres. Local transfer meetings are regularly held between day care centre and primary school teachers.

Common to all of these institutions is that they were established by private initiatives and civil society organizations. In the 1960s and 1970s their status was consolidated by legislation and substantial public funding motivated by social and regional equality. Training of the professionals needed for the development of the services was organized and funded, and networks of services were extended to the entire country. In this way the old welfare state created the universal enabling services that constitute a central institutional foundation for a new welfare state.

7.2 The financial crisis of the welfare state and the fate of enabling services

One of the contradictions faced by the welfare states is the contradiction between the need to increase the quality and provision of public welfare services and the decreasing tax basis caused by changes in demography and a weakening level of economic development. It has been estimated that the working age population in Finland will decrease from 66.5% of the total today to 57.6% in 2040 (Andersen *et al.* 2007: 20). The shift of balance between those contributing and those benefiting from the welfare state is outing the financial sustainability of the system in danger. One of the main remedies suggested has been the privatization of public services to increase the efficiency of provision.

After the economic crisis of 1990–1991, social benefits were cut, and changes in taxation favoured capital incomes. As a result, differences in incomes in the following two decades increased in Finland more quickly than in any other OECD country. Many analysts suggest that a radical shift from a planning economy and welfare state into a competition economy and state has taken place (Hämäläinen and Heiskala 2004; Heiskala 2006). Other commentators think that the transition is less straightforward. In spite of the cuts in social benefits the basic services of the welfare state, among them education, child and family care, and pension systems, have prevailed (e.g. Rinne *et al.* 2002; Antikainen 2010). Support for the welfare state among Finnish citizens has increased in the 1990s and 2000s. In a survey made in 2009, 82% of the respondents agreed with the statement: "Even though the maintenance of social security and other public services is expensive, the Finnish welfare state is always worth these expenses" (Paloheimo 2010: 29).[3]

The development of the governance of Finnish basic education has thus deviated from internationally dominant reforms inspired by neoliberalism, such as the creation of educational markets, privatization, and assessment of schools by national tests. Influential political forces defend the public comprehensive school system as a valuable achievement of the welfare state. The Basic Education Act of 1998 confirmed parents' free choice among the schools within a municipality. However, according to the act, a child has the right to attend her/his neighbourhood school. Extra pupils are accepted only if vacant places are available. The evaluation studies made by the National Board of Education (NBE) are sample-based studies. They allow the analysis and feedback of achievements but not comparisons between schools. Practically no education official or politician in Finland supports the league tables for schools because they think it may increase the differences between schools. In a recent survey study (Rinne *et al.* 2011) 93% of both the rectors and the teachers of

---

[3] Since those who agreed with this statement have different opinions on the level of taxation, Paloheimo makes a distinction between the supporters of a social democratic welfare state (39%) and a streamlined welfare state (38%). The first group regards the securing of the public services as very important or very important and does not regard the lowering of taxes as important in the following election. The latter group regards the securing of public services as very important or very important while also regarding the lowering of taxes as important in the next election (Paloheimo 2010: 35).

Finnish comprehensive schools agreed. Almost as many were of the opinion that the league lists of schools would not do any good for teaching and that they are likely to increase teaching for tests. The Finnish Parliament Standing Committee for Education and Culture has expressed this position several times (Simola *et al.* 2009: 172):

> The publicity concerns only the main results of evaluations. The purpose of the new Basic Education Act is not to publish information directly linked to an individual school or teacher. Publishing the evaluation results cannot in any case lead to the ranking of schools or the categorization of schools, teachers or pupils as weak or good on unfair grounds.

The Education Act of 1998 rejected the use of private pedagogical services at the comprehensive school level and limited the possibilities of establishing private schools. There are 72 private comprehensive schools in Finland, which is 2.2% of the total number of 3263 comprehensive schools. Most of these private schools are either Steiner or Christian schools or schools outside Finland. They strictly follow the national core curriculum. In 2011, 13 applicants applied for permission to establish a private comprehensive school. The government did not give permission to any of them because the applications did not meet the criteria for acceptance, among them regional need, qualified teachers and a well-prepared curriculum.

However, even if the basic school system has been protected from competition and the introduction of markets it is influenced by general economic policy and by policies pursued in other sectors. The achievements of enabling services are dependent on the economic conditions of families. Increased differences in incomes has increased the number of families who are unable to stimulate the formation of intellectual capabilities and motivation in their children.

In the 1980s these differences in incomes in Finland and the share of the proportionally poor were the lowest in the world. In the 1990s, these differences increased in Finland in an unforeseen way. According to a survey conducted by the OECD in 2008, income disparities grew faster in Finland than in any other OECD country in the period from 1995 to 2005. After recession in the years 1994–2000, the incomes of the highest 10% of income earners increased by 62%, while the increase of the lowest decile in the same period was 14% (Taimio 2007: 72). Cuts in social benefits and changes in taxation that favoured capital gains contributed to the increasing differences of incomes and property ownership in Finland. In spite of the rapid growth rate in income disparities, Finland is still a country with low inequality of incomes, and is clearly below the average. Among 30 OECD countries Finland was seventh, while Denmark and Sweden are in a class of their own with the lowest income disparity of all. The division of incomes has contributed to the emergence of problems that weaken the conditions of learning and the development of capabilities. Among them are the increasing differences in health services, the social exclusion of young people and increased poverty of families of children.

Unlike education, the public basic health services have declined in Finland. Three different systems provide health care services: public municipal health centres, occupational health centres for those employed and private clinics, the number of which has rapidly increased during the last two decades. The public health centres – especially in scattered settlements – have difficulties in recruiting medical doctors. In 2011, 80% of the population lived in the regions where they cannot have an appointment in a public health centre within two weeks, although according to the law it should be possible within three days. This is especially problematic for students, the unemployed, pensioners and families with children who cannot afford to use private services and who are outside the occupational health services. The health differences between the social groups have increased. The difference in life expectancy between men in the highest and lowest income fifths increased from 7.4 to 12.5 years in 1988–2007.

The number of those who earn less than 60% of median incomes – often used as a criteria of poverty has increased from 3.2% in 1990 to 7.9% in 2008 (Vaarama et al. 2010: 200). Poverty primarily affected families with children, especially families with one parent, those permanently unemployed who lost their jobs in the economic recession in the 1990s, and young people. While the unemployment in the whole population was 8% in 2010, it was almost 20% in the age group 15–24. One third of this group are youth who have only comprehensive school education. What is most alarming, however, from the point of view of education and the development of the children is the increase in child poverty. The number of children who lived in poor families increased from 30,000 in 1990 to 52,000 in 1995 and to 151,000 in 2007.[4] The child poverty decreased from 1970s to 1994. After that it tripled in 15 years and reached the peak of 13.9% in 2007 (Sauli et al. 2011). Although this share is low compared with the average of 20% in the EU countries in 2009 the development has definitely weakened the developmental possibilities of a part of children and make the task of the day care centres and school more difficult.

---

[4] Helsingin Sanomat 10.4.2011, "Increasing childhood poverty damages families in a serious way," Vaarama et al. 2010: 200).

The development also strengthened the social inheritance of poverty, unemployment, and exclusion (Leinonen 2004). This in turn is visible in the slight but consistent decrease in the PISA results of Finnish students in the 2000s. For example, the proportion of weak readers among Finnish students was 6% (compared with the OECD average of 19%) in the 2000 PISA study, while in 2009 it was 8% (compared with the same OECD average of 19%). This group may be potentially excluded from the knowledge society. In addition, differences between schools – the smallest among the OECD countries in 2000 – have increased from 5% in 2000 to 8% in 2009. These differences have increased more in big cities than in the rest of the country. Several new studies have shown that some boys have alarmingly weak reading skills at the end of comprehensive school.

It is widely agreed that state funding for municipalities has lagged behind the increased obligations to provide the social, health and education services defined by law. The crisis in municipality economics has forced many municipalities to cut expenses and the provision of services. In an inquiry made in 2011 the majority of municipal managers regarded basic education as the primary object of savings. In addition the funding of educational services compete with the rising costs of health care services and the rapidly increased need for elderly care. Thus far, a typical target of savings in basic education has been the hiring of substitute teachers. As a result, one teacher must teach two classes simultaneously, as was vividly described by an experienced Finnish teacher in November 2010:[5]

> I have been working as a teacher for 19 years, and during this time I have seen how great a benefit many students who have concentration dysfunctions or other learning difficulties have received from the opportunity to study in small groups (...). The big cities' refusal to hire substitutes is destroying the education given. For absences of less than three days hiring a substitute is not allowed and we teachers run between our own class and the neighbouring class giving instructions. One of the groups is continually without surveillance. Some of the students do what is written on the blackboard because they want to do it and are able to it. Some of them do not because they are unable to do it, and some do not because they don't want to.

The citation shows how even small cuts in the funding of service provision might lead to a grave deterioration in the quality of services. Kindergarten teachers as well have expressed their frustration with

[5] An anonymous opinion published by *Helsingin Sanomat* 11 November 2010 entitled "As a comprehensive school teacher I constantly suffer a bad conscience."

151

expanding groups due to savings, a problem which affects the quality of care and makes it difficult to meet the special needs of individual children. The group size in preschool education in Finland was higher (16.9) in 2003 than the OECD average (14.8). The corresponding size was 10.3 in Sweden and 6.9 in Denmark. These examples show why public funding is instrumental for the development of these services.

7.3 Higher education policy and the nurturing of absorptive capacities

The focus of the innovation policy in the development of the educational system in Finland in the 2000s has been on tertiary education and on the contribution of university research to the Finnish innovation system. It is, however, unclear to what extent these developmental measures have contributed to the development of the capabilities of students. The Polytechnics Act was passed in Parliament in 2003. Twenty-five polytechnics (or universities of applied science) operating in 80 localities were established in many cases through fusing vocational colleagues. The act explicitly defined that the teaching should respond to the needs of working life and that polytechnics are supposed to collaborate with business firms and other work organizations in their region. The polytechnics are expected to strengthen regional centres of expertise. The regional centre programme was initiated in 1993. The aim of regional centres of expertise is to direct private and public regional resources to selected promising areas of expertise and business activity. Twenty-one centres received funding in 2011.

In the late 1990s and 2000s a major concern of the innovation policy was related to the university system (e.g. Hautamäki 2010). It was regarded as a "weak link" of the national innovation system. The structural reform of the Finnish university system composing three elements was realized in 2010. First, the juridical status of the universities was changed from civil service departments under the guidance of the Ministry of Education and Culture into independent legal personalities in order to give them more autonomy and the right to raise private funding. Second, an attempt was made to form larger and more viable units by increasing collaboration between the nearest regional universities. The most visible of these attempts was – as reported before in section 5.3 – the establishment of Aalto University, originally called an "innovation university" and a "top university", by combining three universities of the capital district: the Helsinki of University Technology, the Helsinki School of Economics and the University of Art and Design.[6] It is premature to evaluate the effects of these measures.

In the 1990s the role of universities in the national innovation system was interpreted primarily in terms of the Bayh-Dole framework. The "third mission" of a university – interaction with the surrounding society and the promotion of the impact of research findings – was added to the University Act in 2004. It was interpreted in terms of securing the provision of important research results and inventions to industry by giving universities the right to patent these results and by establishing and strengthening the so-called intermediary organizations. They take care of patenting and the commercialization of patents. The limitations of this framework have been extensively discussed (e.g. Nelson 2001; Kenney and Patton 2009).

The problem of this framework is that it does not discuss the main contribution of the universities to the economy and innovation, which is the training of professionals able to follow the international development of their respective areas of professional knowledge. The knowledge and capacity of graduates to follow the development of a field constitute an essential foundation for the absorptive capacities of their forthcoming employees, firms and other organizations. The production of the capacity to follow the development of a field of knowledge requires interaction between research and teaching in universities. This interaction contributes to the understanding of what problems and developments in the field are important and which conferences, publications, research traditions, organizations, research groups, and scholars are worth following. This cannot be achieved based on textbook teaching detached from research and international collaboration.

In the 1990s and 2000s several developments in the funding of the Finnish university system loosened the connection between research and teaching. During and after the financial crisis of the early 1990s, direct budget funding of universities was reduced, while the numbers of students simultaneously increased. As a result, in 1995 funding per student in Finland was 60% of the average of the OECD countries (Tiitta 2007: 230). In 1992–2001 the number of students in the university system increased by 33%, master's degrees by 38% and doctoral degrees by 128%, while the number of university teaching staff

[6] All the universities were promised an extra public funding equal to the sum that they were able to raise from private sources. Since Aalto University was an initiative of Finnish industry, it can easily raise extra private funding from firms. The universities that are strong in the humanities, social sciences and pedagogical sciences had difficulties in raising private funding.

decreased by 3% (Patomäki 2005: 96). The student/teacher ratio in Finnish universities grew from 19 in 1990 to 25 in 2000 and was 26 in 2009 (Korkeakoulut 2011). At the same time, the budget funding of the universities was tied to the number of degrees that they produced. This has increased mass and textbook-based teaching and left fewer possibilities for more time-consuming group and project teaching, small group seminars, personal supervising and scholarly discussions.

Paradoxically the worst situation is in the technical sciences. The number of teachers did not reach the 1991 level until 2004 in spite of the increase in the number of students by 43% (Tiitta 2007: 251). It is evident that such a increase in efficiency cannot have been realized without the deteriorization of the quality of teaching, the increase of mass lecturing and less time for personnel supervision of students. Research and teaching personnel find themselves overburdened, stressed and without sufficient time for research or preparation of high quality teaching. The increase of competitive project funding on the cost of budget funding in research tends to weaken the connection between research and teaching: the project researchers rarely teach. This situation is characterized as a "plight" of the university system constituting a bottleneck in the Finnish innovations system: it is doubted whether the universities are any longer capable of educating specialists capable of following and utilizing the results of the cutting-edge research.

The most important structural change in funding in the 1990s was the increase in the proportion of competitive project funding from the Finnish Academy, Tekes, and ministries at the expense of the direct budget funding from state. Competitive funding rose from 24% to 38% of the total funding of the universities. Unintended consequences of this change include, first, a rapid increase in the number of project researchers salaried for short periods who do not contribute to teaching. Second, professors and senior researchers increasingly have to spend their time on proposals and project management at the cost of research and teaching. Also, this change has contributed to the separation of teaching and research: those who teach do not write project proposals or do research. Those who apply for money and do research teach less. This weakened connection between research and teaching undermines the quality of competence creation.

7.4 From investment in human capital to cultivation of human creativity

In order to develop a policy of enabling services, an understanding of the nature of human development and capabilities is needed. With the development of the idea of the knowledge-based economy different disciplines have presented their own definitions of capabilities. The economics of education has introduced *human capital* (Becker 1964/ 1993), welfare economics the *capability approach* (Sen 1993), innovation studies *technological capabilities* (Faberberg and Srholec 2008) or *national innovation capability* (Fuhrman *et al.* 2002), and organizational and business studies *organizational or dynamic capabilities* (Dosi *et al.* 2000).

The last two groups of capability concepts have been constructed to explain the success of firms or nations in competition. Capabilities are specified by listing institutional and organizational conditions or processes that enhance or explain competitive capability. In an attempt to measure the innovation capability of nations Fagerberg and Srholec (2008: 1420), for instance, define nine "aspects" of capability which cover a wide range of institutional state of affairs. The authors define empirical indicators for each of them. The aspects include science and research (measured by number of scientific publications, patents, R&D investments), openness of trade, skills (levels of education), quality of governance (independence of courts, property rights, business friendly regulation) as well as social values such as trust and tolerance. The term capability in this analysis is an explanatory construction that could also be called a condition or a determinant of national competitiveness or innovation.

Organization and management studies discuss capabilities on the level of the firm in terms of absorptive and dynamic capabilities as well as core competencies. Dynamic capabilities refer to "capabilities which allow the firm to create new products and processes, and respond to changing market circumstances" (Teece and Pisano 1994: 541). Key activities related to dynamic capability include searching the changes of markets, technology and competition, developing an alternative business model in order to answer these changes, as well as the orchestration of internal and external resources needed to realize the model (Teece 2009). Organizational capability, therefore, refers both individual and collaborative activities vital for the success of a firm. In innovation studies, Lundvall and his colleagues (Arundel *et al.* 2007) have underlined the significance of organizational arrangements that stimulate learning of the employees and interactive learning. Whereas hierarchical or Taylorist organizations prevent learning and initiative, team-based non-hierarchical forms enhance them.

The literature on organizational learning is abundant and somewhat fragmented (see e.g. Dierkes *et al.* 2001). Its evaluation is out of the scope of this book. One important dividing line between the theories of the field can however be drawn (Miettinen *et al.* 2012). Many researchers regard experience-based tacit learning related to daily work and routines (often called learning by doing) the most important for learning. Others think that such a habitual conception of learning and practice has difficulties in explaining the emergence of agency central for the change of practices (Emirbayer and Miche 1998; Miettinen *et al.* 2012). It largely disregards the role of reflection, critical thinking and imagination in activity as well conscious absorption and further development of new concepts and tools developed elsewhere. The cultural-historical theory of learning in work (Engeström 2005; Miettinen and Virkkunen 2006) and Dewey's theory of problem solving, inquiry and transformation of habits is an example of the latter perspective. These two perspectives lead to different strategies of enhancing the development of capabilities and expertise in working life. As suggested by the case of Finnish special education, in-house and further education organized together with other actors continues to play a crucial role in transmitting the results of research work, initiatives and the solutions developed in different localities to the practitioners of an institutional field.

The theorizing of capabilities in organizational and innovation literature largely neglects the problem of the development capacities in early childhood and in elementary school. This development, however, constitutes an essential foundation for learning and expertise in adulthood. Without strong basic capabilities (literacy, maths, basic understanding of nature and society) later attempts to advance learning and expertise have limited possibilities to achieve substantial results.

The most established way of speaking about human capabilities in policy language is to use the concept of human capital. It emerged within neoclassical economics as a form of capital – comparable to physical and financial capital – that was used to explain both the success of individuals in labour markets and economic growth and welfare. An OECD report (2001b: 18) defines it as "the knowledge, skills and competences and attributes embodied in individuals that facilitate the creation of personal, social and economic well-being." It was first used to explain occupational attainment and differences in earnings between individuals (Becker 1964/1993), and subsequently regional and national economic growth. Since education and training are the most important investments in human capital, the level of education is often used as an indicator of human capital in empirical research. In addition, it has been measured in terms of individual cognitive (reading, maths, and IT-related skills) and non-cognitive skills (study habits, perseverance, social skills) that are operationalized by using results from psychological tests and school achievement tests (e.g. Heckman 2007).

Educational sociologists have analysed the limitations and consequences of the economist concept of human capital (e.g. Block 1990).
This concept deals with the economy as an analytically separate realm of
society that can be understood in terms of its own internal dynamics. It
assumes that individuals act rationally to maximize their preferences,
that is, they calculate the relationship between costs and benefits in
realizing their self-interest. This kind of ahistorical conception of
human behaviour, however, lacks an understanding of human activity
other than exchange of commodities in the market. In addition to the
maximization of rational self-interest, other factors such as moral commitments, recognition from the community, world views and professional ethics influence human activity. Because the human mind has a
social origin, culture constantly moulds the preferences of individuals.

The economist human capital model is insufficient for the politics of
capabilities, because it does not recognize qualitative differences
between educational systems. It is insensitive to dimensions of capabilities that are most important for change and innovation, such as creativity and imagination. A more recent version of human capital policy
(e.g. Carneiro and Heckman 2003) takes into account the social economic position and cultural resources of families as a source of cognitive
development and prefers early childhood interventions and well-
tailored services for unprivileged students to general investments in
the school system. Heckman argues that an accumulating body of
knowledge shows that early childhood intervention for disadvantaged
young children is more effective than interventions that come later in
life. However, interventions can be done in different ways. As was
shown in Chapter 6, for example, intervening in learning problems at
school is a pedagogic and epistemic challenge. It calls for the creation of
multiprofessional expertise, collaboration across boundaries as well as
the consistent development of diagnostic and remediational tools.

The policy of early childhood intervention outlined by the human
capital theory includes a contradiction from the point of view of innovation. In extending the teaching of cognitive skills to early childhood it
threaten to destroy the developmental sources of creativity and imagination. Ruth Lister (2006) has harshly criticized the "child-centred social
investment strategy" outlined by New Labour in the UK in the 1990s. It
has a tendency to define children as "citizen-workers of the future" and
objects of social funding (Lister 2006: 462). The strategy extends or projects the cognitive and social demands of today's working life to early
childhood. In doing so it ignores the fundamental developmental task of
children under school age: the development of self and imagination
through play (Vygotsky 2004). In play and role play children create

imaginary situations and solve moral problems related to human relations. Organized play is experimentation with social relations and the environment. It constitutes an important foundation for a holistic approach to the world in adult life (e.g. Sawyer 2006). Developmental psychologists and students of cognition have convincingly argued that imagination in play is a key source of adult creativity (Carruthers 2002: 229):

> The function of human pretend play is to practice for the sorts of imaginative thinking which will later manifest themselves in the creative activities of adults. The connection between the two forms of behavior, arguably, is that each involves essentially the same cognitive underpinnings – namely, a capacity to generate, and to reason with novel suppositions or *imaginative scenarios*.

Unilateral early enforcement of cognitive skills characteristic to school is likely to deteriorate the formation of individual sources of innovation. This is why many developmental psychologists and professionals of pre-school education have consequently resisted the idea of extending reading and writing education characteristic to school to kindergarten and to early childhood.

This is related to a larger problem of the relationship between the development of the individual and the prevailing culture. School tends to transmit the cultural tradition of today to children who will live in the society of tomorrow. However, "adult wisdom does not provide a teleology for child development. A zone of proximal development is a dialogue between the child and his future; it is not a dialogue between the child and the adult's past" (Griffin and Cole 1984: 62). One of the major challenges of pedagogic interaction is how to combine the "acquiring of culture" and the fostering of the child's potential to create new cultural means and forms. An important means of developing the sources of imagination and initiative is the development of play and narrative pedagogy not only in day care but also in the first grades of basic school (Van Oers 2005; Hakkarainen 2008; Rainio 2010).

The capability approach was developed in the 1960s by the Nobel price winner Amartya Sen as an approach to welfare economics and developmental studies. It aims at breaking the limits of neoliberal thought by defining a set of intrinsically valuable human capabilities that constitute the foundation for welfare, such as "live long, escape avoidable morbidity, be well nourished, be able to read, write and communicate, take part in literary and scientific pursuits and so forth" (Sen 1984: 497). Sen's functional capabilities can also understood as the rights and positive freedoms of individuals. His approach has inspired the development of the United Nation's Human Development Index" (HDI), which measures the human development including health and education.

Sen's theory remains that of an economist in defining functional capabilities as the capacity of utilizing commodities. Salais and Villeneuve (2004) have outlined a capability policy for the European Union inspired by the work of Sen. They (2004: 41) state that "what matters for public policies is what a person can do and be with the resources over which she has command. (...) When faced with the same hazard, people are unequal in their capabilities of doing and being with the same basket of commodities or amount of money." This concept risks tearing capabilities away from the public and culturally shared nature of science, professional expertise, public education, craft, local traditions, as well as from other non-commercial forms of culture. To the extent that the approach reduces human capabilities to the ability to operate with commodities in the market, it impoverishes the sources of development of individual capabilities.

The capability approach, human capital theory as well as theories of organizational and technological capabilities analyse the significance of human capabilities for economic growth and well-being. They, however, do not have much to say how the capabilities of individuals emerge and develop or how their development can be systematically enhanced. This problem is traditionally the subject of developmental psychology and educational sciences, which will be discussed in the following section. In the 19th century pedagogical though development was analysed in terms of all-around development of an individual and *Bildung*. In the first half of 1900th century a concept of general intelligence measured by tests developed based the differential psychology became a dominating view (Hauser 2010). In the latter half of the century the cognitive and constructivist views of thought and intelligence became a leading approach and finally when reaching the turn of millennium the socio-cultural view has gained ground.

7.5 Individual capabilities: From cognitive skills to the development of the self

The dominant psychological and pedagogic view of learning during the last decades of the 1900s has been the cognitive view. It understands learning as information processing in which an individual actively constructs knowledge structures and schemas of action. Over the last two decades a social dimension has been added. Pupils construct knowledge in the school together through dialogues in collaborative projects (Bereiter 2002). At the same time alternatives to the concept of inherited intelligence measured by IQ tests have been suggested. Among them are the theory of multiple intelligences (Gardner, 1993) and the concept of learning to learn (Black *et al.* 2006). The theory of multiple intelligence takes a step towards understanding the variety of human talents. However, it is still an outgrowth of the individualist conception of intelligence that regards talents as measurable individual features (e.g. White 2009). The concept of learning to learn rightly takes up motives, commitment to study and the self-image of a child as important conditions in the learning of skills and capabilities.

It is widely agreed that literacy and numeracy as complex multidimensional learned skills are an essential part of the "general" human capabilities cultivated in school. They are used in problem solving, many life activities, fields of knowledge and in diverse situations in life. They constitute the foundation for the absorptive capacity of firms and public service providers. High-quality literacy is not the same as technical reading capability. It is connected to the lifelong increase in vocabulary, the enlargement of the understanding of multiple uses and meanings of concepts as well as to the constant enlargement of background knowledge. The understanding of words, concepts and background knowledge decisively contributes to reading fluency. "Strategic literacy" (Wolf 2008) is, therefore, also a condition for well-developed thought, imagination, and expertise. It also the foundation for critical, conceptual and theoretical thinking.

However, the development of information and communication technologies will change the nature of literacy and cognitive functions. They provide possibilities that exceed those of written language and literature. First, computer-based models allow in a new way the study interactions of complex phenomena and systems as well as allowing the evaluation of alternative plans for the future. In a world of increased interconnectedness and complexity the capability for dynamic systemic thinking becomes important. Second, the ICT technologies allow communication between individuals as well as distributed collaborative creation of knowledge exemplified by Linux and Wikipedia. Third, they will open access to databases and library collections, that is, to the external memory of the humankind, which will radically expand cognitive capabilities of individuals.[7]

---

[7] Today, an ever-growing assortment of old and new intellectual tools, equipment, and databases, such as calculators, dictionaries, guides (e.g. plant guides or bird guides), cameras with the capability of sending photographs electronically, maps, satellite-connected route guides with timetables, and so on are being embodied in smartphones and tablet computers.

The cognitive conception of capabilities has three limitations. First, it focuses on intellectual capabilities and does not deal sufficiently enough with the development of self, life motives, sphere of values and democratic virtues such as responsibility, tolerance for the ideas of others, and a capacity negotiate differences. Even the educational economics have come to this conclusion. In their review of a number of studies on the effects of schooling on life earnings Bowles and Gintis (2002) concluded that only approximately 20% is due to cognitive skills measured by tests. The rest is due to noncognitive factors such as motives and social skills. Second, the cognitive view tends to limit its view of learning to school learning, that is, what is done in classroom or in an ICT-mediated learning environment. The classical school critic (e.g. Dewey 1906; Whitehead 1947) suggests that the problem of motivation and the limited usability of what is learned in school can be resolved by opening the school to society and by connecting the knowledge to be studied to societal practices outside the school. Third, from the point of view of innovation and knowledge society, the cognitive tradition does not satisfactorily deal with the challenge of creativity and imagination.

Learning, the development of self and creativity are richly intertwined in the concept of *Bildung* developed by German philosophers and pedagogues in the late 18th century and early 19th century (Bruford 1975).[8] *Bildung* is more than education or cognitive development. It refers to the self-realization and growth of an individual, to the overall development of her capabilities and identity through her participation in and contribution to the culture in which she lives. Good (2011) makes a distinction between three dimensions of *Bildung.* First, *in Bildung* an individual finds her unique vocation, a calling to which she is well suited and that contributes to the growth of the culture in which she lives. All individuals have different talents and live in a society in which the unique talents of others compliment their own. The mutual positive interdependency between an individual and her society is realized through the development of her uniqueness and the acceptance of social responsibility as the avenue toward self-development.

They provide access to e-mail, Facebook, e-commerce, bank services, Google as well as to libraries and scientific databases. Such an equipment is simultaneously a small portable material object, an external cultural memory and a generalized means of daily life and communication between people. It radically differs from the key artifact of school learning, the textbook.

[8] The concept was developed by Herder, Goethe, Wilhelm von Humbolt and Hegel (see, e.g., Bruford 1975; Good 2005 and 2011).

Second, since a modern complex society lacks universally accepted values, the widest possible variety of experiences is needed to develop an open and intelligent mind. In pedagogy this is addressed in terms of arousing multiple interests in children. Third, the development of one's capabilities and calling in *Bildung* involves not only a unique pattern of participation in society and culture but also independent and critical thought that allows further development of that culture. Cultural critique is here immanent critique: it criticizes culture on its own terms, on the basis of its highest ideals, not on any abstract universal moral standards. This concept resonates in many respects with the modern sociocultural view of individual development as a co-evolution of the individual mind and culture or more concretely, a co-evolution of the individual and the activities in which she participates (e.g. Valsiner 2000).

Dewey highly appreciated the German idea of the complete development of personality, which takes place by becoming a member of a culture and by contributing to the perfectability of humankind. He, however, found that the idea of *Bildung* was historically realized by the institutions of the rising nation states. Cosmopolitan and humanitarian ideals were captured by national interests "and harnessed to do work whose social aim was definitely narrow and exclusive" (Dewey 1916/ 1985: 103). Dewey found the conflict between nationalism and wider social and cosmopolitan goals a "fundamental problem" of a modern democratic society.

The concept of *Bildung* is a forerunner of the modern sociocultural view of individual development and resonates with the recent attempts to redefine the foundations of prosperity and human well-being in political economy (Jackson 2009: 189):

> To do well is in part about the ability to give and receive love. To enjoy the respect of our peers, to contribute usefully to society, to have a sense of belonging and trust in the community, to help to create the social world and find credible place in it. In short, an important component of prosperity is the ability to participate meaningfully in the life of society.

The modern socio-cultural developmental view of giftedness and creativity has much in common with and develops further the concept of *Building* (Gruber 1981; Feldman *et al.* 1994). Many educational economists follow the tradition of the early twentieth century by suggesting that personality traits measured by tests predict the variety of life outcomes (Almlund *et al.* 2011). Studies of creativity have come to reverse conclusions. Two leading American researchers of creativity, Arnold Getzels and Mihaly Csikszentmihalyi (1967) found in their seminal follow-up study of the development of art students only a very weak connection between the results of the most advanced creativity and intelligence tests and creative achievements. Consequently, they were forced to renounce the idea of creativity as an attribute of an individual (Csikszentmihalyi 1990: 198). According to them, creativity should be understood as a systemic phenomenon, something that emerges from the interactions between an individual, a knowledge domain from which she draws resources and a social field that recognizes her contribution (Csikszentmihalyi 1997: 7):

Edison's and Einstein's discoveries would be inconceivable without the prior knowledge, without the intellectual and social network that stimulated their thinking, and without the social mechanisms that recognized and spread their innovations.

Csikszentmihalyi uses architectural and artistic production in Renaissance Florence as an example of a creative field. Competition with other city states, a flourishing economy and competition between rich families to hire the best architects and artists resulted in an abundance of high-quality art. The artistic productivity in Florence cannot be explained by sudden bursts of artistic giftedness, but by the tasks set by the patrons and demanding customers.

Prominent creativity researchers changed their focus from individual features to productive creativity, that is, to the study of people who have made a recognized contribution to a domain knowledge or to expertise. De Groot (1946/1965) studied grandmasters in chess and compared their thinking to those of expert players. Howard Gruber (1981) studied the creative work of Charles Darwin. Both came to the conclusion that rather than giftedness, motivation and character matter. The grandmasters of chess have lived the game with greater passion than others and have experienced periods of youthful chess monomania (De Groot 1946/1965 348): "a very strong long-term motivation toward self-development in the field in question leads to a rapid accumulation of fertile, differentiated experience." As a result, they simply know more about chess and have a richer knowledge base from which to draw solutions.

Like the concept of *Bildung*, the sociocultural view of development underlines the primacy significance of motivation or "passion" for the development of the mastery of a field (Gruber 1981). Second, it finds that the formation of an expertise is a long process with several levels and phases which calls for extensive collaborations with more experienced colleagues, teachers, tutors and trainers. As a rule of thumb, it takes ten years of deliberate practicing to become an expert in a domain of activity (Ericsson 2006). Third, it finds that creativity is domain-specific, characteristic to a certain area of knowledge, culture or activity and cannot be easily transferred to other domains. Individuals may achieve a high-level of mastery in a domain based on different combinations of basic abilities. Fourth, a creative contribution calls for the mastery of the tradition, its creative transformation as well as novel combinations of cultural resources that thus far have been separate.

The sociocultural view of development suggests a redirection of the capability policy from cognitive skills towards the development of self as a citizen, creative participant in a cultural field, and member of humanity. The central starting point for education should be finding and developing one's calling or one's "own way" to contribute to society and become a recognized member of society. It constitutes the foundation for the development and learning of specific skills. The support of the development of the self, recognizing of the signs of emerging interests and specific talents and nurturing them is possibly the most subtle and demanding dimension of pedagogic work. Encouragement by teachers recurrently arises in the stories of people who have found their place in society.

By what means can the finding of one's calling and the development of one's specific talents be fostered? Measures can be taken in daily schoolwork, by developing the collaboration between service providers and other actors as well as by structural reforms of the school system, especially in secondary education.

Schoolwork itself may increasingly include study projects in which collaboration is done with practitioners and experts and outside the school. It not only increases the sources and quality of the knowledge available and creates social network. It also helps in understanding the different activities as well as the world views and motives of the practitioners with whom the students collaborate. Partners outside school are living models of professional practices and of constructive participation to society (Miettinen 1999b; Miettinen and Peisa 2002). Theatre, sports, literature, nature, environment and other hobby clubs and their interaction with cultural and scientific institutions and associations outside the school should be supported. Student welfare groups could redirect their focus from learning difficulties to the politics of nurturing the variety of individual talents. Of course, new tools must be developed to achieve this reorientation. Associations may again play a key role in achieving this.[9]

---

[9] *The Youth Against Drugs* association (founded in 1988) launched in 2002 a project called *Coordination of Preventive Work*. The target group of the project was the children and young persons who need support to develop their social skills. The project developed a regional model for recognizing these children and helps them to find a regular hobby in which they can interact with their peers and adults. Basic schools and their student welfare groups play an important role in the recognition phase. Another association *Icehearts* (founded in 1996) establishes ice hockey and soccer teams for 6-year old children at risk of exclusion in

The collaboration between school and parents should be strengthened. The Finnish association of parents recently suggested that because the rules for schoolwork concern teachers, pupils, and parents, all of them should participate in the definition of the rules for each age group. Parents represent the different fields of expertise in society and can be used as a resource for understanding different callings and occupations in society.

The collaboration between schools (study counsellors), occupational administration (occupational psychologist and counsellors), social and health care authorities (e.g. youth psychiatry and youth work) as well as recruitment and training of firms and public service providers should be increased. New collaborative means and programmes need to developed to help young people orient working life and civil society. Associations (such as sport clubs) may play in important role in this.

New flexible forms of education responsive to a variety of interests are needed in secondary education. For example, the modules from general and vocational education as well as apprentice and training periods in firms and in public sector can be combined. In Finland a system of regional networks of secondary education is being constructed in which upper secondary schools, vocational schools and employer organizations together create elements for individualized study plans. In addition, the goal of this collaboration is the increased responsiveness of the study contents to the challenges of working life as well as the increased impact of secondary education to regional development. These regional networks may constitute new platforms for the development of individualized enabling services. Much could be learned from the Danish active labour market policy of the 1990s in which the retraining or upskilling of employees was planned locally in collaboration between vocational schools, firms and other local service providers. The state provides funding for the training and helps in institutionalization of promising training solutions such as programmes for industrial operators (IO) and four-year training for process operators (PO). These can be tailored according to local needs and also transferred to other localities (Kristensen and Lilja 2011:122):

> For instance, in North Western-Zealand, human resource managers from plants owned by major Danish firms, vocational training institutions and associations, employee representatives, national union officials, and university

collaboration with day care centres and sport clubs. As a part of this, trainer-educators are committed to working with teams for 12 years. These projects are good examples of tailored non-formal services provided by a hybrid network of families, schools, public service providers, sport clubs, and civic associations.

researchers joined forces to upgrade the entire local labour market through the IO and PO training programmes.

However, The models of "hybrid" collaborative design and the realization of education by several agents are not yet well developed. The separation of theoretical studies in schools and practice periods as rehearsing routine activities in firms tends to persist. New "hybrid" solutions such as joint development projects in which problem solving, development of new procedures and high quality learning are combined, are badly needed.

7.6 Education and capability-cultivating services as a foundation for innovation policy

Investment in education, learning and skills has been a central idea in welfare theory, the economics of innovation and the national innovation theorizing. When a turn from the protective concept of the welfare state towards a "productive", "active", and "enabling" welfare state took place in the 1990s the investment in human capital started to play an ever more central role. According to Anthony Giddens (1998: 117), the central guideline for the new social democracy in the UK is "investment in *human capital* wherever possible, rather than the direct provision of economic maintenance." Education was meant to respond to the demands for a flexible workforce in a post-Fordist economy (e.g. Room 2002; Iversen and Stephens 2008; Hudson and Köhner 2009). It is evident that the development of science and technology, ascending levels of education in the general population as well as globalization all contribute to the increased significance of the capabilities for innovation and economic development.

Both the well-known welfare researcher Gösta Esping-Andersen (2009) and economist James Heckmann have underlined the significance of early childhood for the formation of capabilities. The increased division of incomes and the second demographic transition has lead to a growing disparity of parental resources and to a growing gap between rich and poor children (McLanahan 2004). The second demographic transition began in the 1960s. It includes delays in marriage and fertility, increases in divorce, nonmarital child bearing, maternal employment as well as an increase in the number of single-mother families. Because of this development the disparity in parental resources has increased in terms of the time and money available to support the development of the children (2004: 614). For these reasons Esping-Andersen and Heckmann find that the support of unprivileged families and the day care provision are the key services that contribute to the development of the capabilities of children and prevent unemployment exclusion from working life. Esping-Andersen (2009: 71 and 115) concludes:

> Since cognitive (and non-cognitive) abilities influence school success, and subsequently, adult's life chances, the policy challenge is to ensure a strong start for all children. (...) Remedying skill deficiencies among adults is, however, difficult and costly. The real objective must, accordingly, be to ensure that the coming generations will possess the skills that meet the demands of the knowledge economy.

The significance of education for employment has increased. As a rule of thumb, it can be predicted that someone with no more than a lower secondary degree will fare poorly in tomorrow's labour market (Esping-Andersen 2009: 56). The US data indicates that the wage returns for additional years of schooling have almost doubled since the 1980s. Finland confirms Esping-Andersen's analysis. In 1987, 40% of the workforce had no vocational education. In 2010, the figure was 17%.[10] A recent study (Sipilä *et al.* 2011) shows that young people born in the 1970s who only completed comprehensive school had a six times greater risk of unemployment compared with those who had matriculated. The value of basic education in the labour market started to deteriorate at the beginning of the 2000s.

Education and capability-cultivating services contribute to the innovativeness of a nation in at least three ways. By educating well-qualified citizens and professionals they contribute to the absorptive capacities of firms and other organization. Second, universal educational systems contribute to the development of social capital and trust, that make economic transaction easier and more reliable as well as enhancing creative collaboration between different professionals and social groups. Third, high-quality and versatile vocational and tertiary educational institutions that collaborate with firms and service providers can be adopted to support even unexpected structural changes in production.

7.6.1 Creating foundations for absorptive capacities of firms and other organizations

Absorptive capacity refers to an organization's capacity to follow the development of the knowledge domains that are relevant for the development of its products and services. It consists of the capacity of individuals to follow the development of knowledge in their areas of

---

[10] The morning news of the Finnish Broadcasting Company, 1 February 2011.

speciality. High-quality literacy, or what can be characterized as "expert" or "strategic" literacy – the capability of reading, interpreting and utilizing and combining knowledge from printed and digital texts – constitutes the individual foundation for absorptive capacity.[11] "Strategic literacy" (Wolf 2008) is, therefore, also a condition for well-developed thought, imagination and expertise.

Based on high-quality literacy and numeracy, a deeper knowledge of the field can be acquired. In universities its achievement requires, as suggested before, the integration of research and teaching which provides knowledge of important new directions in the field, journals, and conferences in which the new knowledge is introduced as well as networks of collaboration in the field. An important challenge is whether the collaboration between vocational schools, polytechnics, firms, and service providers will be able to create professional and practitioner and craft absorptive capacities in areas in which front-line scientific research does not play a central role.

7.6.2 The creation of trust and social capital

Studies on social capital, social trust and corruption (Seligman 1997; Ulsener 2008) show that a universal education is highly related to generalized trust and to low corruption in a society (Rothstein and Uslaner 2005: 47): "Spending on universal programmes for education promises long-term opportunities for greater equality of results as higher education opens up opportunities for economic advancement. Education is also one of the strongest determinants of generalized trust." Universal education enhances social solidarity and the perception of a shared fate among citizens. Generalized trust is trust in fellow citizens, institutions and civil servants. In contrast people who have in-group trust only have faith in their own kind and distrust outsiders, creating boundaries between social groups (Ulsener 2008: 49). Students of social capital suggest that generalized trust is a major lubricant of economic collaboration. By making collaboration across organizational and professional boundaries easier, generalized trust enhances the formation of innovation networks and also promotes encounters between people

---

[11] The developmental transition from accuracy to reading fluency with comprehension is a critical turn in learning literacy. Researcher in literacy Maryanne Wolf (2008: 135), for instance, analysed the situation in the US as follows: "Recent reports from the National Reading Panel and the 'nation's report cards' indicate that 30 to 40 percent of children in the fourth grade do not become fully fluent readers with adequate comprehension. This is a devastating figure, made even worse by the fact that teachers, textbook authors, and indeed the entire school system have different expectations for the students from grade 4 on."

with different kinds of expertise and cultural backgrounds. A universal education therefore not only creates the know-how and expertise needed in economic life and in public services, it also contributes to the formation of the generalized trust which functions as a lubricant of horizontal innovative collaboration across boundaries.

The interrelationship between social capital, innovation and economic growth has been studied since the 1990s. Evidence is accumulating that shows that social capital has an effect on economic outcomes, such as growth and investment (e.g. Knack and Keefer 1997). Akçomak and ter Weel (2009) studied the relationship between social capital accumulation and regional economic growth in 102 regions in 14 European countries. They suggest that social capital affects on economic growth through innovations. Social capital and trust foster innovations by facilitating collaboration between researchers and risk investors. They found that (2009: 561) "social capital is a significant determinant of innovation, which in turn explains approximately 15% of per capita income growth in EU regions between 1990 and 2002."

Social psychologists Klaus Helkama and Tuija Seppälä (2004) have studied the connection between the values of people and competitiveness in the OECD countries. They found that the only indicator that predicted the competitiveness of a country was the degree to which the citizens of the country trusted each other. They provided two explanations for this observation. First, where citizens trust each other, the economic environment is predictable. Second, trust makes it possible for diverse ideas to freely collide with each other and give rise to new ideas and projects. The authors point out that social psychological experiments repeatedly show that sharing a reward gives rise to collaboration and trust, and dividing a reward according to individual performance creates distrust and even hostility. They find this to be a strong argument for equality and universal services.

7.6.3 Providing a prerequisite for flexible economic and industrial transformation

Flexibility is a basic requirement of the post-Fordist welfare state (Jessop 1991: 99). A well-organized and high-quality vocational education and university system is able to provide an educated workforce for any field in which new economic activity emerges. Education can be directed to rising areas, as exemplified by the growth in the Finnish ICT sector. The Nokia Corporation was able to negotiate with relevant university departments and polytechnics, and through this was able to meet the rapidly increasing demand for product-development engineers. In a small nation relatively far from the main markets, a country with a harsh climate and an exotic language, the availability of a high-quality, internationally oriented workforce is one of the primary reasons for firms to stay in the country or keep a portion of the design and product development activities in the country.

In their comparison of welfare regimes, Iversen and Stevens (2008: 609) argue that the combination of heavy spending on public education and well-developed vocational training in the Nordic countries has enabled their firms to be very successful in high-value international niche markets, such as specialized machine tools, furniture or high-quality processed agricultural products. Good general skills (literacy, maths, IT-knowledge) are an increasingly important condition for acquiring technical skills related to knowledge-intensive production. The broad acquisition of general skills has also helped the Nordic countries to cope with the rise of services. One may well conclude that investment in the development of day care and education may be a more far-sighted innovation policy than product development support for established firms or attempts to create internationally competitive concentrations of expertise and resources in selected areas of the economy.

8

An enabling welfare state, collective learning, and democracy

Since the focus of this book has been on the significance of human capabilities and education for welfare and innovation, I will draw my conclusions by analysing the different meanings of the concept of the "enabling state." It has been suggested as a solution to the crisis of the first welfare state and as an outline for a new welfare society able to adapt to the globalizing and rapidly changing working life while simultaneously able to ensure the welfare of citizens. A review of definitions of an enabling state also uncovers the contradictory ambitions and tendencies that come up in the discourse on the future of the welfare state.

Political economists have analysed the alternatives to a future welfare state as part of the changing nature of capitalism. It has been characterized as a transition from Fordist to Post-Fordist capitalist accumulation regime and a transition from a Keynesian welfare state to a Schumpeterian competition state (Jessop 2002). Because the potential of capital accumulation based on mass production and consumption is shrinking, the financial capital looks for new sources of profit making in new territories including public services. The competition is being restructured (Jessop 2008: 28) "over innovation policies and how best to subordinate the extra-economic to the demands of economic competition." Wolfgang Streeck (2010) wants to bring capitalism back to comparative institutional analysis by analysing how market relations are extended to new territorial spaces and social spheres. The widening and deepening of market relations raises the question of political and social regulation of markets and the significance of non-market institutions for social order, economic development and welfare. Tim Jackson (2009: 167) characterizes the basic policy alternatives in "the conflicted state" as follows:

There is a real sense here of policy-makers struggling with competing goals. On the one hand government is bound to the pursuit of economic growth. On the other, it finds itself having to intervene to protect the common good from incursions of the market. The sate itself is deeply conflicted, striving on the other hand to encourage consumer freedoms that lead to growth and on the other hand to protect social goods and defend ecological limits.

Robert Jessop (2000) finds that new contradictions are emerging in the knowledge-driven economy. One of them is the contradiction between a growing short-termism in economic calculation and an increased interdependency of economic and extra economic factors such as social capital, trust and learning organizations. Short-termism is in contradiction with "the long term dynamics of 'real competition' rooted in resources (skills, trust, heightened reflexivity, collective mastery of techniques...) that may take years to create, stabilize and reproduce" (2000: 70).

Comparative studies of welfare states have analysed welfare policy in terms of "decommodification", that is, protection of the workforce from the risks and negative consequences of labour markets by the activities of the state (Esping-Andersen 1990). In a In this book, I have discussed the basic education as a field in which the policy of introducing a market and the policy of developing a public school based on the "long term" ideals of educational equality clash as alternative strategies to respond to the demands of knowledge society development and globalization.

8.1 An enabling welfare state: The next stage of the Nordic welfare state?

At least three different conceptions of an enabling state have been suggested. Neil Gilbert (2004 and 2005) has presented a well-articulated neoliberal concept of an enabling welfare state. To him the term refers to the privatization of social services, the introduction of the market to social services as well as a transition from universal services, and transfers to selective targeting. Gilbert shows that the transition in this direction has taken place in all developed economies including the Nordic welfare states. He considers the transition to be inevitable and that it should be developed further. In a market-oriented welfare state, solidarity as social rights on the societal level is replaced by civic responsibilities on the local level. Firms and voluntary associations will increasingly take charge of the services formerly provided by the state and the public sector.

I find this concept of an enabling state insufficient for several reasons. First, like most accounts of the welfare state it focuses on social services and the labour market and does not speak about education and other capability-cultivating services. Second, its programme of replacing public services by private ones is questionable in the case of education and other capability-cultivating services. The results of the OECD PISA studies show that the Finnish public school system is able to achieve excellent results and enhance educational equality at moderate cost. The universality of educational services ensured by the public school system is important for the emergence of social capital and trust in society. Finally, market competition does not favour institutional learning, which is essential for the development of quality services.

The second concept of an enabling state is presented by developmental researcher Donald Curtis (2006). The first element of his view is institutional pluralism, which was also suggested both by the World Bank and New Labour's third way strategy. Government agencies who often suffer from hierarchist bias need to collaborate with the private sector and civil society organizations. The state (Curtis 2006: 152) "may support market and civil society development but operationally remain committed to instruments of command, specifying, targeting, performance monitoring and regulating when not actually directly providing." The second element of his view is the introduction of "the second-order enabling role for the state". The first-order role composed of maintaining infrastructures, a legal framework, and the direction of public funds through the budget. The second-order enabling role entails dialogue with other actors, market, and civil society as well as enhancing experimentation and learning, which make the constant redefinition of standards and shared goals possible. I do not share Curtis's pessimism about the public provision of services, but I find his idea of the second-order role of the state important.

The third concept of the enabling state has been presented by pragmatist institutionalists (Sabel 1994 and 2006; Herrigel 2007; Kristensen 2011a). Charles Sabel (1994) has generalized the significance of the developmental associations of firms. They collect, generalize, and publish information and set standards for the quality of products and services. They provide, therefore, a mechanism of institutional learning. Dorf and Sabel (1998) have developed a pragmatist concept of democracy that they call democratic experimentalism. In it (1998: 267) "power is decentralized to enable citizens and other actors to utilize their local knowledge to fit solutions to their individual circumstances, but in which regional and national coordinating bodies require actors to share their knowledge with others facing similar problems." They find methods for experimentalist inquiry from the practices of post-Fordist business firms exemplified by the Toyota system. Benchmarking, simultaneous engineering and error correction, which together can be called learning by monitoring, enable actors to learn from one another's successes and failures. These are methods of "questioning the prevailing routines" and of finding alternatives through dialogue and interaction (Sabel 2006).

As for public services the pragmatist concept underlines the need for tailoring and for individualized services able to meet the needs of different clients (Sabel *et al.* 2011). I find most of these ideas important and will want to elaborate on them further. I think, however, that methods of learning drawn from the Toyota model of production (benchmarking, error detection, concurrent engineering) are only one important set of possible methods of learning and reflection. New ideas, concepts, and tools may come from research or from unexpected encounters with specialists and practitioners from more remote activities. In my analysis of the Finnish comprehensive school in Chapter 6, research-based and the collaborative development of new tools and instruments proved to be an essential method of collective learning. Nor is it self-evident that the procedures developed in the business environment can be used as such in the provision of public services.

I find good reasons to define an enabling welfare state in relation to the Nordic model of the welfare state and define it as the next stage in its development. It is based on the further development of the public universal capability-producing services created by the welfare state in the 1960s–1980s to meet the demands of a knowledge society and international competition. As Finnish political historian Pauli Kettunen (2006: 64) points out, "a wide spectrum of socially and ethically highly appreciated achievements and objectives are proved to be competitive advantages, including egalitarian institutions of education and welfare." He (ibid.) points out that a change in policy rhetoric can take place simultaneously with remarkable institutional continuity. Old welfare state institutions and industrial relations can be modified to serve the new functions of a "competitive community".

The new enabling welfare state also will take steps to resolve two problems of the old welfare state: detailed bureaucratic control and nationalism. Gunnar Myrdal (1960: 67) anticipated that in the mature phase the welfare state delegates responsibility for detailed public regulations to local and sectional collective authorities (1960: 166):

The assumption is the continued strengthening of provincial and municipal self-governance, and a balanced growth of the infra-structure of effective interest organizations. This would in its turn, presume an intensified citizens' participation and control, exerted in both of these fields.

Enabling state theorists address this transition by underlining the significance of associations, hybrid organizations, and institutional learning that crosses the boundaries between state agents, municipalities, civil society associations, and firms. The problem of nationalism will be commented in the final section of this chapter.

Why can an enabling welfare state be seen as a continuation and the next developmental phase of the Nordic welfare state? At least six reasons can be presented. First, the Nordic model has differed from the other European welfare models because of its strong focus on the provision of high-quality public services to equalize opportunities instead of direct transfer of money to meet the social risks. The proportion of the working age population employed in public health, education, and welfare is 16% on average in Nordic countries, as opposed to a range of 5–8% in other countries (Bernard and Boucher 2007: 224). This explains why Nordic welfare states have been characterized as "forerunners in the shift to the service-based welfare state" (Sabel *et al.* 2011: 19). Services such as child care, education, libraries, and cultural activities have mainly been provided as universal public services. An enabling state further develops the capability-cultivating and civilizing services created by the old welfare state. The special education system of the Finnish comprehensive school analysed in this book is an example of a step towards the provision of individualized enabling services. This individualization, however, is not realized through the market but takes place within the public school system.

Second, the creation of basic services in the 1970s and 1980s was accompanied by the education of professionals who provided the services as well as the development of the research related to these services. As a result of this development today highly competent multiprofessional communities take care of education in the Finnish schools. They are connected through further education and participation in different projects to universities and research institutes. The hybrid and interactive field is instrumental in the further development of the quality of services. Professional, scientific, and civic associations as well as firms are connected to the public service production system. These kinds of hybrid multiorganizational fields are remarkable cultural, epistemic, and practical achievements that further develop the quality of enabling services.

Third, the universal educational system organized by the welfare state has radically changed the educational level of the population. In a comparison between the types of European welfare states, the

175

proportion of the population aged 26–54 in 2003 with at least upper secondary education was 75% in the Nordic countries while it was 60% in Anglo-Saxon, and 39% in Mediterranean countries (Sapir 2006: 379). A well-educated population provides a huge potential of theoretical, professional, and practical knowledge distributed in all spheres of society. It constitutes an enlarging foundation for innovative activity. It underlines the need to democratize innovation and questions the elitist nature of innovation policy. The benchmarking activities in the EU have thus far been limited to interaction between civil servants from ministries. The abundance of expertise in the provision of services underlines the need for direct transnational interaction between local front line service-proving communities of professionals.

Fourth, during the first welfare state, the provision of public services became decentralized. Several reasons contributed to this. The Nordic countries have a strong tradition of local municipality governance. It was an important basis for the local implementation of the universal services of the welfare state (Sellers and Lindström 2007: 625):

> In Nordic countries empowered local government has been much more than a simple out-growth of the welfare state or a product of social democratic policy. Pre-existing local government infrastructures laid the foundation for Social Democratic welfare administration and have helped its continuous survival.

The economic crisis of the 1990s caused cuts in the expenses of state agencies in Finland. The decentralization of governance was also a conscious policy. In the late 1980s and early 1990s more responsibility was given both in Sweden and Finland to municipalities and school communities in the design of the curriculum, in developing methods of teaching, and in the evaluation of students. This was facilitated and coordinated by the state through regulations and research and development projects with the participation of regional and local service providers and research organizations. The decentralized provision of services based on wide national goals constitute a good starting point for developing the "enabling governance" that stimulates local experimentation and the constant updating of goals and standards around good practices.

Fifth, the citizens of the Nordic countries typically are active members of associations. In Denmark and Sweden, nine out of ten people are members of associations. Over 80% of Norwegians and 76% of Finns belong to associations. The corresponding figures are 50% in France, 29% in Germany and Belgium (Kankainen 2009: 8). In addition, the number of registered associations are not showing any signs of diminishing in the Nordic counties. They have been and still are a major means of advancing the interests of citizens, and collaborate with the state. Both the tradition of local democracy and the active participation of citizens in associations constitute a foundation for deepening and extending democracy in service production, innovation, and politics.

Finally, the idea of an enabling welfare state can also be regarded as a reformulation of the idea of the virtuous circle of equality, economic development, and democracy central to the ideology of the Nordic welfare state. A major concern in the virtuous cycle outlined by Gunnar Myrdal was to release the creative forces of the people. "This was a precondition for social equality and welfare, but still more, promoting social equality was seen as a means by which human resources would be released" (Kettunen 1997: 170). Human capital research has confirmed the connection between the level and quality of education and economic development (e.g. Psacharopoulos and Patrinos 2004). Education is also shown to contribute to equality (e.g. Sapir 2006) and through increasing civic engagement to democracy (e.g. Castelló-Climent 2008). In addition, the provision of education and other enabling services seems to require an organization that stimulates local experimentation, participation of stakeholders, and learning across boundaries. This contributes to the growth of democracy in working life and in society.

8.2 State, associations, and institutional learning

The pragmatist theory of enabling state underline the significance of associations for learning and development. They are the loci of collective and institutional learning and development. Empirical studies have shown the significance of associations in different spheres of society and they play a role in the provision of public services such as education, health and social services as well as in industry and business activities. In services production they are a 'natural' organizational form of individualized service provision. Many of the associations emerged to produce services for its members who needed them. In the following the role of developmental associations in civic and political life, in the provision of public services as well as in industry and business life, will be discussed.

The political and ideological associations of working class and agrarian people have been important for the emergence of the Nordic welfare state. In the beginnings of the 1900s local social democratic associations helped school people in political and civil participation: social and political issues were discussed, minutes were written, members were helped and people's halls were constructed, and the sites of cultural and civic activities were set up. They were virtual schools of democracy and collaboration as suggested by such social theorists as Alexander Tocqueville and George Simmel. In addition to theatre, music, and recreation, study circles became a key activity both in social democratic and agrarian local associations in the first decades of the 1900s in Finland. It was the political coalition of these two social groups that later joined forces in the construction of the welfare state based on universal services to ensure social and regional equality in the country. In Finland the term 'civilization policy' is frequently used. The civilization policy programme published by the Association of the Finnish Municipalities in 2007 covered the development of all levels of education, youth work, and the fields of cultural services including library, museums, art activities and sports. Culture is defined in the programme as a service that supports individual development and brings vitality to the region. Cultural services are provided by "multiprofessional networks".

There are about 80,000 associations in Finland in the early 2000s. The number of new registrations has risen steadily since 1920s. During the 1990s, more associations were formed than during any other decade. During the 1990s and 2000s more than 2000 new associations were founded each year (Kankainen 2009: 6). Since the 1990s the political and ideological associations have lost ground. In the early 2000s, 70% of all associations registered were cultural, exercise, or hobby associations (ibid.). The share of cultural and educational associations increased from 10% to 22% in the 1990s (Siisiäinen 1999: 129).

The analysis of the development of the Finnish basic education system in Chapter 6 showed the vital significance of the various professional and civic associations to the development of a field. I made a distinction between four kinds of associations: professional, civic, patient, and method associations. New associations emerged to meet new problems and challenges. For example, the national association for different learners was established in 2002 and the association for developing the Varga-Neményi Method of teaching mathematics in 2005. As new actors emerged and joined the field, interactions between actors in the field were enriched. All the actors in the field contribute in their own particular way to a shared common good, namely the all-round development of every child and the ethos of educational equality.

The methods and forms of learning change in the transition from the "old" welfare state to an enabling state. During the construction period of the services the main methods were professional training and further education. They remain essential today. In further education the latest research results and recent diagnostic tools are transmitted to the teachers and other professionals in the field. After strong multiprofessional communities emerged in schools, and the decentralization of governance required local specification of curriculum and development of methods teaching and evaluation new forms of learning emerged in the 1990s. They include 1) local experimenting and the development of pedagogical solutions and methods in schools; 2) horizontal learning, learning from local solutions through regional groups, organized visits, by articulation of local practices as well as by regional fairs of good practices (section 6.8); 3) multilevel developmental projects with participation from the state, municipalities, and local schools facilitated by universities and initiated by the National Board of Education. The emerging forms and means of institutional learning need both to be studied and systematically further developed. It is a major challenge, for instance, how the promising local solutions should be articulated (described, modelled, presented) to make their efficient distribution possible.

State-subsided voluntary association has traditionally played an important role in the provision of social services. In 2000, 32,000 persons, 11% of the workforce of the social and health sectors in Finland, were salaried by the associations. In the Finnish social service sector and in child care there are strong associations such as the Mannerheim League for Child Welfare, which has a variety of enabling activities: research and publishing, provision of a number of services (such as peer support, serving telephones, professional help), collaboration with academic research and practitioners, and large-scale provision of training. Chapter 6 showed that the Central Union of Child Welfare of Finland played a leading role in the collection, articulation, and dissemination of the theoretical and practical knowledge of learning difficulties and the special education of children in Finland.

Micheal Callon and Vololona Rabeharisao (2008) have studied the contribution of the patient organizations to health care in France. They call them "concerned organizations" organized around a specific problem or disease, its consequences and care. Patients, their parents, their family members and professionals collaborate in these associations. They have multiple functions including mutual help and support, education, funding of research and research activity and finally to political lobbing related to the care and life of conditions the patients. Callon and Rabeharisao (2008: 239) found that these associations participated in the orientation of research, and played a key role (2008: 239) "in the definition of a research and innovation policy in the full sense of the term."

The Juvenile Diabetes Research Foundation established by the parents of diabetic children is one of biggest funders of medical research in the

USA. The funding decisions for research projects are made by a lay committee composed of parents who have been thoroughly educated to understand the current diabetes research. A distinguished Finnish diabetes researcher who has been an evaluator for the Foundation has said that the lay committees often come to conclusions that differ from the recommendations of the scientific committee, "most often in such a way that the committee has a more positive attitude to new areas of research (...) it supports the innovative aspects of the projects."[1]

Callon and Rebeharisoa report the growing importance of the concerned groups in health care in France. They found that 118 of the 213 patient organizations in a data base they analysed had scientific committees and financed research projects. In 2000 Alliance Maladies Rares was established to meet with the upsurge of concerned groups in the health care, scientific, and political scene in France. It has today 141 member organizations and its objective is to promote a research policy coupled with the demands for full citizenship of people with rare diseases.

The history of technology and industry uncovered the significance of "collective invention settings" in which firms distribute and change information about the design and performance of new technology (Allen 1983; Nuvolari 2004; Powell and Gianella 2011). Both in the development of blast furnaces in Cleveland in the late 1800s and in the development of Cornish pumping engines in the early 1800s, information was exchanged directly between firms and through engineering association and their publications. The pragmatist institutionalists regard the collection of production information and the imposing of standards by developmental industrial associations as a central mechanism of institutional learning in industry.

Charles Sabel (1994) analysed the long tradition of developmental associations in Japan starting from the local trade associations in the late 1800s. Such associations as the All-Japan Cotton Spinner's Association co-operatively inspected the quality of products and published monthly information on the efficiency of plants. Less efficient firms consulted with the technically more advanced firms. After the Second World War Engineering Research Associations organized the testing of products comparing them with foreign products and to standardized superior solutions. Sabel found similar associations in all industrialized countries. Berk and Schneiberg (2005) have studied the emergence and activities of associations in American industry in a number of industry sectors in 1900–1925. They found a variety of associations with multiple

---

[1] Professor Olli Simell, 22 February 2007.

functions starting from bargaining and standard setting to education. They (2005: 47) characterize them as collaborative learning associations "which used deliberation, cost accounting, and benchmarking to shift competition from volume and cutthroat pricing to innovation and improvement."

Greenwood *et al.* (2002) analysed the central role of the Canadian Institute of Chartered Accountants in the transformation of accountancy into a multiprofessional business adviser practice. Lounsbury *et al.* (2003) show how first volunteer communities and then a trade association played a central role in the establishment of solid waste recycling practices and in the emergence of the for-profit recycling business. In these cases the interaction of associations with state regulators played an important role in industrial development. Garud and Karnoe (2003) analysed the vital role of the Wind Mill Owner's Association in the emergence and development of the successful Danish windmill industry. It shared knowledge, introduced a key subtechnology (a fail-safe braking system), and published monthly reliability and performance data on turbine models, which forced producers to compete on market-defined evaluation criteria.

State agencies, universities, vocational training institutions, municipalities, association, and firms all played a role in the development of the Danish active labour market policy and in the development of the Finnish comprehensive school and special education. Innovation and organizational studies have looked at the variety of interaction between different actors: between producers and users, between producers and subcontractors, and between firms and universities, between firms and business angels. Associations should be included. The production of ICT-based platforms and databases (such as Wikipedia and Encyclopedia of Life) give rise to new types of communities that have been characterized as commons-based peer-production (Benkler 2006).

8.3 Forms of governance: From competition and control to experimentation and learning

The central idea of the neoliberal conception of an enabling state is that the market is the superior method of coordination of economic activities. According to this idea the public provision of services is hierarchical and inefficient and should be replaced by quasimarkets. State and public agencies will have a double role. First, they purchase services on behalf of the public from a variety of competing providers on a contract basis. Second, they define standards and check that they are complied with in contacts and in service production.

I find a number of reasons why this conception is untenable when applied to education or social and health care services. Finnish basic education provides the evidence. First, the PISA comparisons undeniably show that a public service system is able to produce excellent results at a reasonable cost. It is able to ensure equality better than market-based systems, which tend to increase social segregation. Second, the transition from public service provision to competitive provision is accompanied with control and regulation systems that easily develop into heavily bureaucratic forms of governance. Third, giving up the provision of services leads to a loss of expertise among public agencies. Fourth, the market and competition do not favour collective and institutional learning, which are instrumental in the development of enabling services.

Recent developments in educational politics in the OECD countries indicate that a system that is organized around public schools is likely to produce better and more equal results than a system based on the market and competition. The continuous success of Finnish students in PISA studies, the low differences between the schools and the significantly higher scores of students in lower achievement groups provide evidence for this conclusion (see Table 5.3). The comparison between the two Nordic countries that had very similar schools systems in the 1970s and 1980s, Sweden and Finland, provides additional evidence. Sweden introduced a voucher system to its basic education in 1992 and started to favour the establishment of private schools and the formation of an educational market. Not only does Sweden lag behind Finland in overall distribution of PISA scores, but in PISA 2003 the level of between-school variance in student performance (11%) was more than twice as high as in Finland (5%).[2] In Sweden the maths scores of the socio-economically most disadvantaged students were 44 points below the same group in Finland, whereas in the most advantaged group they were 22 points below the Finnish group (Andersson et al. 2008: 3). According to a study done by the Swedish National Teacher Union the difference between the grades in basic school certificates between the best 10th percentile and the weakest 10th percentile has increased by 31% in the years 1999–2011 (Lärarnas Riksförbund 2012: 4). The study concludes (2012: 12): "a school that is entirely based on competition with a focus on individual freedom has created a division into winners

---

[2] The corresponding variance was 26% in the United States and 62% in the Netherlands.

and losers; in which winner is only in highly relative terms. Even the best students achieve lower." The governance of public services based on strict goals and control by constant assessment has been a central feature of new publics management inspired by neoliberalism, and also of the welfare policy of New Labour in the United Kingdom. In analysing the educational policy of the Labour Party in the 1990s Cristopher Pierson (2006: 190) found "an almost religious faith in the capacity of targets and auditing to produce positive change." There is accumulating evidence that accountability based on high-stakes testing has several adverse effects on school work such as narrowing the curriculum, demoralizing teachers, increasing student drop-outs and diminishing integrity among administrators, teachers, and students (Darling-Hammond 2007; McNeil *et al.* 2008).

One of the arguments of this book has been that decentralizalized school governance based on trust and active agency of multiprofessional school communities contributed to the Finnish PISA success. This form of governance challenges the mainstream educational policy based on test-based external accountability. Pasi Sahlberg (2010: 58) describes the accountability of Finnish school as an intelligent form of accountability:

> Test-based accountability, public ranking of schools based on those tests, and related rewards and sanctions are not contributing to ongoing efforts to sustainable improvement of the quality of public education. More intelligent accountability involves all stakeholders, including students and parents, in discussing and determining the extent that the jointly set goals have been attained. It combines data from student assessments, external examinations, teacher-led classroom assessments, feedback from parents and school self-evaluations.

Five features of the Finnish system of school governance can be pointed out. First, research-based training and continuous further education encourage the development of strong multiprofessional school communities. Together with networks of other actors (universities, municipalities, associations, parents) they are able to take responsibility for the development of the quality of teaching and schoolwork. Second, educational equality and the inclusion of every child is the overall widely shared aim of different agents in the field. It is supported among other things by reverse discrimination. For example, in Helsinki schools with high percentage of immigrant students and students from a low socio-economic background get extra funding. Third, instead of being based on strict goals and constant assessment of students' achievement, governance is based on widely agreed broad aims and principles expressed in the core curriculum. The municipalities and schools are supposed to interpret them and plan how these aims will be achieved. Dewey (1927/1988: 362) expressed this idea by saying that jointly agreed goals are a working hypothesis rather than rules: "Policies and proposals for social action should be treated as working hypotheses, not as programmes to be rigidly adhered to and executed."

Fourth, schools are required to evaluate the progress of students and are expected to take immediate measures to help students who have difficulties or are lagging behind. Evaluation is done primarily by those who are able to provide immediate help to students. National evaluations are based on sampling-based studies which are deliberately designed so that the construction of league lists for schools is not possible. Fifth, the model of governance includes learning across hierarchical levels of the field. The preparation of the latest changes to the Finnish Basic Education Act of 2011 is an example. The National Board of Education, municipalities, and schools that had developed promising practices all played an important role in formulating the principles of reorganizing special education. Two new tools, pedagogical evaluations and learning plans, already experimentally used in some schools, were included in the law.

The idea of narrowing down the duty of the public agency (state, municipality) to that of purchasing and supervising the provision of services will most likely lead to increased bureaucracy (comparable to test-based accountancy in education) as well as to a decline in the expertise of the public agency. This is in conflict with its duty to supervise the quality of services. Neil Gilbert (2004: 121–122), a strong supporter of privatization, discusses the deep problems of bidding in social services. Several studies that have compared profit-oriented and non-profit-oriented services providers reveal that for-profit providers charge less for day care and nursing homes for elderly than non-profit providers when calculated on the basis of costs per consumer. But this advantage quickly fades when considerations of quality of care are introduced. The for-profit organizations had a higher child-to-staff ratio, a lower percentage of teachers with college degrees, and a higher rate of staff turnover. When non-profit organizations are drawn into competition with profit-oriented providers (Gilbert 2004: 120) "they will come under growing pressure to cut service costs by reducing quality in the areas of service that are most difficult to quantify and are least likely to be specified in contractual agreements." The essential qualities in child care or education, such as engagement, affection, and commitment of personnel can hardly be quantified at all. They are strongly dependent on the quality and ethos of professional communities and developmental associations to which the personnel belong.

Supervision of the quality of services or the definition of sensible standards is hardly possible unless those who supervise participate in the development of the services themselves. The development of the governance of Finnish basic education of is an example of change in the nature of multilevel collaborative service provision. The focus turns from the control of the accomplishment of quantified goals into the challenge of joint understanding of the key problems of service provision and development of tools to solve them. Disengagement from development and service provision leads likely to a gradual loss of expertise. This became evident in Finland in the public discussion of the development of public large-scale ICT systems in the 2000s. Many of them have been failures, for example the national patient information system and electronic prescription, developments which started in 2003 and is not ready even today. In most cases subscribers to ICT systems have been unable to define the criteria of usability. Costs have even tripled from the original budgets because of repeated changes and improvement projects which have been a "goldmine" for a few big systems deliverers, as a representative of the National Audit Office of Finland characterized the situation in 2009. An experienced researcher and system developer concluded that the only sensible solution should be that the subscriber is in charge of the usability. For this "subscribers must naturally have good competence and skills to make the necessary solutions, to define and ensure usability, and to direct the design work of the deliverer."[3]

It was suggested that institutional learning and collaborative development of new solutions and tools constitute the key foundation for the quality of enabling services. The market and competition do not enhance institutional learning and collaborative development. In a system based on a competition each organizational actor tries to create unique expertise, to keep it hidden from competitors to invite clients, and to succeed in the competition. This is a part of the problem of controlling and developing quality of services in a system based on various competing autonomous individual contributors (Dunleavy et al. 2005). Peer Hull Kristensen (2011b: 254) commented on this aspect of the Danish system of vocational education, which was created in the 1990s to support the active labour market policy:

> The neo-liberal insistence on introducing market principles and competition within the public sector may ironically prevent the comparative assessment

---

[3] Timo Jokela, "ATK-hankinnoissa vastuu kuuluu tilaajalle," HS, 9 January 2011.

across institutions and localities. It is an enigma that the innovative ways of making local use of training institutions in Denmark were not diffused and revealed to other localities. But the reason was very simple: since the introduction of the new public management, any public training institution competes with others when recruiting students, and if they have found a competitive curriculum that attracts students on a massive scale it is in their interest to keep it as secret as possible to stay competitive measured against other vocational training centres. (...) Nobody seems to accumulate the experience and effectiveness across public organizations and it seems as if public–private partnerships have to invent the 'deep dish' again and again.

In working against horizontal learning, competition undermines the purpose and idea of social experimentation, which as Dewey (1899/ 1976: 569) puts it "other people need not experiment; at least need not experiment so much" and "may have something definite and positive to go by". Institutional learning is easier to achieve in a system organized around strong public services. As Curtis (2006) suggests the central task – or second-order role – of an enabling welfare state is the creation the conditions for collaborative learning and the encouragement of actors to participate in joint efforts of development. It is a change "from command and control to listening and learning" (2006: 161).

8.4 Innovation and democracy: Mobilization of human capabilities

Institutional learning in developmental associations and multiorganizational fields is the basic prerequisites of an enabling state. In pragmatist theory it is also a key for deepening democracy. People are able to develop their capabilities by participating to solving the social problems by developmental communities. This was not the case in the Finnish innovation policy. The strategic intelligence in the Finnish innovation policy has been firmly in the hands of an elite composed of people from R&D funding organizations, ministries, firms as well as selected members of universities and research institutes. The civic and professional associations as well as the practitioners of service providers were excluded from the process.[4]

---

[4] In November 2010 the executive manager of the Finnish Prostate Cancer Association wondered why the representatives of national cancer associations had not been invited to a working group (called by the Minister of Health) that defines a cancer strategy for Finland. They have never been invited to the corresponding groups. He asked why the expertise of patients and their organizations could have been excluded. Hannu Tavio, "Potilasjärjestöt on otettava mukaan syövän hoidon kehitystyöhön," HS, 11 November 2010.

In innovation studies we find a reverse tendency. In his book *Democratizing Innovation* (2005) Erich von Hippel suggested that innovations will be increasingly externalized to user communities. Helga Nowotny speaks about *democratizing of expertise* (2003: 155): expertise spreads throughout society and becomes socially distributed expertise. Because of the radically increased level of education in the industrialized countries the knowledge and capabilities needed for innovation will be extensively available in all spheres of society. These capabilities need to be mobilized through local experimentation and innovation. Enlarged participation in the collaborative transformation of social practices is also a key issue in the development of democracy.

Dewey's concept of democracy is based on an interconnection between the development of the capabilities of individuals, the method of collaborative reflection and the development of viable communities of inquiry and learning. The self-development of an individual is realized through her contribution via the division of labour to the common good of a community. The "procedure" of democracy is the collaborative experimental solving of social problems by communities of inquiry. These communities are "prepolitical" collaborative associations. They constitute the foundation for the successful functioning of state institutions. Philosophers and students of public administration and policy have recently rediscovered the relevance of Dewey's approach (Putnam 1992; Dorf and Sabel 1998; Caspary 2000; Evans 2000; Snider 2000; Shields 2003; and Brown 2009). As a model of participatory democracy, it seems to supply answers to the problems caused by managerialism, hierarchical governance, and the top-down policy making dominated by specialists. It has also been seen as an epistemologically realistic alternative to evidence-based policy making (Sanderson 2009).[5]

According to Dewey, democracy is related to the relationship between the individual, the community and the state. The positive rights of individuals to develop their capabilities depend on how work, community life, and the state are organized. For Dewey, democracy was connected to "the concept of equality defined as the freedom generated by society for individuals to develop fully the potential each has for participation in the common life of all" (Evans 2000: 312).[6]

---

[5] For the relationship of the pragmatist view of democracy to other theories of democracy, see Honneth 1998 and Bohman 1999.

[6] Hegel's insight into the *need for recognition* as the fundamental human motive constitutes an important foundation both for the concept of *Bildung* and for Dewey's concept of democracy. An individual contributes to the life of a community in order to be recognized by other members of the community as a unique and accepted individual. This is compatible with the socio-cultural view of the social origins of self. Axel Honneth (1995) has developed

Dewey's theory of inquiry and reflective learning provides a model of how social problems are collaboratively solved by experimentation (Dewey 1938/1991; Miettinen 2000). His theory of inquiry is simultaneously a theory of learning and a theory of the reconstruction of social practices (Campbell 1992; Burke 1994). When established ways of action do not work or a social problem is faced, reflection on the conditions of the action is needed. A working hypothesis is formulated to change a situation and to find a solution. Efforts to implement the solution in practice finally test the viability of the working hypothesis, and the success of this experiment is evaluated. Dewey's book *School and Society* (1899/1976: 56) presents the principles of his Chicago experimental school. A social experiment produces working models that can be further adapted and developed in other localities.

According to Dewey, reflective collaboration and experimentation take place in an experimental community of inquiry. Dewey was wary of the dominance of specialists in such communities because it tends to exclude the points of view of the people who are directly involved and influenced by a social problem. In today's developed societies, the division between experts and non-experts is becoming ever more problematic. In Finland, it is predicted that 70% of the age cohort will have a tertiary education. A rich pool of professional and scientific expertise will be distributed across the fabric of society. Several studies on decision making and projects have uncovered the limitations of expert knowledge and the virtues of "lay knowledge" (e.g. Wynne 1996; Brown 2000; Yearley 2000; Kleinman 2005). Instead of experts and non-experts, we should instead have different kinds of specialized expertise – theoretical and practical – which need to be mobilized into dialogue in the cooperative process of social inquiry. In collaborative experiments, professionals in different fields, teachers, engineers, social workers etc., as well as clients play key roles.

According to Paul Adler and David Heckscher (2006), because of the increasing socialization of production, trust-based collaborative communities will become an ever more prevalent form of economic and professional activity. Both the increasingly complex problems, products, and services to be dealt with and the increasing cognitive division of labour require the development of collaborative communities. This development was anticipated by Dewey (1916/1985: 92) when he defined the two traits that characterize democracy:

an original philosophical anthropology based on Hegel's theory of the need for recognition and on Mead's social-psychological theory of self.

The first signifies not only more numerous and more varied points of shared common interest, but greater reliance upon the recognition of mutual interests as a factor in social control. The second means not only freer interaction between social groups (once isolated...) but change in social habit – its continuous readjustment through meeting the new situations produced by varied intercourse.

Dewey's concept also has affinities with the associative theories of democracy, which find that associations complement both representative democracy and the activities of state institutions in an essential way (Cohen and Rogers 1992: 426): "Associative governance can provide a welcome alternative or complement to public regulatory efforts because of the distinctive capacity of the associations to gather local information, monitor behaviour, and promote cooperation among private actors." It also converges with the idea of democratic professionalism (Druz 2008: 37) which finds the "forums of middle democracy" important, that is "settings in which citizens come together on a regular basis to reach collective decisions about public issues". A meeting in which school personnel, parents, and students together decide about the rules of the school going is an example of such a forum.

Although the notion of natural scientific experimentation inspired Dewey's method of inquiry, he made a distinction between natural scientific and social experiments (e.g. Caspary 2000). In experiments with human beings, subjects have the capacity to be aware of the experiment and its result, reflect on it, and change their behaviour accordingly. In this way experimentation as a "practical reform of social conditions" becomes a part of participatory democracy (Dewey 1927/1995: 367). An experiment, however, requires systematic knowledge of the conditions of the activity and a working hypothesis in relation to which the consequences of the experimentation are evaluated. Dewey's idea has a family resemblance with Donald Campbell's notion of the "experimenting society", founded upon a commitment to experimentation, innovation, social reality testing and learning (Campbell and Russo 1999: 13).

In social, educational, and organizational studies, experimental or interventionist approaches have been developed to stimulate reflection and local organizational change (e.g. Flyvbjerg 2001; Cobb et al. 2003; Engeström 2005). An example of such an approach is the Change Laboratory method developed at the University of Helsinki and based on cultural-historical activity theory (Engeström et al. 1996; Kerosuo et al. 2010). In applying it to the study of the development of home care services for the elderly in the City of Helsinki, Engeström and his colleagues (2007) do not speak about best practices but about cultivating promising practices into social innovations and of attempts to distribute them systematically. The goal of the three-year project is (2007: 3) "to recognize, cultivate and link the promising new practices of home care for the elderly in the City of Helsinki and develop them further into largely usable models of home care in Helsinki." Representatives of management, planners, foremen, social workers, home care providers, and nurses together with researchers and doctoral students constitute a community of inquiry or, it may more opportune to say, a community for the development of new practices. When planning the new forms of services, one of the key tasks of the intervention was the formation of an agent, that is, a multiprofessional group of workers who agree to take the responsibility for the development and implementation of a specific new tool or service model.

8.5 Transcending the national view: Learning networks across national boundaries

This book has discussed the Nordic model of welfare and innovation. Although global competition has made benchmarking of national models topical, the limits of a national view or technonationalism in a world of increased interconnectedness has constantly been addressed. All the basic ethical values and foundations of the Nordic welfare state grew out of the national context within which they historically emerged. Equality and solidarity do not recognize national boundaries. Democracy is a universal value and economic competition increasingly requires learning from other countries. Education and 'Bildung' means participation in the richness of the world culture and to the achievements of science, technology and professional knowledge that do not recognize boundaries. Neither do environmental problems. Their solution requires transnational decisions and measures.

The recent escalating problems of the indebted countries of the European Union has shown the problem of interconnectedness in a concrete way. These European countries with a severe debt problem must be supported by others to avoid the collapse of a joined financial system. A Finnish commentator, Professor Martti Koskenniemi, finds that this problem caused by the financial markets is a part of the larger political crisis. The competition demanded by the market will require the dismantlement of the present social security and labour law, which would lead to the exacerbation of the social conflicts. The European Union faces a contradiction between maintaining and developing a welfare state and a tendency to cut expenses to increase competitiveness. It can only by solved by deepening political collaboration, according to Koskeniemi. What is needed is an establishment of a strong central power "that is able to decide about the necessary actions related to the internal division of incomes. These actions are needed to balance the European economy without compromising the principle of welfare that covers the whole Union. To begin with it would be necessary to work on eliminating the welfare gap between the North and the South."[7]

By the same token it can be asked whether any national or European actions to maintain welfare are sufficient or ethically sustainable if the division of incomes increases in the world and significant parts of the populations live in poverty. The share of the world population who live in extreme poverty defined in terms of those who use under 1.25 dollars a day for living has declined considerably during the least three decades. The World Bank, however, estimates that 1.4 billion people still today live in extreme poverty. According to the United Nations Developmental Programme, even more live in conditions in which there are severe lacks in basic health care, schooling, and standard of living (Kanniainen 2011: 660).

The problem of global governance transcends the scope of this book. However, the visions of democratic global governance (e.g. Held 2005) or democratic global Keynesianism (Patomäki 2012) can be seen as a consequent step forward from the viewpoint of an enabling welfare society. They suggest that the social and educational policies through which the major differences between social groups within nation states have been equalized could be extended to cover all people in the world. The suggestion (Patomäki 2012: 205) that "Part of the incomes from global taxes could be allocated to fund a global basic education system" seems the most sensible developmental policy in the light of the experience, for example, of the Nordic welfare states as well in the light of the analysis of the catching up processes analysed in innovation studies. It would stimulate economic development and enhance democracy and equality globally. I can well imagine that an International Association for the Global Basic Education with the participation of teachers, researchers, and experienced administrators from all over the world could accumulate knowledge, expertise, and even standards for the organization of viable basic education systems. Since every such system is also strongly based on the local culture and needs, the activity of local organizations is of course decisive. An international multi-professional association

---

[7] Prof. Kimmo Koskenniemi "The crisis calls for the political unification of the EU", HS, 22 December 2011.

inspired by the value of equal educational opportunity might be a strong impartial partner in the dialogue needed to advance global education.

The globalization challenge touches immediately and in many ways on the industrialized nation states including the Nordic countries. The problems of European development have strengthened nationalistic sentiments that might further enhance isolationalism, which is specifically dangerous to small countries dependent on exports and with limited cultural and scientific resources. The major source of the viability of a national culture is its interaction with other cultures. Both expertise and creativity are increasingly distributed: they are based on the dialogue and complementarity of different kinds of knowledge and points of views. Howard Gardner (2004: 254) characterizes the consequence of globalization for education as follows: "Knowledge and the ability needs to interact civilly and productively with individuals with quite different cultural backgrounds – both within one's own society and across the planet." The politics of supporting the exchange of students and favouring working periods of employees in foreign organizations is an essential part of cultivating the capabilities needed in a globalizing world.

A challenge for Finnish society caused by immigration – as for most European countries – is the development a non-discriminatory unitary school where children from different backgrounds learn to respect each other and learn from each other's cultural background. On the other hand, how can the viewpoints and realities of cultures outside Europe and in the margin of the competition between economic great powers be included in education? Should each Finnish school have a twin school in a developing country to have joint projects and dialogue? This would provide an opportunity to teachers, pupils, and parents to learn from different cultural traditions, world views, and realities, and possibly give rise to new kind of initiatives to develop the host communities of the schools.

Benchmarking in the European Union relating to the open coordination method has thus far mainly been realized at the level of collaboration between civil servants in the state administration of the member countries. It, therefore, realizes only in a limited way the ideals of learning by comparing practices and learning by peer review. Horizontal direct collaboration between local service providers with other countries is needed. The network of Finnish and Hungarian teachers, researchers, and teacher trainers around the development of the Varga-Neményi method of teaching mathematics is an example of such transnational collaboration. Another example is the collaboration of the Swedish and Finnish children's art schools with the art school system of the small northern Italian city of Reggio Emilia, "home of what are widely regarded to be the finest preschools in the world" (Gardner 2011: 43). In Reggio Emilia system art is used as a method of inquiring about the world and of developing children's thought and imagination (Edwards *et al.* 1993). Conditions should be created for the development of this kind of international, horizontal peer partnership networks around important and promising social, cultural, and technological innovations.

9

Conclusions: Politics for the cultivation and mobilization of human capabilities

In this final section, policy conclusions are presented concerning the cultivation and mobilization of human capabilities in an enabling welfare state. They are partly based on the analysis of the Finnish capability-cultivating services and partly on the debates of the future of a welfare state and democracy in a knowledge-driven society. From the point of view of innovation policy, the development of the capabilities of the children through education and by social participation constitutes the foundation for interactive learning for adults in working life as well as for the development of the democracy needed to foster innovation.[1]

It has been shown that the development of capabilities, self-image, and social engagement of an individual takes decisive formative steps during early childhood and the first grades of school. Omissions in enhancing learning and development during this period are likely to lead to cumulative difficulties in school and to result in damages in development that are very difficult to compensate for later in childhood and adulthood. From this premise, recommendations concerning capability policy in pre-school and school education can be drawn. First, measures should be taken to decrease the poverty among families with children, since poverty undermines the capacity of the parents to contribute to the development of their children. As welfare researchers and economists of innovation argue, family policy plays a role in enhancing the development of capabilities and in the prevention of exclusion. Improvement

---

[1] They do not preclude the relevance of policy measures that emerge from industrial, science, and technology policy traditions, such as the need to strengthen venture capital institutions, support for the emergence of innovative small firms, the enhancement of interaction between national actors, or to foster the internalization of university research.

and better coordination of the family-related services such as household help, family counselling, child, youth, and family psychiatry, student care at schools as well as child welfare is needed.

Second, the core potential of day care and kindergarten for the development of creative capabilities should be recognized. Day care should not be regarded primarily as a social political means of ensuring the participation of parents in the labour market. It should be emphatically developed as a central institution contributing to the development of the children and particularly to the development of their imagination, thought, and propensity for going to school and social collaboration. Play is the key mechanism for child development before school age. Play develops a holistic approach of encountering the world and it is a primary source for the development of imagination and creativity. Attempts to extend the formal methods of school teaching into day care jeopardizes its development. The child care and pre-school services need to be developed on the basis of play-pedagogy. This calls for both research in day care and play activities as well as high-quality education of kindergarten teachers: a challenge comparable to the construction of the comprehensive school system. The savings made by increasing the size of care groups and replacing educated kindergarten teachers with social workers driven by the crisis of municipality economics impedes this development. The investment in day care should be seen as an investment for the cultivation of the social and creative capabilities needed in a knowledge-driven society.

Third, the collaboration between child and maternity care, social services, and day care should be increased to ensure the early diagnosis and recognition of learning and developmental problems of children possible in order to provide immediate tailored remedial measures to overcome them. The degradation of basic day care services increases the need for expensive rehabilitation and child protection services. Many observers, for instance, find that the considerably higher numbers of charged children in Finland compared with other Northern countries is due to neglect in the basic child care services.

The basic education remains the fundamental institution in the creation of such generic capabilities as strategic functional literacy that makes lifelong learning, critical thought, and the following development of knowledge in a field of expertise possible. The policy of "overcoming the learning difficulties" by tailored support and special education in the comprehensive school should be further developed toward the recognition of the unique capabilities and interests of each child so as to support them in finding their way to participate in society. Pedagogical solutions that are able to combine high-quality learning in specific subjects and a non-discriminatory school community that accepts diversity need to be developed. The measures for preventing bullying, supporting collaboration, and eliminating the negative consequences of competition are needed in order to develop children's tolerance, responsibility, and capacity to negotiate differences. The interaction and collaborative projects between school and other societal activities are needed to foster the motivation of the students and to develop their capacity to use knowledge in different activities of social life. The forms of learning from the solutions developed by single schools and municipalities need to be developed.

As a result of the knowledge society development and the rising level of education, the transition from comprehensive school to secondary education constitutes a major challenge for a welfare society. A considerable minority of the young people who have completed the comprehensive school stay away both from secondary education and from the labour market. Helping these young people to find their place in society is a major challenge for the development of individualized services. In addition the remnants of a double track school system still remains in Finnish secondary education. Very few students from vocational schools go on to enter to tertiary education. Flexible forms of training organized together with schools, firms, recruiting firms, and public authorities tailored to meet the situations of individual young persons is needed to solve the problem of exclusion. Because of the rapid change in the working life these solutions need to be done without jeopardizing the quality of overall education to ensure the possibility for further lifelong learning. The extension of compulsory education to 12 years as well as the creation of a youth school need to be reconsidered. A new level of integration of all around and vocational education as well as dialogue between theory and practice are central epistemic and pedagogical challenges for this school.

The extension of democracy and the mobilization of the theoretical and practical expertise of different domains of society need to be developed in three ways. First, representatives of the relevant professional and scientific communities, associations, and civic organizations as well as the practitioners of work organizations need to be involved in the preparation of social and institutional reforms at a national level. This is needed to ensure the mobilization of necessary expertise, for the efficient implementation of the reforms and for the development of democracy. Forms of multilevel preparation of reforms need to be developed which are able to take into account locally developed promising practices that allow for experimentation. The preparation of the

New Education Act of 2012 through the large-scale participation of schools and municipalities is an example of such a multilevel dialogic reform.

Second, institutional learning needed to develop the quality of enabling service provision. It comprises three elements. First, experimenting in local communities guided by broad guiding values and goals should be encouraged and rewarded. Second, the collaborative development of tools and solutions between universities and research institutes, associations, central and municipal authorities, service providers, and users of the services is needed. The state and the municipalities must ensure that interaction and dialogue between the actors of multi-organizational fields is realized. Forms of horizontal learning between local service providers are needed in order to learn from the promising new practices and to develop them further. Multilevel vertical forms of learning need to be developed in which national, regional, and local actors develop and articulate standards and conceptions together by utilizing the versatility of knowledge and experience of the field.

Third, the forms and instruments of governance that allow and reward local experimenting and institutional learning are needed. The strong forms of accountancy based on pre-given external goals and the following of their achievement by quantitative indicators mostly help in making the provision of well-defined products more efficient. However, they do not stimulate the experimentation and development of new solutions. It is not possible to have indicators or well-defined evidence of something that is emerging or does not yet exist. That is why forms and instruments of governance are needed that are based on reports of experimentation, peer-review, networking, and learning from the promising new models, tools, and practices by benchmarking. Forms of governance and evaluation need increasingly to be fused with and developed for the forms of collaborative learning and development. This is a central challenge for the new second-order role of an enabling welfare state.

References

A Renewing, Human-centric and Competitive Finland: The National Knowledge Society Strategy 2007–215 (2006), Helsinki: Prime Minister's Office. http://www.umic.pt/ images/stories/publicacoes1/Strategia_englanti_181006final.pdf

The Academy of Finland's forward look (2000), "Suomen Akatemian julkaisuja 3/00". Helsinki: Edita. http://www.aka.fi/Tiedostot/Tiedostot/Julkaisut/Linja2000.pdf

Adler, P. A. and Clark, K. B. (1991), "Behind the learning curve: A sketch of the learning process", *Management Science* 17 (3), 267–281.

Adler, P. S. and Heckscher, C. (2006), "Towards collaborative community", in Heckscher, C. and Adler, P. S. (eds), *The Firms as Collaborative Community; Reconstructing trust in the knowledge economy*, Oxford: Oxford University Press, 11–105.

Aho, E., Pitkänen, K., and Sahlberg, P. (2006), *Policy Development and Reform Principles of Basic and Secondary Education in Finland since 1968*, Washington: The World Bank. www.worldbank.org/education

Ahvenainen, O. (1983), *Laaja-alaisen erityisopetuksen ja erityisopettajan toiminnan kartoitus*, National Board of Education, *Research Notes* 42. Helsinki: VAPK.

——Karppi, S., and Åström, M.-L. (1977), *Lasten lukemis- ja kirjoittamishäiriöt*, Jyväskylä: Koulun Erityisplavelu Oy.

Aiginger, K. (2006), "Competitiveness: From a dangerous obsession to a welfare creating ability", *Journal of Industry, Competition and Trade* 6 (2), 161–177.

Akçomak, S. and Ter Weel, B. (2009), "Social capital, innovation and growth: Evidence from Europe", *European Economic Review* 53 (5), 544–567.

Albernathy, W. J. and Wayne, K. (1974), "Limits of learning curve", *Harvard Business Review* September–October 1987 (4), 109–119.

Albert, M. and Laberge, S. (2007), "The legitimation and dissemination process of the innovation system approach: The case of Canadian and Québec science and technology policy", *Science, Technology & Human Values* 32 (2), 221–249.

Alestalo, M. (1999), "The university under the pressure of innovation policy – Reflecting some European and Finnish Experiments", *Science Studies* 12 (1), 44–69.

Ali-Yrkkö, J. (ed.), (2010), "Nokia and Finland in the sea of change", *ETLA Series* B 244, Helsinki: Taloustieto.

——and Hermans, R. (2002), *Nokia Suomen innovaatiojärjestelmässä*, Keskustelunaihe 799, Helsinki: ETLA.

————(2004), "Nokia: A giant in the Finnish Innovation system" in Schienstock, G. (ed.), *Embracing the Knowledge Economy; The dynamic transformation of the Finnish Innovation System*, Cheltenham: Edward Elgar, 106–127.

Allardt, E. (1995), "Kansallinen innovaatiojärjestelmä teknologiapolitiikan ystä-vänä ja tiedepolitiikan haittana [National innovation system as a friend of technology policy and as a foe of science policy]", *Tieteessä tapahtuu* 13 (4), 5–9.

——(1998), "Teknologiaretoriikka suomalaisen todellisuuden konstruoimisen välineenä (Technology rhetoric as a means of contructing the Finnish reality)", *Tiede & Edistys* 23 (2), 85–95.

Allen, R. C. (1983), "Collective invention", *Journal of Economic Behavior and Organization* 4, 1–24.

Allen, T. J. (1977), *Managing the Flow of Technology*, Cambridge, Mass: MIT Press.

Almlund, M., Duckword, A. L., Heckman, J., and Kautz, T. (2011), "Personality psychology and economics", in Hanushek, E. A., Machin, S. J., and Woess-mann, L. (eds), *Handbook of the Economics of Education*, Amsterdam: Elsevier, 1–181.

Amable, B. (2003), *The Diversity of Modern Capitalism*, Oxford: Oxford University Press.

Amir, S. (2007), "National rhetoric and technological development: The Indonesian aircraft industry in the new order regime", *Technology in Society* 29, 283–293.

Andersen, T., Holmström, B., Honkapohja, S., Korkman, S., Söderström, H. T., and J. Vartiainen (2007), *The Nordic Model; Embracing golabization and sharing risks*, Helsinki: Taloustieto.

Anderson, E.-L. and Lundvall, B.-Å. (1988), "Small national systems of innov-ation facing technological revolutions: An analytical framework", in Freeman, C. and Lundvall, B.-Å. (eds), *Small Countries Facing the Technological Revolution*, London and New York: Pinter Publishers.

Andersson, E., Malmberg, B., and Östh, B. (2008), "Schools and neighborhood effects in Swedish regions – Inequalities in education in PISA", Paper presented at the ENHR Conference, Dublin, 6–9 July.

Ansell, C. K. (2011), *Pragmatist Democracy; Evolutionary learning as public philoso-phy*, New York: Oxford University Press.

Antikainen, A. (2010), "The capitalist state and education: The case of structuring the Nordic model", *Current Sociology* 58(4), 530–550.

Apple, M. (2006), *Educating the "Right" Way: Markets, standards, God and equality*, New York: Routledge.

Archibugi, D., Howells, J., and Michie, J. (1999), "Innovation systems and policy in a global economy", in Archibugi, D., Howells, J., and Michie, J. (eds), *Innovation Policy in a Global Economy*, Cambridge: Cambridge University Press, 1–16.

Arrow, K. J. (1962), "The economic implications of learning by doing", *The Review of Economic Studies* 29 (2), 155–173.

Arrowsmith, J., Sisson, K., and Margison, P. (2004), "What can 'benchmarking' offer to the open method co-ordination?", *Journal of European Public Policy* 11 (2), 311–328.

Arundel, A., Lorenz, E., Lundvall, B.-Å., and Valeyre, A. (2007), "How Europe's economics learn: A comparison of work organization and innovation mode for the EU-15", *Industrial and Corporate Change* 16 (6), 1175–1210.

References

Au, W. (2007), "High-stakes testing and curricular control: A quantitative meta-synthesis", *Educational Researcher* 6 (5), 258–267.

Austin, J. (1976), *How to do Things with Words*, Oxford: Oxford University Press.

——(1979), *Philosophical Papers*, Third Edition, Oxford: Oxford University Press.

Balzat, M. (2006), *An Economic Analysis of Innovation. Extending the concept of national innovation system*, Cheltenham: Edward Elgar.

——and Hanusch, H. (2004), "Recent trends in the research on national innovation systems", *International Journal of Technology and Globalization*, Volume 2, 1–2/2006, 158–176.

Bateson, G. (1972), *Steps to an Ecology of Mind*, New York: Balantine Books.

Battilina, J. and D'Aunno (2009), "Institutional work and the paradoxes of embedded agency", in Lawrence, T. B., Suddaby, R., and Leca, B. (eds), *Institutional Work; Actors and agency in institutional studies of organizations*, Cambridge: Cambridge University Press, 31–58.

Bazerman, C. (1999), *The Languages of Edison's Electric Light*, Cambridge, Mass.: MIT Press.

Becker, G. S. (1964/1993), *Human Capital; A theoretical and empirical analysis with special reference to education*, Third Edition, Chicago: the University of Chicago Press.

Benkler, Y. (2006), *The Wealth of Networks; How social production transforms markets and freedom*, Yale: Yale University Press.

Bereiter, C. (2002), *Education and Mind in the Knowledge Age*, Mahvah, NJ.: Lawrence Erlbaum.

Berk, G. and Schneiberg, M. (2005), "Varieties in capitalism, varieties of associations: Collaborative learning in American industry, 1900–1925", *Politics and Society* 33 (1), 46–87.

Bernal, J. D. (1939/1967), *The Social Function of Science*, New York: The Macmillan Company.

Bernard, P. and Boucher, G. (2007), "Institutional competitiveness, social investment, and welfare regimes", *Regulation and Governance* 1 (3), 219–229.

Bertalanffy, L. von (1969), *General System Theory*. New York: George Braziller.

Bhaskar, R. (1987), *Scientific Realism and Human Emancipation*, London: Verso.

Billig, M. (1987), *Arguing and Thinking: A rhetorical approach to social psychology*, Cambridge: Cambridge University Press.

——(1991), *Ideology and Opinions*, London: Sage.

Black, P., McGormic, R., James, M., and Pedder, D. (2006), "Learning how to learn and assessment for learning: A theoretical inquiry", *Research Papers in Education* 21 (2), 119–132.

Block, F. (1990), *Posindustrial Possibilities: A critique of economic discourse*, Berkley: University of California Press.

Bohman, J. (1999), "Democracy as inquiry, inquiry as democratic: Pragmatism. Social science and the cognitive division of labor", *American Journal of Political Science* 43 (2), 590–607.

Bourdieu, P. (1977), *Outline of a Theory of Practice*, Cambridge: Cambridge University Press.

——(1991), *Language and Symbolic Power*, ed. J. B. Thompson, Cambridge: Polity.

Bowker, G. C. and Star, S. L. (1999), *Sorting Things Out; Classification and its consequences*, Cambridge, Mass.: MIT Press.

Bowles, S., and Gintis, H. (2002), "The inheritance of inequality", *Journal of the Economic Perspectives* 16 (3), 3–30.

Braadbaart, O., Yusnandarshah, B. (2008), "Public sector benchmarking: A survey of scientific articles, 1990–2005", *International Review of administrative Sciences* 74 (3), 421–433.

Bresnahan, T., Cambardella, A., and Saxenian, A. L. (2001), "Old economy inputs for new economy outcomes: Cluster formation in the new Silicon Valleys", *Industrial and Corporate Change* 10 (4), 835–860.

Brink, S. (2010), "Striving for excellence and equity: The value of OECD assessment programs for policy in Canada", in Laukkanen, R. (ed.), *PISA, PIAAC, AHELO Miksi ja miten OECD mittaa osaamista?*, Opetus- ja kulttuuriministeriön julkaisuja 2010:17 Helsinki: Yliopistopaino, 19–32.

Brown, M. B. (2009), *Science in Democracy; Expertise, institutions and representation*, Cambridge, Mass.: MIT Press.

Brown, P. (2000), "Popular epidemiology and toxic waste contamination: Lay and professional ways of knowing", in Kroll-Smith, S., Brown, P., and Gunter, V. J. (eds), *Illness and Environment: A reader in contested medicine*, New York: NYU Press, 364–383.

Bruford, W. H. (1975), *The German Tradition of Self-cultivation: Bildung from Humbolt to Thomas Mann*, London: Cambridge University Press.

Bruno, I. (2009), "The 'indefinite discipline' of comparativeness benchmarking as a neoliberal technology of government", *Minerva* 47, 261–280.

Burke, K. (1969), *A Rhetoric of Motives*, Berkeley: University of California Press.

Burke, T. (1994), *Dewey's New Logic; A reply to Russell*, Chicago: University of Chicago Press.

Burkitt, I. (1999), *Bodies of Thought; Embodiment, identity and modernity*, London: Sage.

Burroni, L. and Keune, M. (2011), "Flexicurity: A conceptual critique", *European Journal of Industrial Relations* 17 (1), 75–91.

Callon, M. (1998), "The embeddedness of economic markets in economics", in Callon, M. (ed.), *The Laws of the Markets*, Oxford: Blackwell, 1–57.

——(2006), "What does it mean to say that economics is performative?", CSI Working paper, Series 5. http://www.csi.endsmp.fr/.

——and Rabeharisoa, V. (2008), "The growing engagement of emergent concerned groups in political and economic life: Lessons from French Association of Neuromuscular Disease Patients", *Science, Technology and Human Values* 33(2), 230–261.

Cambrosio *et al.* (1990), "Representing biotechnology: An ethnography of Quebec science policy", *Social Studies of Science* 20, 195–227.

Campbell, D. T. and Russo, M. J. (1999), *Social Experimentation*. Thousand Oaks: Sage Publications.

Campbell, J. L. (1992), *The Community Reconstructs; The Meaning of Pragmatic Social Thought*, Urbana: University of Illinois Press.

——(1998), "Institutional analysis and the role of ideas in political economy", *Theory and Society* 27, 377–379.

References

Canguilhem, G. (1988), *Ideology and Rationality in the History of Science*, Cambridge, Mass.: MIT Press.

Caracostas, P. (1998), "Towards system policy at the European level: Five key challenges for the future", *STI Review 22*, Paris: OECD, 307–321.

Carneiro, P. D. and Heckman, J. J. (2003), "Human capital policy", IZA Working Paper 821.

Carruthers, M. (2002), "Human creativity: Its evolution, its cognitive basis and its connection to childhood's pretence", *British Journal for the Philosophy of Science* 53, 1–25.

Caspary, W. R. (2000), *Dewey and Democracy*, Ithaca: Cornell University Press.

Castelló-Climent, A. (2008), "On the distribution of education and democracy", *Journal of Development Economics* 87, 179–190.

Castells, M. and Himanen, P. (2002), *The Information Society and the Welfare State; The Finnish model*, Oxford: The Oxford University Press.

Ceccarelli, L. (2001), *Shaping Science with Rhetoric; The cases of Dobzhansky, Schrödinger and Wilson*, Chicago and London: University of Chicago Press.

Chaminade, C. and Edquist, C. (2006), "From theory to practice: The use of the systems of innovation approach in innovation policy", in Hage, J. and Meeus, M. (eds), *Innovation, Science, and Institutional Change*, Oxford: Oxford Univeristy Press, 141–160.

Clemens, E. S. and Cook, J. M. (1999), "Politics of institutionalism: Explaining durability and change", *Annual Review of Sociology* 25, 441–466.

Cobb, P., Confrey, J., diSessa, A., Lehrer, R., and Schauble, L. (2003), "Design experiments in educational research", *Educational Researcher* 32, 9–13.

Cohen, J. and Rogers, J. (1992), "Secondary associations and democratic governance", *Politics and Society* 20 (4), 393–472.

Cohen, W. and Levinthal, D. (1990), "Absorptive capacity: A new perspective on learning and innovation", *Administrative Science Quarterly* 35, 128–152.

Constant, E. W. (1989), "Cause and consequence: Science technology and regulatory change in oil business in Texas, 1930–1975", *Technology and Culture* 30, 426–455.

Conway, S. (1995), "Informal boundary-spanning communication in the innovation process: an empirical study", *Technology Analysis and Strategic Management* 7 (3), 327–342.

Cowan, R., David, P. A., and Foray, D. (2000), "The explicit economics of knowledge codification and tacitness", *Industrial and Corporate Change* 9, 211–253.

Crawford, H. (1993), "An interview with Bruno Latour", *Configurations* 2, 247–269.

Csikszentmihalyi, M. (1990), "The domain of creativity", in Ronco, M. A. and Albert, R. S. (eds), *Theories of Creativity*, London: Sage, 190–212.

——(1997), *Creativity*, New York: Harper Perennial.

Curtis, D. (2006), "Mind sets and methods: Poverty strategies and the awkward potential of the enabling welfare state", *International Journal of Public Sector Management* 19 (2), 150–164.

Darling-Hammond, L. (2007), "Race, inequality and educational accountability: The irony of 'No child is left Behind'", *Race, Ethnicity and Education* 10 (3), 245–260.

De Groot, A. (1946/1965), *Thought and Choice in Chess*, The Hague: Mouton Publishers.

de la Porte, C. and Nanz, P. (2004), "The OMC – A deliberative-democratic mode of governance? The case of employment and pensions", *Journal of European Public Policy* 11 (2), 267–288.

DeBresson, C. H., Xiaoping, I., Drejer, I., and Lundvall, B.-Å. (1997), "Innovative activity and learning economy – A comparison of systems in 10 OECD countries", Draft report to the OECD.

Dewey, J. (1899/1976), "The school and society", in Boydston, J. A. (ed.), *The Middle Works, Vol. 1: 1899–1901*. Carbondale: Southern Illinois University Press, 1–109.

——(1906), *The School and the Child; Selections from the educational essays of John Dewey*, ed. by J. J. Findlay, London: Blackie and Son.

——(1916/1985), "Democracy and education", in Boydston, J. A. (ed.), *John Dewey; The Middle Works, 1899–1924, Vol. 9*, Carbondale: Southern Illinois University Press.

——(1922/1988), "Human nature and conduct", in Boydston, J. A. (ed.), *The Middle Works, Vol. 14: 1899–1901*, Carbondale: Southern Illinois University Press.

——(1927/1988), "The public and its problems", in Boydston, J. A. (ed.), *The Later Works of John Dewey, Vol. 2*, Carbondale: Southern Illinois University Press, 235–372.

——(1933/1989), "How we think", in Boydston, J. A. (ed.), *The Later Works of John Dewey, Vol. 8*, Carbondale: Southern Illinois University Press.

——(1938/1991), "Logic, the theory of inquiry", in Boydston, J. A. (ed.), *The Later Works of John Dewey, Vol. 12*, Carbondale: Southern Illinois University Press.

——and Bentley, A. (1949/1989), "Knower and the known", in Boydston, J. A. (ed.), *The Later works of John Dewey, Vol. 16*, Carbondale: Southern Illinois University Press.

Dierkes, M., Antal, A. B., Child, J., and Nonaka, I. (eds). (2001), *Organizational Learning and Knowledge*, New York: Oxford University Press.

DiMaggio, P. J., (ed.), (1982), *The New Institutionalism in Organizational Analysis*, London: University of Chicago Press, 1–38.

——and Powell, W. W. (1983), "The iron cage revisited: Institutional isomorphism and collective rationality on organization fields", *American Sociological Review* 48 (2), 147–160.

———(1991), "The iron cage revisited: Institutional isomorphism and collective rationality in Organizational Fields", in Powell, W. W. and DiMaggio, P. J. (eds), *The New Institutionalism in Organizational Analysis*, Chicago: University of Chicago Press, 63–82.

References

Djelic, M.-L. (2010), "Institutional perspectives: Working towards coherence or irreconcible diversity?", in Morgan, G., Campbell, J., Crouch, C., Pedersen, O. K., and Whitley, R. (eds), *Oxford Handbook of Comparative Institutional Analysis*, Oxford: Oxford University Press, 15–39.

Dobzhansky, T. (1937/1964), *Genetics and the Origins of Species*, New York: Columbia University Press.

Dogson, M., Hughes, A., Foster, J., and Metcalfe, S. (2011), "Systems thinking, market failure, and the development of innovation policy: The case of Australia", *Research Policy* 40, 1145–1156.

Donald, M. (1991), *Origins of Modern Mind. Three stages in the evolution of culture and cognition*, Cambridge, Mass.: Harvard University Press.

——(2001), *The Mind so Rare. The evolution of human consciousness*, New York: W.W. Norton & Company.

Dorf, M. C., and Sabel, C. F. (1998), "A constitution of democratic experimentalism", *Columbia Law Review* 98 (2), 267–473.

Dosi, G., Freeman, C., Nelson, R., Silverberg, G., and Soete, L. (eds), (1988), *Technical Change and Economic Theory*, London: Pinter Publishers.

——, Nelson, R. and Winter, S. (eds), (2000), *The Nature and Dynamics of Organizational Capabilities*, Oxford: Oxford University Press.

Douglas, M. (1981), *How Institutions Think*, New York: Syracuse University Press.

Dunleavy, P., Margetts, H., Bastow, S., and Tinkler, J. (2005), "New public management is dead–Long live digital-era governance", *Journal of Public Management Research and Theory* 16, 467–494.

Dzur, A. W. (2008), *Democratic Professionalism; Citizen participation and the reconstruction of professional ethics, identity and politics*, Pennsylvania: The University of Pennsylvania Press.

Edquist, C. (1997), "Systems of innovation approaches – Their emergence and characteristics", in Edquist, C. (ed.), *Systems of Innovation; Technologies, institutions and organizations*, London: Pinter, 1–35.

——(2005), "Systems of innovation: Perspectives and challenges", in Fagerberg, J., Mowery, D., and Nelson, R. (eds), *The Oxford Handbook of Innovation*, Oxford: Oxford University Press, 181–207.

——and Lundvall, B.-Å. (1993), "Comparing the Danish and Swedish systems of innovation", in Nelson, R. (ed.), *National Innovation Systems; A comparative analysis*, New York: Oxford University Press, 265–298.

——, Luukkonen, T., and Sotarauta, M. (2009), "Broad-based innovation policy", in *Evaluation of the Finnish National Innovation System – Full report*, Helsinki: Taloustieto Ltd, 11–69.

Edwards, C., Forman, G., and Gandini, L. (eds), (1993), *The Hundred Languages of Children: The Reggio Emilia approach to early childhood education*, Norwood, NJ: Ablex Publishing.

Eklund, M. (2007), *Adoption of the Innovations System Concept in Sweden*, Stockholm: Uppsala Studies in Economic History 81.

Emirbayer, M. and Mische, A. (1998), "What Is Agency?", *American Journal of Sociology*, 103 (4), 962–1023.

Engeström, Y. (1987), *Learning by Expanding: An Activity Theoretical Approach to Developmental Research*, Helsinki: Orienta Konsultit.

——(2001), "Expansive learning at work: Toward an activity theoretical reconceptualization", *Journal of Education and Work* 14 (1), 133–156.

——(2005), "Developmental work research: Expanding activity theory in practice", in George Rückriem (ed.), *ICHS, International cultural-historical human sciences*, Vol. 12, Berlin: Lehmans Media.

——,Engeström, R., and Vähäaho, T. (1999a), "When the center does not hold: The importance of knotworking", in Chaicklin, M., Hedegarrd, M., and Jensen, U.-J. (eds), *Activity Theory and Social Practice*, Aarhus: Aarhus University Press, 345–374.

——Miettinen, R., and Punamäki, R.-L. (eds), (1999b), *Perspectives on Activity Theory*, Cambridge: Cambridge University Press.

——,Virkkunen, J., Helle, M., Pihlaja, and Poikela, R. (1996), "Change laboratory as a tool for transforming work", *Lifelong Learning in Europe* 1 (2), 10–17.

——,Niemelä, A.-L., Nummijoki, J., and Tukia, H. (2007), "Vanhusten syrjäytymisen ehkäiseminen kotihoidossa: lupaavien hankkeiden jalostamishanke", *Väliraportti I. Helsingin terveyskeskus*, Helsingin yliopiston Toiminnan teorian ja kehittävän työntutkimuksen yksikkö. Heinäkuu.

Eriksson, K. A. (2005), "Innovaatiojärjestelmä ja hallinnan kieli. (Innovation system and the language of governance)", *Politiikka* 47 (2), 105–116.

Ericsson, K. A. (2006), "The influence of experience and deliberate practice on the development of superior expert performance", in Ericsson, K. A., Charness, N., Feltowich, P.-J. and Hoffman, R. R. (eds), *The Cambridge Handbook of Expertise and Expert Performance*, Cambridge: Cambridge University Press, 683–703.

Esping-Andersen, G. (1990), *The Three Worlds of Welfare Capitalism*, Cambridge: Polity Press.

——(2009), *The Incomplete Revolution; Adapting to woman's new roles*, Cambridge: Polity Press.

Etzkowitz, H. and Leydesdorff, L. (2000), "The dynamics of innovation: From national systems and "mode 2" to a triple helix of university-industry-government relations", *Research Policy* 29, 109–123.

Evaluation of the Finnish National Innovation System – Full Report (2009), www.tem.fi/files/24929/InnoEvalFi_FULL_Report_28_Oct_2009.pdf

Evans, K. G. (2000), "Reclaiming John Dewey. Democracy, pragmatism, and public administration", *Administration and Society* 32 (3), 308–328.

Fagerberg, J. (2005), "Innovation. A guide to the literature", in Fagerberg, J., Mowery, D., and Nelson, R. (eds), *Oxford Handbook of Innovation*, Oxford: Oxford University Press, 1–26.

——and Srholec, M. (2008), "National innovation systems: Capabilities and economic development", *Research Policy* 37 (9), 1417–1435.

——,Mowery, D. C., and Verspagen, J. (2009), *Innovation, Path Dependency and Policy*, Oxford: Oxford University Press.

Fairclough, N. (1992), *Discourse and Social Change*, Cambridge: Polity Press.

Feldman, D. H. and Csikszentmihalyi, M., Gardner, H. (1994), *Changing the World: A framework for the study of creativity*, Westport: Praeger.

Finlayson, A. (2004), "Political science, political ideas and rhetoric", *Economy and Society* 33 (4), 528–549.

Finland's national innovation strategy (2008), http://ec.europa.eu/invest-in-research/pdf/download_en/finland_national_innovation_strategy.pdf

Finnemore, M. (1993), "International organizations as teachers of norms: The United Nations Educational, Scientific, and Cultural Organization and science policy", *International Organization* 47 (4), 565–597.

Fleck, J. (2000), "Artifact-activity: The coevolution of artefacts, knowledge and organization in technological innovation", in Ziman, J. (ed.), *Technological Innovation as an Evolutionary Process*, Cambridge: Cambridge University Press, 248–266.

Fleck, L. (1979), *Genesis and Development of a Scientific Fact*, Chicago: University of Chicago Press.

Flyvbjerg, B. (2001), *Making Social Science Matter: Why social inquiry fails and how it can succeed again*, Cambridge: Cambridge University Press.

Forrester, J. W. (1968), *Principles of Systems*, 2nd ed., Waltham, MA: Pegasus Communications.

Freeman, C, (1979), "The determinants of innovation: Market demand, technology and the response to social problems", *Futures*, June, 206–215.

——(1987), *Technology Policy and Economic Performance: Lessons from Japan*, London: Pinter.

——(2002), "Continental, national, sub-national innovation systems–complementarity and economic growth", *Research Policy* 31, 191–211.

——and Lundval B.-Å., (ed.) (1988), *Small Countries Facing the Technological Revolution*, London: Pinter.

Fuegi, D. and Jennings, M. (2004), *International Library Statistics: Trends and commentary based on Libecon data*. http://www.libecon.org/pdf/InternationalLibraryStatistic.pdf

Furman, J. L., Porter, M. E., and Stern, S. (2002), "The determinants of national innovative capability", *Research Policy* 31 (6), 899–933.

Galison, P. (1997), *Image and Logic: A material culture of microphysics*, Chicago, Ill: The University of Chicago Press.

Galton, F. (1869/2009), *Hereditary Genius: An inquiry into its laws and consequences*, Charleston, SC: Forgotten Books.

Gardner, H. (1993), Multiple Intelligences: The theory in practice, New York: Basic Books.

——(2004), "How education changes?", in Suáres-Orozco, M. and Baolian, D. (eds), *Globalization; Culture and education in the new millennium*, Berkeley: University of California Press, 235–258.

——(2011), "From progressive education to educational pluralism", in Elmore, R. F. (ed.), *I Used to Think . . . and Now I Think; Twenty leading educators reflect on the work of school reform*, Cambridge, Mass.: Harvard Education Press, 41–48.

Garud, R. and Karnoe, P. (2003), "Bricolage versus breakthrough: Distributed and embedded agency in technology entrepreneurship", *Research Policy* 32, 277–300.

Gerlils, H. (2006), *Dynamic Innovations Systems in the Nordic Countries?*, Vol. 2, Denmark, Finland, Iceland, Norway and Sweden, Stockholm: SNS Förlag.

Getzels, J. W. and Csikszentmihalyi, M. (1976), *The Creative Vision; A longitunal study of problem finding in art*, New York: John Wiley & Sons.

Ghemawat, P. (1985), "Building strategy on the experience curve", *Harvard Business Review* 63 (2), March–April, 143–149.

Gibbons, M., Limoges, C., Nowotny, H., Schwartzman, S., Scott, P., and Trow, M. (1994), *The New Production of Knowledge; The dynamics of science and research in contemporary societies*, London: Sage.

Giddens, A. (1998), *The Third Way: The renewal of social democracy*, Cambridge: Polity.

Gilbert, N. (2004), *Transformation of the Welfare State; The silent surrender of public responsibility*, Oxford: Oxford University Press.

——(2005), *The "Enabling State?" from Public to Private Responsibility for Social Protection: Pathways and pitfalls*, OECD Social, Employment and Migration Working Papers 26, Paris: OECD.

Godin, B. (1997), "The rhetoric of a health technology: The microprocessor patient card", *Social Studies of Science* 27, 865–902.

——(1998), "Writing performative history: The new Atlantis?", *Social Studies of Science* 28(3), 465–483.

——(2002), "Technological gaps: An important episode in the construction of science and technology statistics", *Technology in Society* 24, 387–413.

——(2006), "The value of science: Changing conceptions of scientific productivity, 1869–circa 1970", *Social Science Information* 48 (4), 547–586.

——(2007), "National innovation system: The system approach in historical perspective. Project on the history and sociology of STI Statistics", *Science, Technology, and Human Values* 34 (4), 476–501.

Good, J. A. (2005), *A Search for Unity in Diversity: The "permanent Hegelian deposit" in the philosophy of John Dewey*, Landham, MD: Lexington Books.

——(2011), *The German Bildung Tradition*. http://www.philosophy.uncc.edu/ mielrid/SAAP/USC/pbt1.html 12.3.2001

Goodwin, C. (1995), "Seeing in depth", *Social Studies of Science* 25, 237–234.

Gould, S. J. (1987), "Panda's thumb of technology", *Natural History* 1, 14–43.

——(1988), *The Mismeasure of Man*, London: Penguin Books.

Graham, C. and Neu, D. (2004), "Standardized testing and the construction of governable persons", *Journal of Curriculum Studies* 36 (3), 295–319.

Graham, L. J. and Jahnukainen, M. (2011), "Wherefore art you, inclusion? Analyzing the development of inclusive education in New South Wales, Alberta and Finland", *Journal of Education Policy* 26 (2), 261–286.

Greenwood, R., Oliver, C., Sahlin, K., and Suddaby, R. (2008), "Introduction", in Greenwood, Oliver, Sahlin and Suddaby (eds), *The Sage Handbook of Organizational Institutionalism*, Los Angeles: Sage, 1–46.

——Suddaby, R., and Hinings, C. R. (2002), "Theorizing change: The role of professional associations in the transformation of institutionalized fields", *Academy of Management Journal* 45 (1), 58–80.

References

Griffin, P. and Cole, M. (1984), "Current activity for the future: The Zo-ped", in Rogoff, B. and Wertsch, J. (eds), *Children's Learning in the "Zone of Proximal Development"*, San Francisco: Jossey-Bass, 45–64.

Gross, A. C. (1996), *The Rhetoric of Science*, Cambridge, Mass.: Harvard University Press.

Gruber, H. E. (1981), *Darwin on Man; A psychological study of scientific creativity*, Chicago: University of Chicago Press.

Grupp, H. and Schubert, T. (2010), "Review and new evidence on composite innovation indicators for evaluating national performance", *Research Policy* 39 (1), 67–78.

Häikiö, M. (2001), *Nokia Oyj:n historia* (The history of Nokia pcl.), Volumes 1–3. Helsinki: Edita.

——(2002), *Nokia: The Inside Story*, Helsinki: Edita.

Hakkarainen, P. (2008), "The challenge and possibilities of a narrative learning approach in the Finnish early childhood education system", *International Journal of Educational Research* 47, 292–300.

Hall, P. and Soskice, D. (eds). (2001), *Varieties of Capitalism; Institutional foundations of comparative advantage*, Oxford: Oxford University Press.

Hämäläinen, T. and Heiskala, R. (2004), *Sosiaaliset innovaatiot ja yhteiskunnan uudistumiskyky* (Social innovations and the society's capacity for renewal), Helsinki: Edita.

———(2007), (eds), *Social Innovations, Institutional Change and Economic Performance: Making sense of structural adjustment processes in industrial sectors, regions and societies*, Cheltenham: Edward Elgar.

Hargrave, T. J. and Van de Ven, A. H. (2009), "Institutional work as creative embrace of contradictions", in Lawrence, T. B., Suddaby, R., and Leca, B. (eds), *Institutional Work: Actors and agency in institutional studies of organizations*, Cambridge: Cambridge University Press, 120–140.

Hargreaves, A. and Shirley, D. (2009), *The Fourth Way*, Thousand Oaks, CA: Corwin Press.

Hart, D. (2006), "Changing systems of innovation in theory and practice", Paper presented in the SPRU 40th Anniversary Conference, University of Sussex, 11–13 September 2006.

Hartley, K. (1966), "The learning curve and its application to the aircraft industry", *Journal of Industrial Economics* 13, 122–128.

Hasselbladh, H. and Kallinikos J. (2000), "The project of rationalization: A critique and reappraisal of neo-institutionalism in organization studies", *Organization Studies* 21 (4), 679–720.

Hauser, R. M. (2010), "Causes and consequences of cognitive functioning across the life course", *Educational Researcher* 39 (2), 95–109.

Hautamäki, A. (2010), *Sustainable Innovation; A new age of innovation and Finland's innovation policy*, Sitra Reports 87, Helsinki: Sitra.

Heckman, J. J., (2007), "The economics, technology, and neuroscience of human capital formation", *PNAS* 104 (33), 1350–1355.

References

Heiskala, R. (2006), "Kansainvälisen toimintaympäristön muutos ja Suomen yhteiskunnallinen murros", in Heiskala, R. and Luhtakallio, E. (eds), *Uusi jako. Miten Suomesta tuli kilpailukyky-yhteiskunta?*, Helsinki: Gaudemus, 14–42.

——and Luhtakallio, E. (eds), (2006), *Uusi jako. Miten Suomesta tuli kilpailukyky-yhteiskunta?* (The new deal. How Finland became a competition society?), Helsinki: Gaudemus.

Hekkert, M. P., Suurs, R. A. A., Negro, S. O., Kuhlman, S., and Smits, R. E. H. M. (2007), "Functions of innovation systems: A new approach for analyzing technological change", *Technological Forecasting and Social Change*, 74 (4), 413–432.

Held, D. (2005), *Democracy and Global Order; From the modern state to cosmopolitan governance*, London: Polity.

Helkama K., and Seppälä, T. (2004), Arvojen muutos Suomessa 1980-luvulta 2000-luvulle, Helsinki: Sitra, 1–21.

Herrigel, G. (2007), "Roles and rules: Ambiguity, experimentation and new forms of stakeholderism in Germany", *Industrielle Beziehungen* 15 (2), 11–132.

Herrmann, A. M. and Peine, A. (2011), " 'When national innovation system' meets 'varieties of capitalism' arguments on labour qualifications", *Research Policy* 40 (5), 687–701.

Hewstone, M. (1989), *Causal Attribution; From cognitive processes to collective beliefs*, Oxford: Basil Blackwell.

Himanen, P. (2004), *Välittävä, kannustava ja luova Suomi: Katsaus tietoyhteiskuntamme syviin haasteisiin* (A Caring, Supportive and Creative Finland: A review of the profound challenges facing our knowledge society), Eduskunnan Kanslian julkaisu 4, Helsinki: Eduskunnan Kanslia.

——(2007), *Suomalainen unelma. Innovaatioraportti*, Helsinki: Teknologiateollisuuden 100-vuotissäätiö.

Hodgson, G. M. (1997), "The ubiquity of habits and rules", *Cambridge Journal of Economics* 21, 663–684.

——(2004), *The Evolution of Institutional Economics*, London: Routledge.

Honkapohja, S. and Koskela, E. (2001), "The economic crisis of the 1990s in Finland", in Kalela, J., Kiander, J., Kivikuru, U.-M., Loikkanen, H. A., Simpura, J. (eds), *Down from the Heavens, Up from the Ashes*, Helsinki: VATT Publications 27(6), 52–101.

Honneth, A. (1995), *The Struggle for Recognition; The moral grammar of social conflicts*, Cambridge: Polity Press.

——(1998), "Democracy as reflective cooperation: John Dewey and the theory of democracy today", *Political Theory* 26 (6), 763–783.

Hopmann, S. T. (2008), "No child, no school, no state left behind: Schooling in the age of accountability", *Journal of Curriculum Studies* 44(4), 417–456.

——, Brinek, G., and Retzl, M. (eds) (2007), *PISA zufolge PISA–PISA according to PISA. Hält PISA, was er verspricht? Does PISA keep what is promises?*, Wien: Lit Verlag.

Hosoya, S. and Ushida, S. (2006), "Accepting diversity in both background and ability: A comparative study of Finland and Japan". http://opac.kanto-

References

gakuin.ac.jp/cgi-bin/retrieve/sr_bookview.cgi/U_CHARSET.EUC-JP/NI10000615/ Body/04hosoya.html, accessed in 04/30/2012

Hudson, J. and Kühner, S. (2009), "Towards productive welfare? A comparative analysis of 23 ORCD countries", *Journal of European Social Policy* 19 (1), 34–46.

Hughes, T. P. (1988), *Networks of Power; Electrification of western world, 1880–1930*, Baltimore: The John Hopkins University Press.

Husso, K. and Kangaspunta, S. (1999), "Innovaatiojärjestelmä ja tutkimuksen kaupallistaminen: keskustelua OECD:n piirissä", *Kansantaloudellinen Aikakauskirja* 95(3), 577–589.

Hutchins, E. (1995), *Cognition in the Wild*, Cambridge, Mass.: The MIT Press.

Hyytinen, A., Paija, L., Rouvinen, P., and Ylä-Anttila, P. (2006), "Finland's emergence as a global information and communication technology player: Lessons from the Finnish wireless cluster", in Zysman, J. and Newman, A. (eds), *How Revolutionary was Digital Revolution?*, Stanford: Stanford Business Books, 56–77.

Ilyenkov, E. V. (1977), *Dialectical Logic; Essays on its history and logic*, Moscow: Progress Publishers.

Istance, D. (2003), "Schooling and lifelong learning: Insights from OECD analyses". *European Journal of Education* 38 (1), 85–99.

Iversen, T. and Stephens, J. D. (2008), "Partisan politics, the welfare state, and three worlds of human capital formation", *Comparative Political Studies* 41 (4/5), 600–637.

Jääskeläinen, J. (2001), *Klusteri tieteen ja politiikan välissä. Teollisuuspolitiikasta yhteiskuntapolitiikkaan* (Cluster – between science and policy. From industrial policy to social policy), Helsinki: ETLA Publications A 33.

Jackson, T. (2009), *Prosperity without Growth; Economics for finite planet*, London: Earthscan.

Järvinen, R., Lampinen, A., Ikäheimo, H., Voutilainen, E., and Kairavuo, K. (2003), "Matikkamaa – Mattelandet", *Dimensio* 1, 24–28.

Jeppeson, R. L. (1991), "Institutions, institutional effects, and institutionalism", in Powell, W. W. and DiMaggio, P. J. (eds), *The New Institutionalism in Organizational Analysis*, London: University of Chicago Press, 143–163.

Jessop, R. (1991), "The welfare state in transition from Fordism to Post-Fordism", in Jessop, R., Kastendiek, H., Nielsen, K., and Pedersen, O. K. (eds), *The Politics of Flexibility. Restructuring state and industry in Britain, Germany and Scandinavia*, Aldershot: Edward Elgar, 82–105.

——(2000), "The crisis of the National Spatio-temporal Fix and the Ecological Dominance of globalization Capitalism", *International Journal of urban and regional studies* 24, 323–360.

——(2002), *The Future of the Capitalist State*, Cambridge: Polity Press.

——(2008), "A cultural political economy of competitiveness and its implications for higher education", in Jessop, B., Fairclough, N., and Wodak, R. (eds), *Education and Knowledge-based Economy in Europe*, Rotterdam: Sense Publishers, 13–39.

Johnson, B. (2010), "Institutional learning", in Lundvall, B.-Å. (ed.), *National Systems of Innovation; Toward a theory of innovation and interactive learning*, London: Anthem Press, 21–45.

Julkunen, R. (2007), "Sitran hyvinvointihautomosta", *Yhteiskuntapolitiikka* 72 (1), 72–79.

Kamin, L. J. (1974), *The Science and Politics of IQ*, Potomac, Md.: Erlbaum.

Kankainen, T. (2009), "Voluntary associations and trust in Finland", *Research on Finnish Society* 2, 5–17.

Kanniainen, V. (2011), "Köyhyyden anatomia Suomessa: taloustieteellisiä näkökohtia", *Yhteiskuntapolitiikka* 76, 658–668.

Kansallinen teollisuusstrategia, (1993), *Kauppa- ja teollisuusministeriön julkaisuja 1/1993*, Tampere: Tammer -Paino.

Kaufmann, A. and Tödling, F. (2001), "Science-industry interaction in the process of innovation: The importance of boundary crossing between systems", *Research Policy* 30, 791–804.

Kekkonen, U. (1952), *Onko maallamme malttia vaurastua?* Helsinki: Otava.

Kenney, M. and Patton, D. (2009), "Reconsidering the Bayh-Dole act and the current university invention ownership model", *Research Policy* 38, 1407–1422.

Kerosuo, H., Kajamaa, A., and Engeström, Y. (2010), "Promoting innovation and learning trough change laboratory: An example from Finnish health care", *Central European Journal of Public Policy* 4 (1), 110–131.

Kettunen, P. (1997), "The society of virtuous circles", in Kettunen, P. and Eskola, H. (eds), *Models, Modernity and the Myrdals*, Helsinki: Renvall Institute Publications 8, 153–173.

——(1998), "The Nordic welfare state in Finland", *Scandinavian Journal of History* 26, 225–247.

——(2002), Suunnitelmataloudesta kansalliseen innovaatiojärjestelmään (From planned economy to national innovation system), in Bolmberg, H., Hannikainen, M., and Kettunen, P., *Lamakirja – näkökulmia 1990- luvun talouskriisiin ja sen historiallisiin konteksteihin*, Turku: Kirja-Aurora, 15–43.

——(2004), "The Nordic model and consensual competitiveness in Finland", in Castrén, A-M., Lonkila, M., and Peltonen, M. (eds), *Between Sociology and History; Essays on microhistory, colletiove action and nation-building*, Helsinki: SKS/Finnish Literature Society, 289–309.

——(2006), "The power of international comparison: A perspective of making and challenging of the Nordic welfare state", in Cristenssen, N. F., Petersen, K., Elding, N., and Haave, P. (eds), *The Nordic Model of Welfare; A historical reappraisal*, Copenhagen: Museum Tusculanum Press, 31–66.

——(2008), *Klobalisaatio ja kansallinen me*, Tampere: Vastapaino.

Kivirauma, J. (1989), *Erityisopetus ja suomalainen oppivelvollisuuskoulu vuosina 1921–1985*, Turun Yliopiston julkaisuja, C: 74. Turku: Turun Yliopisto.

——and Ruoho, K. (2007), "Excellence through special education? Lessons from the Finnish school reform", *Review of Education* 53, 283–302.

Kleinman, D. J. (2005), *Science and Technology in society; From biotechnology to the internet*, Malden, MA: Blackwell Publishing.

References

Knack, S. and Keefer, P. (1997), "Does social capital have an economic payoff? A cross-country investigation", *Quarterly Journal of Economics* 120 (2), 1215–1288.

Knorr-Cetina, K. (2001), "Objectual practice", in Schatzki, T., Knorr-Cetina, K., and von Savigny, E. (eds), *The Practice Turn in Contemporary Theory*, London and New York: Routledge, 175–188.

Korkeakoulut 2011 – yliopistot ja ammattikorkeakoulut (2011), *Opetus- ja kulttuuriministeriön julkaisuja* 2011:10, Helsinki: OKM.

Kosellek, R. (1982), "Begriffsgeschichte and social history", *Economy and Society* 11 (4), 409–427.

Koski, H., Rouvinen, P., and Ylä-Anttila, P. (2002), "ICT cluster in Europe: The great central banana and the small Nordic potato", *Information Economics and Policy* 14, 145–165.

Kristensen, P. H. (2011a), "The co-evolution of experimentalist business systems and enabling welfare states: Nordic countries in transition", in Kristensen, P.H. and Lilja, K. (eds), *Nordic Capitalisms and Globalization; New forms of economic organization and welfare institutions*, Oxford: Oxford University Press, 1–46.

——(2011b), "Developing comprehensive, enabling welfare states for offensive experimentalist business practices", in Kristensen, P. H. and Lilja, K. (eds), *Nordic Capitalisms and Globalization; New forms of economic organization and welfare institutions*, Oxford: Oxford University Press, 220–258.

——and Lilja, K. (2011), *Nordic Capitalisms and Globalization; New forms of economic organization and welfare institutions*, Oxford: Oxford University Press.

Kröger, K. (1995), "Maalaiskunnan murros ja kamppailu päivähoidosta. Maaseudun uusi aika", *Maaseutututkimuksen ja –politiikan aikauslehti* 2 (2), 26–37.

Krücken, G. (2002), "Panta rei-rethinking science, rethinking society", *Science as Culture* 11 (1), 125–130.

Kuitunen, S. and Lähteenmäki-Smith, K. (2006), "Eliittien pelikenttä? Terknologiapolitiikan malli ja periaatteet Suomessa" (The Finnish technology policy model: Beyond the elite playground?), *Politiikka* 88 (2), 99–114.

Kupiainen, S., Hautamäki, J., and Karjalainen, T. (2009), *The Finnish Education System and PISA*, Helsinki: Ministry of Education Publication, 46.

Kuusi, P. (1961), *60-luvun sosiaalipolitiikka*, Porvoo: WSOY.

Lampinen, A. and Korhonen, H. (2010), "Suomessa opitaan matematiikkaa Varga-Nemenyi menetelmän mukaan", *Dimensio* 2, 24–28.

Langlois, R. N. and Everett, M. J. (1994), "What is evolutionary economics?", in Magnusson, L. (ed.), *Evolutionary and Neo-Schumpeterian Approaches to Economics*, Boston: Klüwer, 11–47.

Lärarnas Riksförbund (2012), En skola för alla eller endast för en del? Lärarnas Riksförbund. Undersökningar, May 3rd 2012. http://www.lr.se/opinionpaverkan/undersokningar/arkiv/en Downloaded 1 June 2012.

Lascoumes, P. and Le Gales, P. (2007), "Introduction: Understanding public policy through its instruments – From the nature of instruments to the sociology of public policy instrumentation", *Governance: An international Journal of Policy, Administration, and Institutions* 20 (1), 1–21.

Lasten erityishuolto ja – opetus Suomessa (1954), Lastensuojelun Keskusliitto, Helsinki: Kirja-Mono Oy.

Latour, B. (1992), "Where are the missing masses? The sociology of a few mundane artifacts", in Bijker, W. and Law, J. (eds), *Shaping Technology/ Building Society. Studies in sociotechnical change*, Cambridge, Mass.: MIT Press, 225–264.

——(1994), "On technical mediation: Philosophy, sociology, genealogy", *Common Knowledge* 3, 29–64.

——and Woolgar, S. (1979), *Laboratory Life: The social construction of scientific facts*, Beverly Hills: Sage Publications.

Leadbeater, C. (2002), *Innovate from Within; An open letter to the new cabinet*, London: Demos.

Lehenkari, J. and Miettinen, R. (2002), "Standardization work in the construction of a large technological system: The case of Nordic Mobile Telephone System", *Telecommunication Policy* 26 (3–4), 109–127.

Leinonen, J. (2004), *Families in Struggle – Child mental health and family well-being in Finland during the economic recession of the 1990s. The importance of parenting*, Helsinki: University of Helsinki, Faculty of Behavioural Sciences.

Leitch, H. and Davenport, S. (2005), "The politics of discourse: Marketization of the New Zealand science and innovation system", *Human Relations* 58 (7), 891–912.

Lektorsky, V. A. (1980), *Subject Object Cognition*, Moscow: Progress.

Lemola, T. (1990), "Teknologiapolitiikan muuttuva maisema", in Lemola, T., Loikkanen, T., Lovio, R., Miettinen, R., and Vuorinen, P. (eds), *Teknologiatutkimuksen näkökulmia ja tuloksia*, Helsinki: Tekes, 90–112.

——(2001), "Tiedettä, teknologiaa, ja innovaatioita kansakunnan parhaaksi. Katsaus Suomen tiede- ja teknologiapolitiikan lähihistoriaan" (Review of the recent history of the Finnish science and technology policy), Espoo: VTT:n teknologian tutkimuksen ryhmä, Työpapereita 57/01.

——(2003), "Transformation of Finnish science and technology policy", *Science Studies* 16(1), 52–67.

——(2004), "Finnish science and technology policy", in G. Schienstock (ed.), *Embracing the Knowledge Economy; The dynamic transformation of the Finnish innovation system*, 268–284, Cheltenham: Edward Elgar.

Levin, B. and Fullan, M. (2008), "Learning about system renewal", *Educational management, Administration and Leadership* 36 (2), 289–303.

Lister, R. (2006), "Investing in the citizen-workers of the future: Transformation of citizenship and the state under new labor", in Pierson, C. and Castles, F. (ed.), *The Welfare State Reader*, Cambridge: Polity, 455–472.

Lorenz, E. and Lundvall, B.-Å. (2009), "European systems of competence building", in Lorenz, E. and Lundvall, B.-Å. (eds), *How Europe's Economies Learn*, New York: Oxford University Press, 1–25.

Lounsbury, M., Ventresca, M., and Hirch, P. M. (2003), "Social movements, field frames and industry emergence: A cultural-political perspective to US recycling", *Socio-Economic Review* 1, 71–104.

References

Lovio, R. (1989), *Suomalainen menestystarina. Tietoteollisen verkostotalouden läpimurto*, Helsinki: Hanki ja Jää.

——(1993), "Evolution of firm communities in new industries", *Acta Academiae Oeconomicae Helsingiensis*, Series A:92.

Lowe, R. (2007), *The Death of Progressive Education; How teachers lost control of the classroom*, London: Routledge.

Löwy, I. (1992), "The strenght of loose concepts – boundary concepts. Federative experimental strategies and disciplinary growth. The case of immunology", *History of Science* 30, 371–396.

Luhmann, N. (1998), *Observations on Modernity*, Stanford, CA: Stanford University Press.

Lundvall, B.-Å. (1985), "Product innovation and producer-user interaction", *Industrial Development Research Series* 31, Aalborg: Aalborg University Press.

——(1988), "Innovation as an interactive process: From user producer interaction to the national system of innovation", in Dosi, G., Freeman, C., Nelson, R., Silverberg, G., and Soete, L. (eds), *Technical Change and Economic Theory*, London: Pinter Publishers, 349–370.

——(1992), *National Systems of Innovation; Towards a theory of innovations and interactive learning*, London: Pinter Publishers.

——(1994), "The learning economy", *Journal of Industry Studies* 1 (2), 23–41.

——(1998), "Nation states, social capital and economic development – A systems approach to knowledge creation and learning", Paper presented at The International Seminar on Innovation, Competitiveness in Central America: A systems of innovation Approach, San José, Costa Rica, 22 and 23 February 1999.

——(1999), "Innovation policy and economic theory", in Schienstock, G. and Kuusi, J. (eds), *Transformation Towards a Leaning Economy; The challenge for the Finnish Innovation system*, Helsinki: SITRA 213, 397–419.

——(2004), "National innovation system – Analytical concept and development tool", Paper to be presented in the DRUID Tenth Anniversary Summer Conference in Copenhagen, Denmark, 29 November.

——(2006), "Innovation systems between policy and research", Paper presented in the "Innovation Pressure Conference", Tampere, Finland, 16–17 March.

——(2007), "National innovation system: Analytical focusing device and policy learning tool", Östersund: Swedish Institute for Growth Policy Studies, Working Paper 2007:004.

——and Borrás, S. (1997), "The globalizing learning economy. Implications for innovation policy", Report based of seven projects under the: TSER project, DG XII, Commission of European Union.

——Johansson, B., Andersen, E. S., and Dalum, B. (2002), "National systems of production, innovation and competence building", *Research Policy* 31, 213–231.

Luria, A. R. (1973), *The Working Brain; An introduction to neuropsychology*, London: Penguin books.

Lyytinen, H., Erskine, J., Kujala, J., Ojanen, E., and Richardson, U. (2009), "In search of a science-based application: A learning tool for reading acquisition", *Scandinavian Journal of Psychology* 509, 668–675.

MacIntyre, A. (1984), *After Virtue; A study in moral theory*, Notre Dame, Indiana: University of Notre Dame Press.

MacKenzie, D. (2006), "Is economics performative? Option Theory and the construction of derivate markets", *Journal of the History of Economic Thought* 28 (1), 29–55.

Madaus, G. F., Russel, F., and Higgins, M. (2009), *The Paradoxes of High Stakes Testing: How they affect students, their parents, teachers, principals, schools and society*, Charlotte, N.C.: Information Age Publication Inc.

Mahony, J. and Thelen, K. (2010), *Explaining Institutional Change; Ambiguity, agency and power*, Cambridge: Cambridge University Press.

Mannheim, K. (1943), *Diagnosis of Our Time; Wartime essays of a sociologist*, London: Routledge & Kegan Paul.

Maturana, H. R. and Varela, F. J. (1992), *The Tree of Knowledge: The Biological Roots of Human Understanding*. Boston: Shambhala.

Mazur, J. E. and Hastie, R. (1978), "Learning as an accumulation: A reexamination of the learning curve", *Psychological Bulletin* 85, 1256–1274.

McKelvey, M. (1991), "How do national systems of innovations differ? A critical analysis of Porter, Freeman, Lundvall and Nelson", in Hogson, G. and Screpanti, E. (eds), *Rethinking Economics*, Aldershot: Edward Elgar, 117–137.

——(1997), "Using evolutionary theory to define systems of innovations", in Edquist, C. (ed.), *Systems of Innovation; Technologies, institutions and organizations*, London: Pinter.

McLanahan, S. (2004), "Diverging destinies: How children are faring under the second democgraphic transition", *Demography* 41 (4), 607–627.

McNeil, L. M., Coppola, E., Radican, J., and Vasquez Heilig, J. (2008), "Avoidable losses: High-stakes accountability and the dropout crisis", *Education Policy Analysis Archives* 16 (3), 1–45.

Metcalfe, S. (1995), "The economic foundations of technology policy: Equilibrium and evolutionary perspectives", in Stoneman, P. (ed.), *Handbook of the Economic of Innovation and Technology Change*, Oxford: Blackwell Publishers, 25–46.

Meyer, R.E. (2010), "New sociology of knowledge: Historical legacy and contribution to current debates in institutional research", in Greenwood, Oliver, Sahlin and Suddaby (eds.) *The Sage Handbook of Organizational Institutionalism*, Los Angeles: Sage, 519–538.

Miettinen, R. (1999a), "The riddle of things: Activity theory and Actor-network theory as approaches of studying innovations", *Mind, Culture, and Activity* 6 (3), 170–195.

——(1999b), "Transcending traditional school learning: Teachers work and the networks of learning", in Engeström, Y., Miettinen, R., and R.-L. Punamäki, (eds), *Perspectives on Activity Theory*, Cambridge: Cambridge University Press, 325–244.

——(2000), "The concept of experiential learning and John Dewey's theory of reflective thought and action", *International Journal of Lifelong Education* 19 (1), 54–72.

Miettinen, R. (2001), "Artifact mediation in Dewey and in cultural-historical activity theory", *Mind, Culture, and Activity* 8 (4), 297–308.

——(2002), *National Innovation System; Scientific concept or political rhetoric.* Helsinki: Edita.

——(2006), "Epistemology of material transformative activity: John Dewey's pragmatism and cultural-historical activity theory", *Journal for the Theory of Social Behaviour* 36 (4), 389–408.

——(2009), *Dialogue and Creativity; Activity theory in the study of science, technology and innovations,* Berlin: Lehmanns Media.

——Eela, R., and Rask, M. (1999), "The emergence and institutionalization of technology assessment in Finland", *Science Studies* 12 (2), 48–63.

——Paavola, S., and Pohjola, P. (2012), "From habituality to change: Contribution of activity theory and pragmatism to practice theories". *Journal for the Theory of Social Behaviour* 42 (3), 345–360.

——and Peisa, S. (2002), "Integrating school-based learning with the study of change at work: The alternative enterprise method", *Journal of Education and Work* 15 (3), 303–319.

——and Virkkunen, J. (2005), "Epistemic objects, artifacts and organizational change", *Organization* 12 (3), 437–456.

————(2006), "Learning in and for work and the joint onstruction of mediational artifacts: an activity theoretical view", in Antonacopoulou, E., Jarvis, P., Anderson, V., Elkjaer, B., and Hoeyrup, S. (eds), *Learning, Working and Living; Mapping the terrain of working life learning,* Palgrave: Routledge, 154–169.

Mjoset, L. (2005), "Can grounded theory solve the problems of its critics?" *Sociologisk Tidskrift* 13, 379–408.

Moscovici, S. (1984), "The myth of the lonely paradigm: A rejoinder", *Social Research* 51 (4), 939–967.

——(2008), *Psychoanalysis; Its image and its public,* Cambridge: Polity Press.

Mowery, D. C. and Rosenberg, N. (1993), "The U.S. national innovation system", in Nelson, R. (ed.), *National Innovation Systems; A comparative analysis,* New York: Oxford University Press, 29–75.

Mowery, D. C. and Ziedonis, A. (1998), "Market failure or market magic? Structural change in the US national innovation system", *STI Review* 22. Paris OECD, 101–136.

Myrdal, G. (1960), *Beyond the Welfare State,* New Haven: Yale University Press.

——(1961), *Beyond the Welfare Society; Economic planning in the welfare states and its international implications,* London: Yale University Press.

Mytelka, L. K. and Smith, K. (2002), "Policy learning and innovation theory: An interactive and co-evolving process", *Research Policy* 31, 1467–1479.

Nee, V. (2005), "The new institutionalisms in economics and sociology", in Smelsel and Swedberg (eds), *Handbook of Economic Sociology,* Princeton: Princeton University Press, 49–74.

Nelson, R. (1987), *Understanding Technological Change as an Evolutionary Process,* North Holland: Amsterdam.

——(1993), "Technical innovation and national systems", in Nelson, R. (ed.), *National Innovation Systems; A comparative analysis*, New York: Oxford University Press, 3–21.

——(2000), "Knowledge and innovations systems", in *OECD, Knowledge Management in Learning Society; Education and skills*, Paris: OECD, 115–124.

——(2001), "Observations of the on the Pots-Bayh-Dole-Act rise of patenting at American universities", *Journal of Technology Transfer* 26 (1–2), 13–19.

——(2002), "Bringing institutions into evolutionary growth theory", *Journal of Evolutionary Economics* 12, 12–78.

——and Nelson, K. (2002), "On the nature and evolution of human knowledge", *Research Policy* 31, 719–733.

——and Rosenberg, N. (1993), "A retrospective", in Nelson, R. (ed.), *National Innovation Systems; A comparative analysis*, New York: Oxford University Press, 505–523.

——and Winter, S. G. (1977), "In search of useful theory of innovation", *Research Policy*, 6 (1), 36–76.

————(1982), *An Evolutionary Theory of Economic Change*, Cambridge, Mass.: The Belknap Press.

Nichols, S. L., and Berliner, D. C. (2007), *Collateral Damage: How high stakes testing corrupts America's schools*, Cambridge, Mass.: Harvard Education Press.

Niiniluoto, I. (1996), "Teknologiapolitiikka, arvot ja kansalaiset", *Tiedepolitiikka* 4/96, 37–44.

Niosi, J., Saviotti, P., Bellon, B., and Crow, M. (1993), "National systems of innovations: In search of a workable concept", *Technology in Society* 15, 207–227.

Nonaka, I. and Takeuchi, H. (1995), *The Knowledge-creating Company; How Japanese companies create the dynamics of innovation*, New York: Oxford University Press.

Normann, R. (2001), *Reframing Business; When the map changes the landscape*, Chichster: John Wiley & Sons.

Noro, A. (2000), "Aikalaisdiagnoosi sosiologisen teorian kolmantena lajityyppinä" (Diagnosis of era as the third type of sociologic theory), *Sosiologia* 4, 321–329.

North, D. C. (1990), *Institutions, Institutional Change and Economic Performance*, Cambridge: Cambridge University Press.

Nowotny, H. (2003), "Democratizing expertise and socially robust knowledge", *Journal of Public Policy* 30 (3), 151–156.

Nurmio, A. and T. Turkki (eds) 2010, *Vibrant Finland; Report of Finnish vitality development programme*. Helsinki: Sitra. www.sitra.fi/julkaisu/2011/report-vibrant-finland-0

Nuvolari, A. (2004), "Collective invention during the British Industrial Revolution: The case of the Cornish pumping engine", *Cambridge Journal of Economics* 28 (3), 347–363.

OECD (1992), *Technology and the Economy; The key relationships. TEP: The Technology, Economy Programme*. Paris: OECD.

——(1997a), *National Innovations Systems*. Paris: OECD.

217

References

OECD (1997b), *Promoting Public Understanding of Science and Technology*. Paris: OECD.

—— (1998), *Technology, Productivity and Job Creation; Best policy practices*. Paris: OECD.

—— (1999a), *Managing National Innovation Systems*. Paris: OECD.

—— (1999b), *Boosting Innovations: The cluster approach*. Paris: OECD.

—— (2001a), *Knowledge and Skills for Life: First results from PISA 2000*. Paris: OECD.

—— (2001b), *The Well-being of Nations; The role of human capital*. Paris: OECD.

—— (2001c), *Innovative clusters. Drivers of national innovation systems*. Paris: OECD.

—— (2002), *Dynamising National Innovation System*. Paris: OECD.

—— (2005), *Governance of Innovation Systems. Volume 1: Synthesis report*. Paris: OECD.

—— (2009), *Science, Technology and Industry Scoreboard 2009*. Paris: OECD.

—— (2010a), *PISA 2009 Results: What students know and can do. Student performance in reading, mathematics and science*. Paris: OECD.

—— (2010b), *Finland: Slow and steady reform for consistently high results*. In *Strong performers and successful reformers in education: Lessons for PISA for the United States*. Paris: OECD, 117–135.

Oinas, P. (2005), "Finland: A success story?" *European Planning Studies* 13 (8), 1227–1244.

Opetusministeriö (2007), "Yliopistojen tutkimustulosten hyödyntäminen", *Opetusministeriön työryhmämuistoita ja selvityksiä 2007:10*, Helsinki: Yliopistopaino.

Palmberg, C. (2002), "Technological systems and competent procurers – The transformation of Nokia and Finnish telecom industry revisited", *Telecommunication Policy* 26 (3–4), 129–148.

—— and Martikainen, O. (2005), "Nokia as an incubating entrant: Case of Nokia's entry to the GSM", *Innovation: Management, policy and practice* 7 (1), 61–78.

Paloheimo, H. (2010), "Hyvinvointivaltion kannatus ja äänestyskäyttäytyminen", in H. Taimio (ed.), *Hyvinvointivaltion suunta – nousu vai lasku?*, Helsinki: TSL, 20–39.

Patomäki, H. (2005), *Yliopisto OYJ – tulosjohtamisen ongelmat ja vaihtoehdot* (The Univercity Inc. – the problems of and alternatives to the management by results), Helsinki: Gaudeamus.

—— (2012), *Eurokriisin anatomia. Mitä globalisaation jälkeen?*, Helsinki: Into Kustannus.

Perelman, C. (1982), *The Realm of Rhetoric*, Notre Dame, Ind.: University of Notre Dame Press.

—— and Olbrechts-Tyteca, L. (1958/1971), *The New Rhetoric; A treatise on argumentation*, Notre Dame, Indiana: University of Notre Dame Press.

Peruskoulun Opetussuunnitelman Perusteet (1985), Helsinki: Kouluhallitus.

—— (1994), Helsinki: Opetushallitus.

Pernaa, V. (2007), "Sivistyspolitiikan suurjärjestelmien rakentaminen", in Pernaa, V. and Tiitta, A., *Sivistyksen ja tiedon Suomi*, Helsinki: Edita, 10–145.

—— and Tiitta, A. (2007), *Sivistyksen ja tiedon Suomi*, Helsinki: Edita.

Piaget, J. (1950/1971), *The Psychology of Intelligence*, London: Routledge & Kegan.

Pierson, C. (1991), *Beyond the Welfare State; The new political economy of welfare*, Cambridge: Polity Press.

———(2006), *Beyond the Welfare State; The new political economy of welfare*, Cambridge: The Polity Press.

———and Castles, F. (2007a), "The labor legacy: Looking Back with the Australian Labor Party", *Government and Opposition* 42 (4), 564–592.

———(eds), (2007b), *The Welfare State Reader*, Cambridge: Polity Press.

Pol, E. and Ville, S. (2009), "Social innovation: Buzz word or enduring term?", *The Journal of Socio-Economics* 38, 978–985.

Potter, J. (1996), *Representing Reality: Discourse, rhetoric and social construction*, London: Sage.

Powell, W. W. and Colyvas, J. A. (2008), "Microfoundations of institutional theory", in Greenwood, Oliver, Sahlin and Suddaby (eds) *The Sage Handbook of Organizational Institutionalism*, Los Angeles: Sage, 276–298.

Powell, W. W. and Gianella, E. (2011), "Collective invention and invention networks", in Hall, B. H. and Rosenberg N. (eds), *Handbook of the Economics of Innovation*, Vol. 1, Amsterdam: Elsevier, 575–605.

Psacharopoulos, G., Patrinos, H. A. (2004), "Returns to investment in education: A further update", *Education Economics* 12 (2), 111–134.

Putnam, H. (1992), "A reconsideration of Deweyan pragmatism", in Putnam, H., *Renewing Democracy*, Cambridge, Mass.: Harvard University Press, 180–200.

Rainio, A. (2010), *Lionhearts of the Playworld; An ethnographic study of the development of agency in play activity*, University of Helsinki, Institute of Behavioural Sciences, Helsinki: Studies of Education Sciences 233.

Rask, M. (2001), "Arvot teknologiapolitiikan taustalla" (Values behind technology policy), *Espoo: VTT, Teknologian tutkimuksen ryhmä*, Työpapereita 55.

Ravitch, D. (2010), *The Death and Life of the Great American School System*, New York: Basic Books.

Research and Innovation Policy Council of Finland (2010), *Research and Innovation Policy Guidelines for 2011–2015*. http://www.minedu.fi/export/sites/default/OPM/Tiede/tutkimus_ja_innovaationeuvosto/julkaisut/Review2011-2015.pdf

Rinne, R., Kivirauma, J., and Simola, H. (2002), "Shoots of revisionist education policy or just slow readjustment?", *Journal of Education Policy* 17 (6), 643–658.

Rinne, R., Simola, H., Mäkinen-Streng, M., Silmäri-Salo, S., and Varjo, J. (2011), *Arvioinnin arvo. Suomalaisen perusopetuksen laadunarviointi rehtoreiden ja opettajien kokemana*, Jyväskylä: Yliopistopaino.

Ritaluoto A. J. (1996), *Soikoon musiikki laadukkaasti*, Helsinki: Kirjapaino Mercur Oy.

Rogowski, R. (ed.) (2008), *The European Social Model and Transitional Labour Markets – law and policy*, Farnham: Ashgate.

Rothstein, B. and Uslaner, E. M. (2005), "All for all: Equality, corruption, and social trust", *World Politics* 58, 41–72.

Room, G. (2002), "Education and welfare: Recalibrating the European debate", *Policy Studies* 23 (1), 37–50.

———(2005), *The European Challenge; Innovation, policy learning and social cohesion in the new knowledge economy*, Bristol: The Policy Press.

Rose, N. and Miller, P. (2010), "Political power beyond the state: Problematic of government", *The British Journal of Sociology* 61, 271–303.

References

Rosenberg, N. (1982), *Inside the Black Box; Technology and economics*, Cambridge: Cambridge University Press.

Rosensweig, P. (2007), *The Halo Effect and Eight other Business Delusions that Deceive Managers*, New York: Free Press.

Rothwell, R. (1986), "Innovation and reinnovation: A role or the user", *Journal of Marketing Managament* 2 (2), 109–123.

Ruoppila, I., Röman, K., and Västi, M. (1968), *KTL:n diagnostisia lukukokeita peruskoulun II ja III luokalle*, Jyväskylä: KTL julkaisuja 41/1968.

Sabel, C. (1994), "Learning by monitoring: The institutions of economic development", in Smelser, N. J. and Swedberg, R. (eds), *The Handbook of Economic Sociology*, New York: Princeton University Press, 137–165.

——(2006), "A real time revolution in routines", in Hekscher, C. and Adler, P. (eds), *The Firm as a Collaborative Community: Reconstructing trust in the knowledge economy*, USA: Oxford University Press, 106–156.

——and Saxenian, A. L. (2008), *A Fugitive Success; Finland's economic future*, Sitra Reports 80, Helsinki: Edita Prima Ltd.

——and Zeitlin, J. (2008), "Learning from difference: the new architecture of experimentalist governance in the EU", *European Law Journal* 14 (3), 271–327.

————(2010), *Experimentalist governance in the European Union; Towards a new architecture*, Oxford: Oxford University press.

————Miettinen, R., Kristensen, P.-H. and J. Hautamäki (2011), *Individualized Service Production in the New Welfare State: Lessons from the special education in Finland*, Sitra Studies 62, Helsinki: Sitra.

Sahlberg, P. (2010), "Rethinking accountability in knowledge society", *Journal of Educational Change* 11, 45–61.

——(2011), *Finnish Lessons: What can the world learn from educational change in Finland?*, New York: Teacher's College Press.

Salais, R. and Villeneuve, R. (2004), *Europe and the Politics of Capabilities*, Cambridge: Cambridge University Press.

Sanderson, I. (2009), "Intelligent policy making for a complex world: Pragmatism, evidence and learning", *Political Studies* 57, 699–719.

Sapir, A. (2006), "Globalization and the reform of European social models", *JCMS* 44 (2), 369–390.

Sauli, H., Salmi, M., and Lammi-Taskula, J. (2011), "Kriisistä kriisiin: lapsiperheiden toimeentulo 1995–2009", *Yhteiskuntapolitiikka* 76, 535–544.

Saviotti, P. P. (1994), "Innovation systems and evolutionary theories", in Edquist, C. (ed.), *Systems of Innovation; Technologies, institutions and organizations*, London: Pinter, 180–199.

Sawyer, R. K. (2006), "Educating for innovation", *Thinking Skills and Creativity* 1, 41–48.

Schatzki, T. R. (2002), *The Site of the Social*, Pennsylvania: Pennsylvania University Press.

Schleicher, A. (2007), "Can competences assessed by PISA be considered the fundamental school knowledge 15-year-olds should possess?", *Journal of Educational Change* 8, 349–357.

Schröter, A. (2009), "New rationales for innovation policy? A comparison of the systems of innovation policy approach and neoclassical perspective", Jena Economic Research papers 2009–033. http://papers.ssrn.com/sol3/papers.cfm?abstract_id=1418651

Science and Technology Council of Finland (1990), *Review 1990; Guidelines of science and technology policy in the 1990s*, Helsinki: Valtion Painatuskeskus.

——(1993), *Towards an Innovative Society; A development strategy for Finland*, Helsinki: Printing Centre.

——(1996), *Finland: A knowledge-based society*, Helsinki: Edita.

——(2000), *The Challenge of Knowledge and Know-how*, Helsinki: Edita.

——(2003), *Know-how, Innovations and Globalization*, Helsinki: Science and Technology Policy Council.

——(2006), *Science, Technology, Innovations*, Helsinki: Science and Technology Policy Council.

——(2008), *Review 2008*, Helsinki: Helsinki University Press.

Scoppio, G. (2002), "Common trends of standardisation, accountability, devolution and choice in the educational policies of England, U.K., California, U.S.A., and Ontario, Canada", *Current Issues of Comparative Education* 2 (2), 130–141.

Scott, R. W. (2008a), *Institutions and Organizations; Ideas and interests*, Third Edition, Los Angeles: Sage Publications.

——(2008b), "Approaching adulthood: The maturing of institutional theory", *Theory and Society* 37, 427–442.

Seligman, A. (1997), *The Problem of Trust*, Princeton: Princeton University Press.

Sellers, J. M. and Lindström, A. (2007), "Decentralization, local government, and the welfare state", *Governance: An international journal of policy, administration, and institutions* 20 (4), 609–632.

Sen, A. (1984), *Resources, Values and Development*, Oxford: Basil Blackwell.

——(1993), "Capability and well-being", in Nusbaum, M. and Sen, A. (eds) *Quality of Life*, Oxford: Clarendon Press, 30–53.

Sharif, N. (2006), "Emergence and development of National Innovation Systems concept", *Research Policy* 35 (5), 745–766.

Shields, P. M. (2003), "The community of inquiry: Classical pragmatism and public adminstration", *Administration and Society* 35 (5), 510–538.

Shinn, T. (1999), "Change or mutation? Reflections on the foundations of contemporary science", *Social Science Information* 38 (1), 149–176.

Siisiäinen, M. (1999), "Voluntary associations and social capital in Finland", in Van Deth, J. W., Maraffi, M., Newton, K., and Whiteley, P. F. (eds) *Social Capital and European Democracy*, London: Routledge, 120–143.

Simola, H. (2005), "The Finnish miracle of PISA: Historical and sociological remarks on teaching and teacher education", *Comparative Education* 41 (4), 455–470.

——and Rinne, R. (2010), "Kontingenssi ja koulutuspolitiikka: vertailevan tutkimuksen teoreettisia edellytyksiä etsimässä", *Kasvatus* 4, 316–330.

——,Rinne, R., Varjo, J., Pitkänen, H., and Kauko, J. (2009), "Quality assurance and evaluation (QAE) in Finnish compulsory schooling: National model or just unintended effect of radical decentralization?", *Journal of Education Policy* 24 (2), 163–178.

References

Sipilä, N., Kestilä, L., and Marikainen, P. (2011), "Koulutuksen yhteys nuorten työttömyyteen. Mihin perustutkinto riittää 2000-luvun alussa?", *Yhteiskunta-politiikka* 76 (2), 121–134.

Skinner, Q. (1978), *The Foundations of Modern Political Thought. Vol. 1: The Renaissance*, Cambridge: Cambridge University Press.

Sleeper, R. W. (2001), *The Necessity of Pragmatism; John Dewey's conception of philosophy*, Urbana: University of Illinois Press.

Smolander, J. (2004), "Neoliberalism or economic nationalism? Changes in the welfare policy of Finnish and Swedish conservatives during the 1970s and 1980s", in Lehtinen, A. and Vainio-Korhonen, K. (eds), *History and Change; Studia Historica* 71. Helsinki: Finnish Literature Society, 239–252.

Snider, K. F. (2000), "Expertise or experimenting? Pragmatism and American public admistration, 1920–1950", *Administration and Society* 32 (3), 329–354.

Soete, L., Verspagen, B., and ter Weel, B. (2010), "Systems of innovation", in Hall, B. H. and Roseberg, N. (eds), *Handbook of the Economics of Innovation*, Vol. 2, Amsterdam: North-Holland, 1159–1180.

Star, S. L. and Griesemer, J. R. (1989), "Institutional ecology, 'translations' and boundary objects: Amateurs and professionals in Berkeley's Museum of verte-brate zoology", 1907–39, *Social Studies of Science* 19, 387–420.

Stokes D. E. (1997), *Pasteur's Quadrant; Basic science and technological innovation*, Washington, D.C.: Brookings Institution Press.

Storper, M. (1997), *The Regional World; Territorial development in global economy*, New York: The Guilford Press.

Strang, G. N. (2005), "Cross-national differences and accounting for social class inequalities in education", *International Sociology* 20 (4), 483–505.

Streeck, W. (2010), "Institutions in history: Bringing capitalism back", in Morgan, G., Cambell, J. L., Crouch, C., Pedersen O. K., and Whitley, R. (eds) *The Oxford Handbook of Comparative Institutional Analysis*, Oxford: Oxford University Press, 659–686.

——and Thelen, K. (2005), "Introduction: Institutional change in advanced political economies", in Streeck, W. and Thelen, K. (eds), *Beyond Continuity: Institutional change in advanced political economies*, Oxford: Oxford University Press, 1–39.

Sum, N-L. (2010), "A cultural political economy of transnational knowledge brands: Porterian "competitiveness" discourse and its recontextualization in Hong Kong/Pearl River Delta", *Journal of Language and Politics* 9 (4), 546–573.

Summa, H. (1989), "Hyvinvointipolitiikka ja suunnitteluretoriikka: Tapaus asunto-politiikka" (Welfare policy and planning rhetoric: The case of housing policy). *Yhdyskuntasuunnittelun täydennyskoulutuskeskus*, Helsinki: Teknillinen korkeakoulu.

Suomi Innovaatiotoiminnan kärkimaaksi (2005), Sitra. Helsinki: Edita Prima Oy.

Taimio, H. (ed.) (2007), *Talouskasvun hedelmät – kuka sai ja kuka jäi*, Helsinki: TSL.

Tainio, R. and Lilja, K. (2003), "The Finnish business system in transition: Out-comes, actors and their influence", in Czarniawska, B. and Sevón (eds), *The Northern lights: Organization theory in Scandinavia*, Malmö: LiberAbstract, 69–78.

Taipale, I. (2007), *100 Social Innovations from Finland*, Helsinki: Hakapaino.

Taking European knowledge Society Seriously (2007), Report of the Expert Group on Science and Governance to the Science, Economy and Society Directorate, Directorate-General for Research, European Comission, Ulrike Felt (rapporteur), Brian Wynne (chairman), Belgium: European Communities.

Teece, D. and Pisano, G. (1994), "The dynamic capabilities of firms: An introduction", *Industrial and Corporate Change* 3 (3): 537–556.

Teece, G. J. (2009), *Dynamic Capabilities and Strategic Management*, Oxford: Oxford University Press.

Thelen, K. (2010), "Beyond comparative statistics: Historical institutional approaches to stability and change in political economy of labor", in Morgan, G., Campbell, J. L., Crouch, C., Pedersen, O. K., and Whitley, R. (eds), *The Oxford Handbook of Comparative Institutional Analysis*, Oxford: Oxford University Press, 41–61.

Tiitta, A. (2007), Tiede- ja teknologiapolitiikka Suomessa 1970–2006, in Pernaa, V. and Tiitta, A. *Sivistyksen ja tiedon Suomi,* Helsinki: Edita, 146–281.

Tikkanen, P. (2008), *Helpompaa ja hauskempaa kuin luulin. Matematiikka suomalaisten ja unkarilaisten perusopetuksen neljäsluokkalaisten kokemana* (Easier and funnier than I expected. Mathematics experienced by the Finnish and Hungarian fourth graders of the basic school), PhD dissertation, Jyväskylä Studies in Education, Psychology and Social Research 337. Jyväskylä: University of Jyväskylä.

Toulmin, S. (1958/2003), *The Uses of Argument*, Cambridge: Cambridge University Press.

Turnbull, D. (2000), *Masons, Tricksters and Cartographers*, Amsterdam: Harwood Academic Publishers.

Tuunainen, J. (2002), "Reconsidering the Mode 2 and the Tripple Helix: A critical comment based on a case study", *Science Studies* 15 (2), 36–58).

Ulsener, E. M. (2008), *Corruption, Inequality and the Rule of Law*, Cambridge, Mass.: Cambridge University Press.

Vaarama, M., Moisio, P., and Karvonen, S. (2010), "Hyvinvointipolitiikka 2010 – luvulla", in Vaarama, M., Moisio, P., and Karvonen, S. (eds), *Suomalaisten hyvinvointi 2010*, Helsinki: National Institute for Health and Welfare, 278–286.

Välijärvi, J., Linnakylä, P., Kupari, P., Reinikainen, P., and Affman, I. (2002), *The Finnish Success in PISA – And some reasons behind it,* Jyväskylä: Kirjapaino Oma Oy.

Välimäki, A-L. and Rauhala, P.-L. (2000), "Lasten päivähoidon taipuminen yhteiskunnalliasiin murroksiin Suomessa", *Yhteiskuntapolitiikka* 65 (5), 387–405.

Valsiner, J. (2000), *Culture and Human Development*, London: Sage Publications.

Van Oers, B. (2005), "The potentials of imagination", *Inquiry* 24 (4): 5–18.

Veblen, T. (1914/1990), *The Instinct of Workmanship, and the States of Industrial Arts*, New Brunswick: Transaction Publishers.

Victor, B. and Boynton, A. C. (1998), *Invented Here: Maximizing your organization's internal growth and profitability*, Boston: Harvard Business School Press.

Vig, N.-J. and Paschen, H. (eds), (2000), *Parliaments and Technology; The development of technology assessment in Europe*, Albany: State University of New York Press.

Von Bertalanffy, L. (1971), *General Systems Theory: Foundations, development, applications*, London: Allen Lane.

Von Hippel, E. (1976), "The dominant role of users in the scientific instrument innovation process", *Research Policy* 5 (3): 212–239.

——(1986), "Lead users: A source of novel product concepts", *Management Science* 32: 791–805.

——(1988), *Sources of Innovation*, New York: Oxford University Press.

——(2005), *Democratizing Innovation*, Cambridge, Mass.: MIT Press. http://web.mit.edu/evhippel/www/books.htm

Vuoden 1971 (1973), *Koulutuskomitean mietintö 1973*. Helsinki: Valtion Painatuskeskus.

Vygotsky, L. (1979), *Mind in Society: The development of higher psychological processes*, ed. M. Cole, V. John-Steiner, S. Scribner, and E. Souberman, Cambridge, Mass.: Harvard University Press.

——(1934/1987), *Thought and Language*, Cambridge, Mass.: The MIT Press.

——(2004), "Imagination and creativity in childhood", *Journal of Russian and East European Psychology* 42 (1), 9–97.

Warren, J., Hauser, R., and Sheridan, J. (2002), "Occupational stratification across the life course", *American Sociological Review* 67, 432–455.

Weingart, P. (1997), "From "Finalization" to "Mode 2": Old Wine in New Bottles", *Social Science Information* 36 (4), 591–613.

Wertsch, J. V. (1985), *Vygotsky and the Social Formation of Mind*, Cambridge, Mass.: Harvard University Press.

White, J. (2009), "Illusory intelligences", in Cigman, R. and Davis, A. (eds), *New Philosophies of Learning*, West Sussex: Wiley-Blackwell, 241–259.

Whitehead, A. N. (1947), *The Aims of Education*, London: Williams & Norgate.

Whitley, R. (2007), *Business Systems and Organizational Capabilities; The institutional structuring of competitive competence*, Oxford: Oxford University Press.

Wolf, M. (2008), *Proust and Squid; The story of the reading brain*, Cambridge: Icon Books.

Wynne, B. (1996), "May the sheep safely graze? A reflexive view of expert-lay knowledge-divide", in Lash, S., Szerszynski, B., and Wynne, B. (eds), *Risk, Environment and Modernity: Towards a new ecology*, London: Sage Publications, 44–83.

Yearley, S. (2000), "Making systematic sense at public discontents with expert knowledge: Two analytical approaches and 2 case studies", *Public Understanding of Science* 9, 105–122.

Ylä-Anttila, P. (1996), "Beyond cluster studies – Internationalization of business and national policies", in Kuusi, O. (ed.), *Innovation Systems and Competitiveness*, Helsinki: ETLA Series B 125, 91–102.

Ziman, J. (ed.) (2000), *Technological Innovation as an Evolutionary Process*, Cambridge: Cambridge University Press.

Name Index

Name Index

Subject Index